JN296717

Econometric Analysis of
Nonstationary and Nonlinear Relationships

Econometric Analysis of Nonstationary and Nonlinear Relationships

Feng Yao

[Kagawa University Economic Studies, Monograph Series 16]

SHINZANSHA
Hongo, Tokyo
2001

Published by Shinzansha Publishing Company
6-2-9 Hongo, Bunkyo-ku, Tokyo 113-0033, Japan
Tel: (03)-3818-1019
Fax: (03)-3838-0344
http://www.shinzansha.co.jp

On behalf of the Institute of Economics and
the Economic Society, Kagawa University
2-1 Saiwai-cho, Takamatsu 760-8523, Japan
Tel: (087)-832-1950
Fax: (087)-832-1952

First published 2002, Tokyo

©*Feng YAO 2002*

All right reserved. Except for the quotation of short passages for the purposes of criticism and review, no part of this publication may be reproduced, stored in a retrieval system, or transmitted, in any form or by any means, electronic, mechanical, photocopying, or otherwise, without the prior permission of the author.

Printed in Japan by Shobi Printers.
Bounded by Daisan Bookbinders.

ISBN 4-1657-3 c3333 hardback

Preface

The main goal of this book is to provide an incentive for the rigorous econometric analysis of causal relationships in time series. We know that science has at least two principal aims: prediction and explanation. Prediction provides knowledge of what happens, and the explanation furnishes knowledge about why things happen as they do. Causal analysis is concerned with both prediction and explanation. Causal concepts are in every branch of science. The concept of causality pervades our thinking about ourselves, our environment, and the whole of the universe we live in. What happens at one place and time may have a significant influence on what happens at other places and times because causal influences can propagate through time and space. The explanation of a phenomenon essentially involves locating and identifying its cause or causes, as there really is a causal structure in the world in which we live. There are many things and laws in the world of whose existence we are not aware, and the more we know about the world that we live in, the more we can control our destiny.

Daily practical planning involves causal considerations. We plant seeds in springtime in order to reap food or flowers later on. Sometimes, governments attempt to use interest rates to control the speed of development of the national economy. Memory (which has a very wide meaning here, such as DNA, human memory, animal memory, and computer memory storage) allows the influence of past events to be transmitted to the present. Earlier experiences and activities may affect our current as well as future behavior. The idea of causality is invariably present in the development of technology. In this book, we attempt to present an econometric approach and some related ideas that may be conducive to achieving desirable effects and avoiding undesirable ones.

Econometrics, being a branch of economics, aims to give empirical content to economic relations. Chow (1983) stated that econometrics is the art and science of using statistical methods for the measurement of economic relations. There have many other definitions of econometrics, but there does not exist a generally accepted answer of what is econometrics. The main reason is that econometricians wear many different hats. The foremost, they are economists, capable of utilizing economic theory to improve their empirical analyses of the problems they address. At times they are mathematicians, formulating economic theory in ways that make it appropriate for statistical testing. At times they are applied statisticians, spending hours and days with the computer trying to estimate economic relationships or predict economic events. Finally, at times they are theoretical statisticians, applying their skills to the development of statistical techniques appropriate to the empirical problems characterizing the science of economics. In this sense, it is often said that econometrics is whatever econometricians do. This book will try to describe the studies in nonlinear and nonstationary processes, summarizing newly developed statistical methods of cointegration and causality as well as information criteria and showing their applications to the analysis of dynamic economic system.

Since the formation of the Econometric Society in the early 1930's, the development of econometric theory has contributed to the explanation of economic phenomena, and practical economic phenomena have also stimulated the development of econometric theory. Because economics is a non-experimental science that often affords weak data, the empirical evidence provided by econometrics is sometimes inconclusive. For this reason, Econometrics has experienced an uneven development. In the highly developed domestic and international economy of the recent years, economic relations have become very complex. Many economic time series are non-stationary and sometimes non-linear. To further our understanding of economic phenomena, the investigation of economic relations must go beyond the early stages of linear and/or stationary processes. A simple linear correlation analysis cannot satisfy the needs of economists or econometricians. To investigate the economic phenomena and answer the questions in the modern information society, more precise, realistic, and, many times, complex econometric methods are needed. We need to study the causal relations of economic phenomena. The remarkable progress attained by computer science in these decades has made it possible to study the more complex nonlinear and nonstationary processes. Furthermore, thanks to the considerable technical and methodological progress in econometrics, the empirical work in economics has become broader and more attractive.

This book focuses on the econometric analysis of nonstationary and nonlinear relationships and summarizes the new results on inference and computational methods obtained by the author in recent years. This book is mainly divided into two parts. The first part contains the econometric analysis of nonstationary processes, and the second one is concerned with the analysis of nonlinear processes. In the first part, we discuss causal measures of time-series based on a autoregressive moving-average (ARMA) model, especially give a detail discussion based on the cointegrated vector autoregressive (VAR) model. We also investigate the cointegration and causal relationships of some macroeconomic data. Furthermore, the long-run and short-run relationships in macroeconomic data are revealed from the point of view of one-way effect causal measures in the frequency domain and the time domain. Many of these results have been published recently. Concerning nonlinear processes, we discuss the identification of the Box-Cox transformation (BCT) model in the second part. Comparisons of the identification for the BCT model are drawn using information criterion methods and the nested χ^2 test. Then, on the basis of this research, we introduce a mixed estimator to identify the BCT model.

During the past ten years, I have had very enriching experiences from which I have learned much. First, I would like to express my heartfelt appreciation to my advisor, Prof. Y. Hosoya, for his guidance and many helpful suggestions in the course of this study. My thanks also to Professors T. Kuriyama, H. Hori, Y. Tsukuda, N. Terui, and A. Suzuki for their kind help during my stay at the Tohoku University campus. I also wish to thank Professors M. Hatanaka, N. Kunitomo and Y. Yajima of Tokyo University, M. Taniguchi of Osaka University, K. Maekawa of Hiroshima University, T. Yanagawa of Kyushu University, X.S. Zhang of the Chinese Academy of Science, Dr. J.L. Lin of Academia Sinica (Taiwan), W.F. Ding and R. Zhao of Northwest University, Mr. C.S. Wang, Mrs. J.L. Cheng, Mr. D.Y. Bu, and Mr. D.B. Li of the State Information Center, and other scholars who attended many conferences and workshops with the author. My appreciation goes to all for their valuable comments.

As a foreign researcher for more than ten years in this country, I am also indebted to Mrs. and Prof. Hosoya, Mrs. M. Yamazaki, and other kind Japanese friends for their generous help and, particularly, for their support during my campus life at Tohoku University. Having been a research fellow (1993-1995) of the Tohoku Kaihatu Memorial Foundation for three years, I am deeply indebted to President N. Ishida and Chairman K. Kameda.

My recent research was partially supported by: the Japanese Ministry of Education Scientific Research Grant (No.(B)(2)-10045016, 1998-2000); the Special Research Expenses (for Youth Scientist, 1996) of Kagawa University; the Special Research Expenses (1997) presented by the faculty of Economics; the Japanese Ministry of Education Scientific Grant for Promoting the Improvement of Education (1998); and the Project Expenses (1999) of the Department of Economics, Kagawa University. All the members of Faculty of Economics, particularly Professors F. Abe, T. Ihara, T. Inoue, K. Ohyabu, T. Ohno, H. Shishido, D.Z. Zeng, H. Takatsuka, K. Choi, P.J. Guo, Reiju H. Mihara, S. Hara, T. Hirai, H. Hisamatsu, Y. Hoshino, H. Fujii, A. Fujihara, Ravindra Ranade, Y. Yamamura, and Y. Yokoyama for their valuable discussions. Professors S. Inoue, R. Kobayasi, A. Takahashi, L. Lrong, T. Yamasita, T. Yanagisawa, S. Yasui, H. Seto, and S. Hosokawa should have earned my respect and gratitude for their cooperation and help since 1996. I would like to thank Miss R. Kanazawa, Mrs. M. Sato, Mrs. S. Nisihara, and Miss. S. Katayama of Tohoku University for their generous help. Thanks are also due to Mr. T. Sodeyama, Managing Director of Shinzansha Publishing Company, for his cooperations during publishing this book in English.

Lastly, I would like to express my deep thanks to my family, for their understanding and total support of my life and research in Japan.

This book was latex'd. The figures were plotted by the use of Microsoft Excel, Mathematica of Wolfram Research, and Kaleida Graph of Synergy Softeware. The computation in this manuscript was programmed by FORTRAN and conducted by ACOS-6/NVX and SX-4 of Tohoku University Computer Center.

Augest, 2000

YAO Feng
Saiwai-cho Campus
Kagawa University, Japan

*To my wife Dr. Jimin Hu
and our lovely son
Zeyu* (澤宇 たくう)

CONTENTS

Preface v

Chapter 1. Introduction 1

Part I
Econometric Analysis of Nonstationary Processes

Chapter 2. An Overview of Causal Analysis 13
   2.1 Granger's Condition for Non-causality 14
   2.2 Causal Measures in the Time Domain and the Frequency Domain 19

Chapter 3. Hosoya's Causal Measures 23
   3.1 The Measure of One-way Effect 24
   3.2 Causal Measures for Nonstationary Processes 30
   3.3 The Measures of Association and Reciprocity 36

Chapter 4. Cointegration and Statistical Tests 41
   4.1 Integration and Cointegration 41
   4.2 VAR Model and Error Correction Form 45
   4.3 Statistical Analysis of Cointegrated Vectors 48

Chapter 5. Causal Analysis of Cointegrated Processes 55
   5.1 Causal Measures for Cointegrated ARMA Processes 56
   5.2 Wald Tests of the One-way Effect 60

Chapter 6. Cointegrated Model Identification 67
  6.1 Preliminary Analysis 67
  6.2 Empirical Cointegrated Relations 72
  6.3 Evaluation of the Identified Models 77

Chapter 7. Empirical Causal Relationships 87
  7.1 Estimation and Explanation of the Causal Measures 87
  7.2 Causal Relations of Japanese Macroeconomic Data 90
  7.3 Causality Between Japanese and Chinese Data 101
    7.3.1 Cointegrated Model Identification 101
    7.3.2 Empirical Measures of the One-way Effect 106

Part II
Econometric Analysis of Nonlinear Processes

Chapter 8. The BCT Model and Cross-entropy Risk 115
  8.1 The Box-Cox Transformation 116
  8.2 Estimation of Cross-entropy Risk and the GIC 119

Chapter 9. Identification Methods for Nonlinear Processes 125
  9.1 Inference of the GIC for BCT Model 126
  9.2 Nested χ^2 Test for the BCT Model 131

Chapter 10. Numerical Evaluation of the GIC and the AIC 135
  10.1 Simulation Models 136
  10.2 Monte Carlo Experiments by the GIC and the MLE 137
  10.3 Comparison of the GIC and AIC 143

Chapter 11. Information Criteria and the Nested χ^2 Test 151
  11.1 Comparison of the Three Methods 152

11.2 The Nested χ^2 Test and the Mixed Estimate 156
11.3 Some Empirical Examples 159

Chapter 12. Nonlinear Model Simulation 167
  12.1 The Information Criteria for Model Choice 168
    12.1.1 Models and Simulations 168
    12.1.2 Evaluation of the Simulation Results 177
    12.1.3 Conclusions 180
  12.2 The Nested χ^2 Test and the AIC for Model Choice 186
    12.2.1 Models and Simulations 186
    12.2.2 Evaluation of the Simulation Results 197
    12.2.3 Conclusions 201

References 213

List of Abbreviations 224

Econometric Analysis of
Nonstationary and Nonlinear Relationships

Chapter 1

Introduction

Unlike many of the time series in natural sciences, most economic time series frequently exhibit a trending behavior or other characteristics, which implies that they are intrinsically nonstationary. For example, income and consumption typically display a growth component as well as cyclical behaviour; and many financial time series in general have no fixed mean. Many econometricians have followed the suggestions of Box and Jenkins (1970) to take the successive difference of the variables to transform nonstationary time series into stationary time series when constructing time series models. Even though such a procedure has an advantage in that the conventional $\sqrt{T}$ convergence and limiting normal distribution of the estimator hold, differencing the data also removes the information about long-run relationships among economic variables.

Granger (1981) [see also Granger and Weiss (1983), Engle and Granger (1987)] proposed the concept of cointegration, according to which econometricians have carefully formulated models that integrate the short-run dynamics and long-run relations of the variables. Two or more time series are said to be cointegrated if one linear combination of the series has a lower order than the individual series. It has been shown that a time series model with cointegration has a representation as an error-correction model (ECM) and vice versa, which underscores the importance of nonstationary processes for econometric modeling. The explosion of interest in cointegration analysis has been of both a theoretical and an applied nature, and the diffusion of cointegration techniques has been very rapid.

Chapter 1. Introduction

An important factor contributing to this diffusion is that cointegration provides a formal link between the use of ECMs and vector autoregressive (VAR) models of dynamic economic relationships. Hsiao (1997) recently presented a basic framework linking the multiple time series model and the dynamic simultaneous equation model and discussed the implications under long-run cointegrating relations. This work presents the conditions for identifying both the short-run dynamics and long-run equilibrium conditions. Furthermore, it derives the limiting properties of the estimators under cointegration.

We will mainly discuss a general p-dimensional integrated order one Gaussian VAR process $\{Z(t)\}$ which is represented in the error-correction form,

$$\Delta Z(t) = \alpha \beta^* Z(t-1) + \sum_{j=1}^{a-1} \Gamma(j) \Delta Z(t-j) + \varepsilon(t), \qquad (1.1)$$

where $\{\varepsilon(t)\}$ is Gaussian white noise process with mean 0 and positive definite non-degenerate covariance matrix Σ, α and β are $p \times r$ matrices (r is called cointegration rank and $r \leq p$). The r-dimensional cointegration vector β has the property that even $Z(t)$ itself is not stationary, $\beta^* Z(t)$ becomes stationary.

As for the cointegration test, the maximum likelihood (ML) in a fully specified error correction model (MLECM) by Johansen (1988, 1991, 1995) is a representative one. Gonzalo (1994) compared five representative cointegration test methods and showed that MLECM has clearly better properties than the others (see Chapter 3 for details). The MLECM ensures that coefficient estimates are symmetrically distributed and median unbiased and that hypothesis tests are conducted using standard asymptotic χ^2 tests. None of the other proposed methods offers these properties. For this reason, we applied Johansen's ML method to the model identification in this book.

The study of causal relationships among a set of time series variables has been one of the most important problems in the literature, especially in the field of economic and business investigations. To solve the problem in deciding the direction of causality between two related variables and also whether or not feedback is occurring, Granger (1963, 1969) introduced a famous definition of non-causality. Sims (1972) introduced a definition for bivariate process expressed in MA form. Hosoya (1977) gave a very general proof of that the causality definitions presented by Granger (1969) and by Sims (1972) are equivalent.

For the purpose of analyzing the feedback relationship between two multivariate time series, Geweke (1982) proposed the measures to quantify the degree of causality from one time series to another in the time domain and the frequency domain. Hosoya (1991) gave three sensible definitions of the causality measure both in the frequency domain and the time domain for a second-order stationary process. These causal measures are constructed by partition of the spectral density matrix. Toda and Phillips (1993) proposed some operational procedures for conducting Granger causality tests that are based on the Gaussian ML estimation of ECMs. Granger and Lin (1995), using the definition provided by Hosoya (1991), heuristically derived an extended measure for a bivariate cointegrated process. Hosoya (1997) extended all his previously presented causality measures (1991) to a nonstationary vector ARMA model. These new causal measures are constructed by a spectral density matrix in which the intercept and the time trend have been removed from the original data process. The key point of Hosoya's causal measure construction for a non-stationary process is that the intercept, time trend dummy variables, and other exogenous variables, do not affect the causal relation [see Hosoya (1997)].

Yao and Hosoya (2000) presented an approach to test a variety of causal characteristics expressed in terms of the measures of a one-way effect for cointegrated vector time series. Using the Wald test statistics, their study also provides a method of confidence-set construction for causal measures. Their approach includes testing Granger's non-causality as an instance of its multiple applications. In addition, Mosconi and Giannini (1992) provided the likelihood ratio test of non-causality between a pair of cointegrated time series based on the Johansen model and inference.

Cointegration and causal relations among a set of time series have been one of the main focuses of the empirical analysis of economic relationships. Earlier representative work on the empirical analysis of causal relations of macroeconomic data was conducted by Sims (1972), who investigated a bivariate system in a monetary aggregate and current dollar GNP with quarterly data of the U.S. He pointed out that unidirectional causality from money to income agrees with the postwar U.S. data and rejects the hypothesis that causality is unidirectional

Chapter 1. Introduction

from income to money. In a quite frequently cited paper that refers to the U.S. data, Stock and Watson (1989) showed that money, as measured by the narrow M1 aggregate, has a statistically significant marginal predictive value for real income, as proxied by industrial production. In contrast to earlier researchers, Stock and Watson's results showed the money-income relationship even in the presence of a short-term interest rate. Frideman and Kuttner (1993), applying the Stock and Watson test to a different sample, pointed out that the conclusions of Stock and Watson (1989) are not robust. Lütkepohl and Reimers (1992), using the Wald test for Granger's non-causality in a bivariate cointegrated finite-order AR process, investigated the short- and long-term interest rates in the U.S.

As for the other empirical analysis of cointegration and causality relationships of macro economic data, see for example, Sims (1980), Hsiao (1982), Johansen and Juselius (1992, 1994), Juselius (1994, 1995). The empirical investigation of Japanese money and income can be seen in Morimune and Zhao (1997), Tsukuda and Miyakoshi (1998), where they mainly used the standard F test and the Wald test presented by Toda and Phillips (1993) and Sims *et al.* (1990). So far, although many empirical analyses have been conducted in the econometric literature, most of them seem concerned only with Granger's non-causality. Work by Yao and Hosoya (1995, 2000) and Yao (1996a) has differed from other empirical work so far presented. On the basis of a cointegrated system and using a one-way effect approach, which has expanded the meaning of Granger's non-causality, we have shown the inference and calculation procedure of one-way effect causal measures for cointegrated Gaussian processes in levels of the VAR(a) model in detail. Yao and Hosoya (2000) presents a characterization of the causal structure of the recent Japanese macroeconomy on the basis of the proposed method and the derived evidence. These results will be discussed in the following chapters.

The calculation algorithm of one-way effect causal measures for cointegrated Gaussian processes in levels of the VAR(a) model is shown in the following flowchart (Figure 1.1). Only the technical procedure is shown until the spectral density matrix $f(\lambda)$ is constructed. For further details, see Chapters 3, 4, and 5.

Even though we will not discuss these topics in detail in this book, recent work by Hosoya and Takimoto (2000) should be mentioned. In their work, the problems of the causal relation based on cointegrated system in the presence of trend breaks are solved. Yao (1996b) presented an algorithm to estimate the causal measure of the one-way effect for the cointegrated VAR model with trend breaks but did not discuss a concrete test of cointegration rank. Yao (2000) provided an approach to the test of measuring a one-way effect for a cointegrated vector time series in the presence of trend breaks.

For the analysis of non-Gaussian process, we discussed the method of Box-Cox transformation (BCT) [see Box-Cox (1964)]. As a special power transformation, for any positive variable Y, the BCT is defined by

$$Y^{[\lambda]} = \begin{cases} \frac{Y^\lambda - 1}{\lambda} & \lambda > 0 \\ 0 & \lambda = 0 \end{cases} \qquad (1.2)$$

where λ is an unknown parameter called the BCT parameter. As the transformed variables can be included in a linear function so that the generalized models of the form

$$Y^{[\lambda_0]} = \alpha_1 X_1^{[\lambda_1]} + \alpha_2 X_2^{[\lambda_2]} + \cdots + \alpha_p X_p^{[\lambda_p]} \qquad (1.3)$$

can be specified and estimated. For $\lambda_0 = 1, 0,$ and -1, $Y^{[\lambda_0]}$ enters into model (1.3) linearly, as log and as the reciprocal of Y. The estimation procedure itself chooses the transformation which best fits the data.

For different models derived from (1.3), see Spitzer (1982). For a discussion of the interpretation of estimated coefficients in the BCT models, see Huang and Kelingos (1979). But all of the work on the BCT model so far are only discussed the fixed order (or the fixed independent variables) models [see for example, Zarembka (1990) and the references therein].

In view of the information criterion methods, Yao (1992, 1994) discussed the simultaneous identification of the order and the BCT parameter of the BCT regression model. One of the information criterion methods for the simultaneous identification of the BCT regression model is an extension of Akaike's information criterion (AIC) [Akaike (1973)]; the other is the general information criterion (GIC) [Hosoya (1983), Yao (1992), Yao and Hosoya (1994)]. The GIC developed here is different from Takeuchi's GIC [see Takeuchi (1976)] in the sense that the BCT parameter constitutes an argument of the model identification criterion. This idea is first proposed by Hosoya (1983). The Monte Carlo experiments

Chapter 1. Introduction

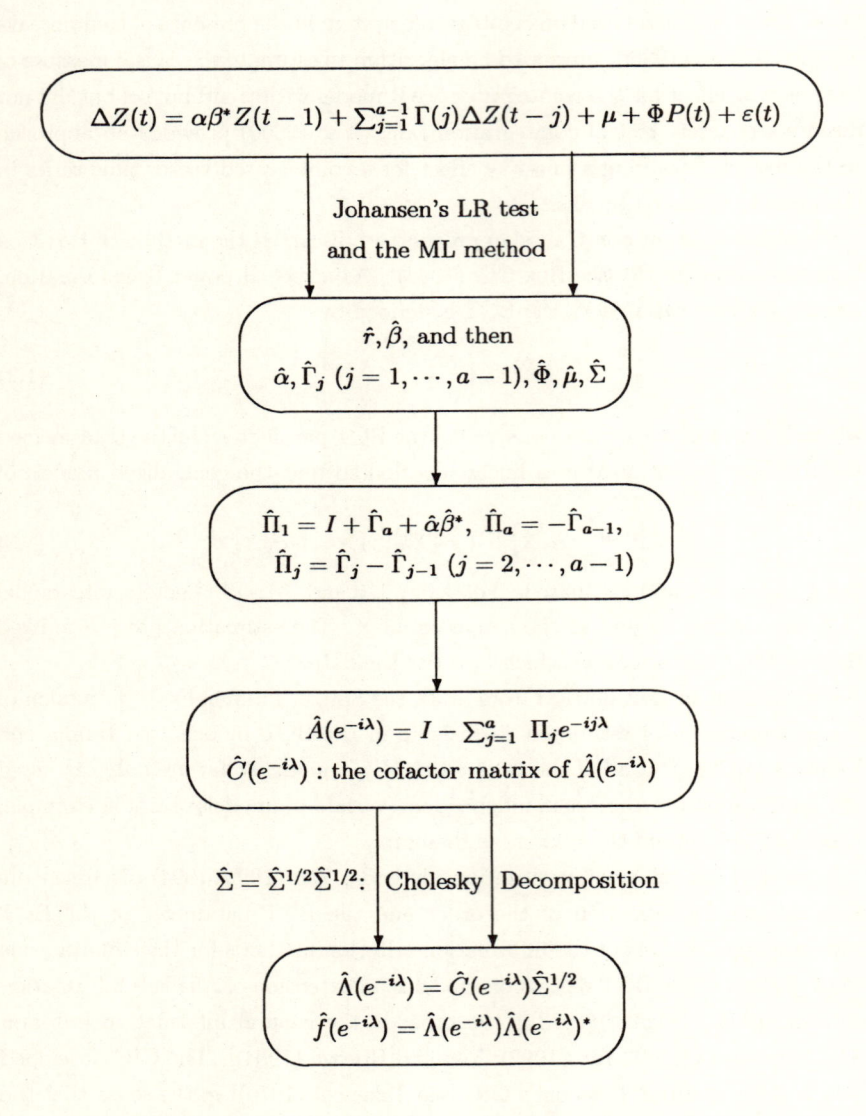

$$\Delta Z(t) = \alpha\beta^* Z(t-1) + \sum_{j=1}^{a-1} \Gamma(j)\Delta Z(t-j) + \mu + \Phi P(t) + \varepsilon(t)$$

Johansen's LR test and the ML method

$\hat{r}, \hat{\beta}$, and then $\hat{\alpha}, \hat{\Gamma}_j$ $(j = 1, \cdots, a-1), \hat{\Phi}, \hat{\mu}, \hat{\Sigma}$

$$\hat{\Pi}_1 = I + \hat{\Gamma}_a + \hat{\alpha}\hat{\beta}^*, \quad \hat{\Pi}_a = -\hat{\Gamma}_{a-1},$$
$$\hat{\Pi}_j = \hat{\Gamma}_j - \hat{\Gamma}_{j-1} \ (j = 2, \cdots, a-1)$$

$$\hat{A}(e^{-i\lambda}) = I - \sum_{j=1}^{a} \Pi_j e^{-ij\lambda}$$
$\hat{C}(e^{-i\lambda})$: the cofactor matrix of $\hat{A}(e^{-i\lambda})$

$\hat{\Sigma} = \hat{\Sigma}^{1/2}\hat{\Sigma}^{1/2}$: Cholesky Decomposition

$$\hat{\Lambda}(e^{-i\lambda}) = \hat{C}(e^{-i\lambda})\hat{\Sigma}^{1/2}$$
$$\hat{f}(e^{-i\lambda}) = \hat{\Lambda}(e^{-i\lambda})\hat{\Lambda}(e^{-i\lambda})^*$$

Figure 1.1 Flowchart for Estimating Spectral Density Matrix

point out that in the estimation of the BCT parameter, the GIC method is a little precise than the AIC method. Just as we expected, the GIC as an extension of the general MLE plays the same role in the identification of the fixed-order BCT model. Applications to the analysis of the Tokyo stock price index and one textile experiment are described.

Hosoya (1989) proposed the nested χ^2 test for the purpose of identifying the model out of a hierarchy of statistical models. The approach has the advantage of controlling the overall error-rate of misidentification. Yao (1994) applied Hosoya's nested χ^2 test [Hosoya (1989)] to the identification of the BCT model. It is shown that, in general, the AIC and the GIC do not make a notable difference in the BCT model identification; rather, the notable differences appear when the regressor set is determined by the nested χ^2 test. The nested χ^2 method tends to underestimate the order with comparably larger probability when the disturbance variance is large compared with the magnitude of variation of the regressor part. On the other hand, the AIC, as well as the GIC, tends to overestimate the order of the BCT model in general. The simulation experiments as well as the empirical examples demonstrate that the parameters estimated by the nested χ^2 test have reasonable behavior compared with the information-criterion approaches. A new approach that combines the AIC and the nested χ^2 test is introduced.

Yao (1996c, 1998) presented some of the simulation results of the nested χ^2 test in the simultaneous identification of the BCT model. His study focuses on the investigation of fitting a BCT polynomial regression model to data generated by a nonlinear model which does not belong to the same family of the BCT regression models. Two nonlinear models are introduced there, one is the exponential regression model, and the other is the logistic regression model. The performances of the AIC and the GIC as well as of the nested χ^2 test applied to the simultaneous identification of the BCT model are compared.

For the analysis of the cointegration and causal relationship of the non-Gaussian process, the Box-Cox transformation may be applied. Let's consider a p-dimensional AR(a) model with BCT given by a first order difference form

$$\Delta Z^{[\lambda]}(t) = \alpha\beta^* Z^{[\lambda]}(t-1) + \sum_{i=1}^{a-1} \Gamma(j)\Delta Z^{[\lambda]}(t-i) + \varepsilon(t), \qquad (1.4)$$

Chapter 1. Introduction

where $\lambda = (\lambda_1, \lambda_2, \cdots, \lambda_p)^*$, and $Z^{[\lambda]}(t)$ denotes the p-dimensional process $Z(t)$ with the BCT whose i-th element is defined by $z_i^{[\lambda_i]}(t)$, $i = 1, 2, \cdots, p$ [see the BCT defined in (1.2)], $\Delta Z^{[\lambda]}(t)$ is defined by $Z^{[\lambda]}(t) - Z^{[\lambda]}(t-1)$. It is need to make the identification of the BCT parameter $\hat{\lambda}$ and also the order $\hat{a}$ as well as the estimated $p \times r$ matrix $\hat{\beta} = \hat{\beta}(\hat{\lambda}, \hat{a}, \mathcal{Q})$, where $\mathcal{Q}$ represent all the other information needed in the estimation of β. The $\hat{\beta}$ should have the property that $\hat{\beta}^* Z^{[\lambda]}(t)$ is stationary and $\varepsilon(t)$ is Gaussian even though $Z(t)$ itself and $\hat{\beta}^* Z(t)$ are non-stationary. The treatment of such inference procedures are left for the future.

This book is organized as follows: Chapter 2 through Chapter 7 discuss the cointegration and causal relationship of nonstationary process. Chapter 8 to Chapter 12 focus on the nonlinear process by the Box-Cox transformation from the point of view of the methods of information criteria and the nested χ^2 test.

An overview of non-causality is presented in Chapter 2, where we mainly discuss the definition of Granger's non-causality [Granger (1969)] and Sims' causal definition [Sims (1972)] as well as the relation of the two definitions given by Hosoya (1977). Then, we give a summary of Geweke's causal measures [Geweke (1982, 1984)] in the time domain and the frequency domain. Hosoya's causal measures in the time domain and the frequency domain for second-order stationary processes [Hosoya (1991)] and their extension [Hosoya (1997), Yao and Hosoya (2000)] are summarized in Chapter 3. The literature work of integrated order 1 process based on cointegrated VAR model is summarized in Chapter 4 [Johansen (1988, 1991, 1995)]. The latest results of causal measures for nonstationary processes [Hosoya (1997)] and the Wald test [Yao and Hosoya (2000)] are summarized in Chapter 5. Chapter 6 shows the empirical analysis of cointegrated model identification. For the purpose of further causal analysis, the estimates of the necessary parameters for some selected Japanese macroeconomic time series are listed. The empirical causal measures of one-way effect in the frequency domain are discussed in Chapter 7. The estimated measures of bivariate and trivariate as well as four-variate AR models with constant term and seasonal dummies are listed in this chapter. In view of numerical integration, the overall measures of one-way effect are also calculated for the macroeconomic data as indicated. The results in Chapter 7 and 8 are based on the work of Yao (1996a, 1996b, 1999), Yao and Hosoya (1995,

2000), Hosoya and Yao (1999).

Chapter 8 gives an overview of the theory and applications related to the BCT. In the same chapter, based on the estimation of cross-entropy risk, the inference of the GIC is shown. The results shown in this chapter are the basic work on the investigation of the non-Gaussian process done by the author. In Chapter 9, we show the inference of the GIC and the nested χ^2 test for the identification of the BCT model. The numerical evaluation of the information methods used in the identification of the BCT model is summarized in Chapter 10, where we mainly compare the performances of the GIC and AIC for the BCT model. The numerical evaluation of the performances of the information criteria methods and the nested χ^2 method are shown in Chapter 11. In the same chapter, we also discuss a constructed mixed test statistic for the identification of the BCT model. Finally, we discuss the applications of these methods to the analysis of earthquake, consumption data of China, and the Tokyo stock price index. The results in Chapter 8 to 11 are mainly based on the results of Yao (1992, 1994, 1995, 1996a), Yao and Hosoya (1994). Chapter 12 summarizes the Monte Carlo simulations of fitting the BCT polynomial regression model to the data generated from a potential regression model and a logistic regression model. The performances of the AIC and the nested χ^2 test are discussed. The results in this chapter are based on those obtained by Yao (1996c, 1998).

The following notations are used in this book. Denote $\mathcal{J}$ the set of all integers, and $\mathcal{J}^+$ the set of all positive integers. Let $\{X(t); t \in \mathcal{J}\}$ and $\{Y(t); t \in \mathcal{J}\}$ be respectively real p_1 and p_2 dimensional processes with mean 0 defined on a probability space. Denote by $\mathcal{H}$ the Hilbert space given by the closure in the mean square of the linear hull of $\{x_j(t); t \in \mathcal{J}, j = 1, 2, \cdots, p_1\}$ and $\{y_j(t); t \in \mathcal{J}, j = 1, 2, \cdots, p_2\}$ in the space where all random variables with finite variance, $x_j(t)$ and $y_j(t)$ denotes the j-th component of the vector valued $X(t)$ and $Y(t)$, respectively. Denote by $\mathcal{H}\{X(s)\}$ and $\mathcal{H}\{X(\infty)\}$ respectively the linear closed subspace of $\mathcal{H}$ generated by $\{x_j(t); t \leq s, j = 1, 2, \cdots, p_1\}$ and $\{x_j(t); t \in \mathcal{J}, j = 1, 2, \cdots, p_2\}$. Notations such as $\mathcal{H}\{Y(s)\}$ and $\mathcal{H}\{Y(\infty)\}$, and of other arguments are defined in the same way. The projection of a random vector $Z = (z_j; j = 1, 2, \cdots, r)$ onto $\mathcal{H}(\cdot)$ implies the componentwise projection; namely if $\bar{z}_j$ is the projection of z_j onto $\mathcal{H}(\cdot)$, then the projection of Z onto $\mathcal{H}(\cdot)$ means the vector $\bar{Z}$, whose j-th

Chapter 1. Introduction

component is $\bar{z}_j$. If each component z_j belongs to $\mathcal{H}(\cdot)$, the random vector Z is said belong to $\mathcal{H}(\cdot)$. The difference $Z - \bar{Z}$ is termed the residual of the projection of Z onto $\mathcal{H}(\cdot)$. The subscripts and prime attached to $X(t)$ and $Y(t)$ denote the projection subspace which is concerned with and the upper bar denotes the projection. For example, $X_{-1,\cdot}(t), X_{-1,-1}(t), X_{-1,0}(t)$ are the residuals of the projection of $X(t)$ onto $\mathcal{H}\{X(t-1)\}, \mathcal{H}\{X(t-1), Y(t-1)\}$ and $\mathcal{H}\{X(t-1), Y(t)\}$ respectively, $\bar{X}_{-1,\cdot}(t), \bar{X}_{-1,-1}(t), \bar{X}_{-1,0}(t)$ are the corresponding projections. The prime denotes that $X(t)$ and $Y(t)$ are projected onto subspaces of $\mathcal{H}\{X(\infty), Y_{0,-1}(\infty)\}$ and $\mathcal{H}\{X_{-1,0}(\infty), Y(\infty)\}$ respectively so that $X'_{-1,-1}(t)$ and $X'_{\cdot,\infty}(t)$ are the residuals of the projection of $X(t)$ onto $\mathcal{H}\{X(t-1), Y_{0,-1}(t-1)\}$ and $\mathcal{H}\{Y_{0,-1}(\infty)\}$, whereas $Y'_{-1,-1}(t)$ and $Y'_{\cdot,\infty}(t)$ are the residuals of the projection of $Y(t)$ onto $\mathcal{H}\{X_{-1,0}(t-1), Y(t-1)\}$ and $\mathcal{H}\{X_{-1,0}(\infty)\}$.

Throughout the book, A^* indicates the conjugate transpose of a complex matrix A and the notation is retained for a complex number or for a real matrix, so that in the former case A^* is the conjugate of A and in the latter A^* is the transpose of A. For $p = p_1 + p_2$, the partition of a $p \times p$ matrix A,

$$A = \begin{pmatrix} A_{11} & A_{12} \\ A_{21} & A_{22} \end{pmatrix},$$

always implies that A_{11} is a $p_1 \times p_1$ submatrix, A_{22} is a $p_2 \times p_2$ submatrix. Let B be an $m \times n$ matrix and a_j its j-th column, then the vec operator transforms matrix B into a vector by stacking the columns of the matrix one underneath the other, i.e. $vecB$ is the $m \cdot n \times 1$ vector. $v(C)$ denotes the $n(n+1)/2$ vector that is obtained from $vecC$ by eliminating all supradiagnoal elements of a square $n \times n$ matrix C. In this way, for symmetric C, $v(C)$ contains only the generically distinct elements of C. For a 3×3 matrix A, $vecA = (a_{11}\ a_{21}\ a_{31}\ a_{12}\ a_{22}\ a_{32}\ a_{13}\ a_{23}\ a_{33})^*$, and $v(A) = (a_{11}\ a_{21}\ a_{31}\ a_{22}\ a_{32}\ a_{33})^*$. For a pair of random vectors X and Y, $Cov(X)$ and $Cov(X,Y)$ indicate the covariance of X and of $vec(X,Y)$ respectively. The trace of a square matrix C is denoted by trC and the determinant is denoted by $detC$. The Kronecker product of any $m \times n$ matrix A and $p \times q$ matrix B is denoted by $mp \times nq$ matrix $A \otimes B$. The lag operator denoted by L and $Lx_t = x_{t-1}$. The difference operator $\Delta = 1 - L$ so that $\Delta x_t = x_t - x_{t-1}$. The equality symbol $\equiv$ is used for definition.

Part I

Econometric Analysis of Nonstationary Processes

Chapter 2

An Overview of Causal Analysis

To solve the problem of deciding the direction of causality between two related variables and whether or not feedback has occurred, Granger (1969) introduced a famous definition of non-causality. Since then, several statistical tests of non-causality as in the Granger's definition have been proposed. There are two representative tests. The first one is Granger's test of zero restriction of certain coefficients of an autoregressive representation, and the second one is Sims' test [Sims (1972)] of zero restriction of some coefficients in the moving average representation of bivariate process. Hosoya (1977) gave a very general evidence that the causal definitions presented by Granger (1969) and by Sims (1972) are equivalent. Pierce and Haugh (1977) described some of the test problems in Granger's definition. Nelson and Schwert (1982) evaluated the results. Later Granger (1980, 1990) gave a further explanation of his causal definition, arguing that the tests are not altered if back filters are applied to the data but some kinds of seasonal adjustments or measurement errors can cause problems.

For the purpose of analyzing the feedback relationship between two multivariate time series, Geweke (1982) proposed measures of quantify the degree of causality from one time series to another in time domain and frequency domain. He showed under certain condition (invertibility) that his measure in the time domain can be represented by the integration of his measure in the frequency domain. Hosoya (1991) gave three sensible definitions of causal measures both in the frequency domain and the time domain. These causal measures are just what

Chapter 2. An Overview of Causal Analysis

many people have tried to obtain, i.e., the causal measure in the time domain is equals to the integration of causal measure in the frequency domain (see Chapter 3 for details). Hosoya (1997) extended all his measures to a nonstationary vector ARMA model (see Section 5). Toda and Phillips (1993) recommended some operational procedures for conducting Granger causality tests that are based on the Gaussian maximum-likelihood (ML) estimation of ECM. The theory allows for stochastic and deterministic trends as well as arbitrary cointegration. Toda and Phillips (1994) provided a theoretical overview of Wald tests for Granger causality in levels of vector autoregressions (VAR's) and Johansen-type ECM. For VAR models, the theory extends on their earlier work on trivariate systems. In such models, the results for inference are not very encouraging. Explicit information on the number of unit roots in the system and the rank of a certain sub-matrix in the cointegration space are needed in order to determine the appropriate limit theory in advance. Pretesting these conditions involves major complications in levels of VAR's. Even if the information were to be available, the limit theory would frequently involve both nuisance parameters and non-standard limit distributions, a situation where there is no satisfactory statistical basis for conducting the tests. Toda and Phillips (1994) explained that Granger causality tests in ECM's suffer from nuisance parameter dependencies asymptotically and, in some cases, non-standard limit theory.

2.1 The Granger Condition for Non-causality

The definition of causality and other related topics are introduced in this section. The problem is how to devise definitions of causality and feedback, which permit tests for existence of causality and feedback. Such a definition was proposed in earlier papers [Granger and Hatanaka (1964)]. In earlier works about causality in economic systems, Basman (1963), Simon (1953), Strotz and Wold (1960), Wiener (1956), and Salmon (1982) were particularly concerned with the problem of determining the causal interpretation of simultaneous equation systems, usually with instantaneous causality. These earlier studies concentrated on the form that the parameters of the equations should take in order to discern definite causal

2.1. The Granger Condition for Non-causality

relationships.

The concept of causality in Granger's sense is purely a statistical criterion defined in terms of predictability. The stochastic elements and the natural time ordering of the variables play relatively minor roles in the theory. The stochastic nature of the variables and the direction of the flow of time are central discussed. The theory is, in fact, not relevant for nonstochastic variables and will rely entirely on the assumption that the future cannot cause the past. Its origins may be found in a suggestion by Wiener [1956]. This is the reason we sometimes called the Granger causality as the Wiener-Granger causality.

For a stationary stochastic process $A(t)$ and an integer k, let $A_{[k]}(t)$ represent the set $\mathcal{H}\{A(t-k)\}$. It is clear that $\mathcal{H}\{A(1)\}$ represent the set of past values $\{A(t-j); j=1,2,\cdots,\infty\}$ and $\mathcal{H}\{A(0)\}$ represent the set of past and present values $\{A(t-j); j=0,1,\cdots,\infty\}$.

Denote the optimum unbiased, least-squares predictor of $A(t)$ using the set of values $B(t)$ by $P_t(A|B)$. Thus, for instance, $P_t(X|X_{[1]})$ will be the optimum predictor of $X(t)$ using only the past $X(t)$. The predictive error series will be denoted by $\varepsilon_t(A|B) = A(t) - P_t(A|B)$. Let $\sigma^2(A|B)$ be the variance of $\varepsilon_t(A|B)$. Granger's definitions of causality, feedback, and so forth, will be very general in nature.

Let $U(t)$ be all the information in the universe accumulated and let $U(t) - Y(t)$ denote all this information apart from the specified series $Y(t)$.

Definition 1: *Causality. If*

$$\sigma^2(X|U_{[1]}) < \sigma^2(X|(U-Y)_{[1]}),$$

we say that Y cause X, denoted by $Y(t) \Rightarrow X(t)$. We say that $Y(t)$ is causing $X(t)$ if we are better able to predict $X(t)$ using all available information than if the information apart from $Y(t)$ had been used.

Definition 2: *Feedback. If*

$$\sigma^2(X|U_{[1]}) < \sigma^2(X|(U-Y)_{[1]})$$

and

$$\sigma^2(Y|U_{[1]}) < \sigma^2(Y|(U-X)_{[1]}),$$

Chapter 2. An Overview of Causal Analysis

we say that feedback is occurring, which is denoted $Y(t) \Leftrightarrow X(t)$, i.e., feedback is said to occur when $Y(t)$ is causing $X(t)$ and also $X(t)$ is causing $Y(t)$.

Definition 3: *Instantaneous Causality.* If

$$\sigma^2(X|U_{[1]}, Y_{[0]}) < \sigma^2(X|U_{[1]}),$$

we say that instantaneous causality $Y(t) \Leftrightarrow X(t)$ is occurring. In other words, the current value of $X(t)$ is better predicted if the present value of $Y(t)$ is included in the prediction than if it is not.

Definition 4: *Causality Lag.* If $Y(t) \Leftrightarrow X(t)$, we define the (integer) causality lag m to be the least value of k such that

$$\sigma^2(X|U_{[1]} - Y_{[k]}) < \sigma^2(X|U_{[1]} - Y_{[k+1]}).$$

Thus, knowing the values $\{Y(t-j); j = 0, 1, \cdots, m-1\}$ will be of no help in improving the prediction of $X(t)$.

These definitions have assumed that only stationary series are involved. In the nonstationary case $\sigma^2(X|U_{[1]})$ etc., will depend on time t and in general the existence of causality may alter over time. The definitions can clearly be generalized to be operative for a specified time t. One could then talk of causality existing at this moment of time.

Sims (1972) showed that the Granger condition for non-causality can be characterized by simple conditions on the parameters of the moving-average or the distributed-lag representation of bivariate second-order stationary processes. He used the moving average representation of the process $\{X(t), Y(t)\}$, gives a definition of causality in terms of Hilbert space argument. We show the two main theorems bellow with no proofs [Sims (1972)].

Theorem 2.1. *Y does not cause X in Granger's definition if, and only if, in the MA representation,*

$$\begin{pmatrix} X(t) \\ Y(t) \end{pmatrix} = \begin{pmatrix} a & b \\ c & d \end{pmatrix} \begin{pmatrix} U(t) \\ V(t) \end{pmatrix} \tag{2.1}$$

a or b can be chosen to be identically zero.

The $U(t)$ and $V(t)$ in model (2.1) are mutually uncorrelated white noise processes with unit variance, a, b, c and d vanish for $t < 0$.

Theorem 2.2. *When the joint process $\{X(t), Y(t)\}$ has an autoregressive representation, Y can be expressed as a distributed lag function of current and past X*

2.1. The Granger Condition for Non-causality

with a residual which is not correlated with any $X(s)$, past or future if, and only if, Y does not cause X in Granger's sense.

As far as the relationship of the two definitions given by Granger (1969) and Sims (1972), Hosoya (1977) gave a very general proof of that the Granger condition is equivalent to Sims condition.

The Granger condition for non-causality is generalized as this: For a bivariate process $\{(X(t), Y(t)); t \in \mathcal{J}\}$, $Y(t)$ does not cause $X(t)$ if the projection of $X(t)$ on $\mathcal{H}\{X(t-1), Y(t-1)\}$ belong to $\mathcal{H}\{X(t-1)\}$ for all t. Let the projection of $X(t)$ on $\mathcal{H}\{X(t-1)\}$ be $\bar{X}(t)$ and let $\varepsilon(t) = X(t) - \bar{X}(t)$, then it following:

Lemma 2.1. *The above Granger condition is equivalent to that*

$$\varepsilon(t) \perp \mathcal{H}\{X(t-1), Y(t-1)\}$$

for all t.

Proof: Suppose that $\varepsilon(t) \perp \mathcal{H}\{X(t-1), Y(t-1)\}$. Because of the relations

$$\bar{X}(t) \in \mathcal{H}\{X(t-1)\} \subset \mathcal{H}\{X(t-1), Y(t-1)\},$$

the projection of $\bar{X}(t)$ on $\mathcal{H}\{X(t-1)\} \subset \mathcal{H}\{X(t-1), Y(t-1)\}$ is $\bar{X}(t)$ itself. Since the projection of $\varepsilon(t)$ on $\mathcal{H}\{X(t-1), Y(t-1)\}$ is 0, the projection of $X(t)$ on $\mathcal{H}\{X(t-1), Y(t-1)\}$ is $\bar{X}(t)$ which belongs to $\mathcal{H}\{X(t-1)\}$. The reverse implication of the assertion is obvious. □

In general, the decomposition $Y(t) = \gamma(t) + \eta(t)$, where $\gamma(t) \in \mathcal{H}\{X(t-1)\}$ and $\eta(t) \perp \mathcal{H}\{X(t-1)\}$ may be called the distributed-lag representation of the process $Y(t)$. In terms of this generalized sense, the Sims condition for $\{Y(t)\}$ not causing $\{X(t)\}$ is that $\eta(t)$, in the above decomposition is orthogonal to $\mathcal{H}\{X(\infty)\}$ for all t

Theorem 2.3. *The Granger condition is equivalent to the Sims condition.*

Proof: The Granger condition implies the Sims condition. Let $\gamma(t)$ be the projection of $Y(t)$ on $\mathcal{H}\{X(t)\}$, and put $\eta(t) = Y(t) - \gamma(t)$. Since it is evident that $\eta(t) \perp \mathcal{H}\{X(t)\}$, the problem is to show that $X(t+a) \perp \eta(t)$ for any $a \geq 1$. As is seen by the iterative application of the above lemma, it follows from the Granger condition that

$$X(t+a) = \bar{X}(t+a-1) + \varepsilon(t+a)$$

Chapter 2. An Overview of Causal Analysis

$$\begin{aligned}&= \bar{X}(t+a-2) + \varepsilon(t+a) + \varepsilon(t+a-1) \\ &= \bar{X}(t) + \sum_{i=0}^{a-1} \varepsilon(t+a-i), \end{aligned} \qquad (2.2)$$

where $\bar{X}(t+a-i) \in \mathcal{H}\{X(t+a-i)\}$ and $\varepsilon(t+a-i+1) \perp \mathcal{H}\{X(t+a-i), Y(t+a-i)\}, i = 0, 1, \cdots, a$. Set $k(t) = \bar{X}(t)$ and $\varepsilon(t+a) = \sum_{i=0}^{a-1} \varepsilon(t+a-i)$, then it is concluded that, if the Granger condition holds, there exists a decomposition $X(t+a) = k(t) + \varepsilon(t+a)$, where $\varepsilon(t) \in \eta(t)$ and $\varepsilon(t+a) \perp \mathcal{H}\{X(t), Y(t)\}$. The relations $\varepsilon(t+a) \perp Y(t)$ and $\varepsilon(t+a) \perp \gamma(t)$ imply that $\varepsilon(t+a) \perp \eta(t)$; consequently $\eta(t) \perp X(t+a)$.

To prove the reverse implication, suppose now that the distributed-lag representation of $Y(t)$ satisfies the Sims condition. That condition says that the subspace $\mathcal{H}\{Y(t)\}$ is included in the vector sum $\mathcal{H}\{X(t)\} \oplus \mathcal{H}\{X(\infty)\}^\perp$, therefore

$$\mathcal{H}\{X(t), Y(t)\} \subset \mathcal{H}\{X(t)\} \oplus \mathcal{H}\{X(\infty)\}^\perp.$$

Let $\bar{X}(t)$ be the projection of $X(t+1)$ on $\mathcal{H}\{X(t)\}$, and put $\varepsilon(t) = X(t+1) - \bar{X}(t)$. Suppose γ be an element of $\mathcal{H}\{X(t)\}$; then it is decomposed as $\gamma = v_1(t) + v_2(t)$ where $v_1(t) \in \mathcal{H}\{X(t)\}$ and $v_2(t) \in \mathcal{H}\{X(\infty)\}^\perp$. Since $\varepsilon(t) \in \mathcal{H}\{X(t+1)\}$, it follows that $\varepsilon(t) \perp \mathcal{H}\{Y(\infty)\}^\perp$. The relations $\varepsilon(t) \perp v_1(t)$ and $\varepsilon(t) \perp v_2(t)$ imply that $\varepsilon(t) \perp \gamma$. Since γ is arbitrary, $\varepsilon(t) \perp \mathcal{H}\{Y(t)\}$. Thus $\varepsilon(t)$ is orthogonal to $\mathcal{H}\{X(t), Y(t)\}$; in view of lemma 2.1, the process $\{X(t), Y(t)\}$ satisfies the Granger condition. □

Granger's causality is typically defined in terms of the predictability of a vector of variables one period ahead. The following discussions will help us to distinguish the properties of "long-run (non)causality" and "short-run (non)causality". Even though this book will not discuss this point in detail, we will summarize the main topics related to the extension of Granger's definition in the remainder of this chapter.

Lütkepohl (1993) proposed definitions based on the noncausality between two variables in terms of the nonpredictibility at any number of periods ahead. He noted that, for multivariate models where a vector of auxiliary variables Z is used in addition to the interested variables X and Y, it is possible that Y does not cause X in Granger's sense but can still help to predict X several periods

2.2. Causal Measures in the Time Domain and the Frequency Domain

ahead. For example, the values of $\{Y(t-j); j \in \mathcal{J}\}$ may help to predict $X(t+2)$, even though they are useless to predict $X(t+1)$. Causality at a given horizon h involves forecasts at horizon h which may depend on autoregressive coefficients in a complex way. To address this issue formally, Hsiao (1982) introduced indirect causality relationships and spurious causality concepts. As a continuation of Hsiao's research agenda, Dufour and Renault (1998) proposed a systematic study and characterization of indirect effects and associated lagged causality relationships. They defined some more general notations of causality: causality at any given horizon h, where h is a positive integer and can be infinite. The "long-run causality" (h large) and "short-run causality" (h small) may be studied in this way.

2.2 Causal Measures in the Time Domain and the Frequency Domain

The study of causal relationships among a set of time series has been one of the most important problems in the literature, especially in the field of economic and business investigations. By extending some known results, Geweke (1982) introduced a decomposition of prediction variance for multiple time series that is useful in the interpretation of macroeconomic time series [Geweke (1983)]. Based on the limiting values of Gaussian likelihood-ratio statistics, a measure of linear dependence between multiple time series was defined and additively decomposed into two measures of directional linear feedback and a measure of instantaneous linear feedback. The measures of directional linear feedback were, in turn, additively decomposed by frequency. These measures are consistent with the measure of information proposed by Gelfand and Yaglom (1959) and quantify the definitions of feedback introduced by Granger (1963) and Caines and Chan (1975). They are non-negative; the measure of linear dependence is zero if and only if the two series are orthogonal, and the measures of directional feedback are zero if and only if causality is unidirectional in the sense of Granger (1969) and Sims (1972).

Consider a wide-sense stationary, purely nondeterministic, multiple time series

Chapter 2. An Overview of Causal Analysis

of dimension $p = p_1 + p_2, \{Z(t); t \in \mathcal{J}\}$. The series has the moving average representation

$$Z(t) = \sum_{i=1}^{\infty} B_i \varepsilon(t - i) = B(L)\varepsilon(t), \qquad (2.3)$$

where the B_i are square summable and $B_0 = 0$. Let $f_Z(\lambda)$ denote the spectral density of Z at frequency λ, and assume that there exists $c > 0$ such that for almost all $\lambda \in (-\pi, \pi]$,

$$c^{-1}I \leq f_Z(\lambda) \leq cI. \qquad (2.4)$$

This assumption guarantees (Rozanov 1967) the existence of the autoregressive representation

$$A(L)Z(t) = \sum_{i=1}^{\infty} B_i Z(t - i) = \varepsilon(t), \qquad (2.5)$$

where the $A(L)$ are square summable and $A(0) = I$.

Suppose now that $Z(t)$ has been decomposed into $p_1 \times 1$ and $p_2 \times 1$ vectors $X(t)$ and $Y(t)$, $Z(t)^* = (X(t)^*, Y(t)^*)$. Let $Z_{[1]}(t) = \{Z(t-i); i = 1, 2, \cdots\}$, and adopt a similar notation for the subvectors. From (2.4), any subvector of $Z(t)$ has AR and MA representations. We define

$$\begin{aligned}
\Sigma_1 &= Var(X(t)|X_{[1]}(t)), \\
T_1 &= Var(Y(t)|Y_{[1]}(t)), \\
\Sigma_2 &= Var(X(t)|X_{[1]}(t), Y_{[1]}(t)), \\
T_2 &= Var(Y(t)|X_{[1]}(t), Y_{[1]}(t)), \\
\gamma &= Var(Z(t)|Z_{[1]}(t)).
\end{aligned}$$

Here and elsewhere, conditional variance is taken to be the variance about the linear projection.

Theorem 2.4. *The measures of linear feedback from Y to X, linear feedback from X to Y, and instantaneous linear feedback are defined to be, respectively,*

$$F_{Y \to X} = log(|\Sigma_1|/|\Sigma_2|), \qquad (2.6)$$

$$F_{X \to Y} = log(|T_1|/|T_2|), \qquad (2.7)$$

$$F_{Y \cdot X} = log(|\Sigma_2| \cdot |T_2|/|\gamma|). \qquad (2.8)$$

2.2. Causal Measures in the Time Domain and the Frequency Domain

The measure of linear dependence is defined as

$$F_{Y,X} = \log(|\Sigma_1| \cdot |T_1|/|\gamma|) \tag{2.9}$$

and

$$F_{Y,X} = F_{Y \to X} + F_{X \to Y} + F_{X \cdot Y}.$$

These measures were motivated by forming the population analog of LR statistics (under the assumption that $\varepsilon(t)$ is Gaussian) for tests of the hypothesis that feedback of the stated type does not exist.

The measures of directional linear feedback $F_{Y \to X}$ and $F_{X \to Y}$ can be decomposed by frequency. We review this process in some detail for $F_{Y \to X}$. Let the AR representation for $\{X(t)\}$ and $\{Y(t)\}$ be

$$\begin{pmatrix} A_{11}(L) & A_{12}(L) \\ A_{21}(L) & A_{22}(L) \end{pmatrix} \begin{pmatrix} X(t) \\ Y(t) \end{pmatrix} = \begin{pmatrix} U(t) \\ V(t) \end{pmatrix}, \tag{2.10}$$

and the corresponding MA representation be

$$\begin{pmatrix} X(t) \\ Y(t) \end{pmatrix} = \begin{pmatrix} B_{11}(L) & B_{12}(L) \\ B_{21}(L) & B_{22}(L) \end{pmatrix} \begin{pmatrix} U(t) \\ V(t) \end{pmatrix} = B(L)\varepsilon(t) \tag{2.11}$$

with $A_{11}(0) = B_{11}(0) = I_{p_1}$, $A_{22}(0) = B_{22}(0) = I_{p_2}$, $Var(U(t)) = \Sigma_2$, and $Var(V(t)) = T_2$.

Observe that the lag operators here are not partitions of those in (2.3) or (2.5), and the variances involved are not related in any simple way to $Var(\varepsilon(t))$. Let $C = Cov(U(t), V(t))$,

$$D = \begin{bmatrix} I_{p_1} & 0 \\ -C^* \Sigma_2^{-1} & I_{p_2} \end{bmatrix}, \tag{2.12}$$

$B^\dagger(L) = B(L)D^{-1}$, $V^\dagger(t) = V(t) - C^*\Sigma_2^{-1}U(t)$, and renormalize (2.11) to

$$\begin{pmatrix} X(t) \\ Y(t) \end{pmatrix} = \begin{pmatrix} B^\dagger_{11}(L) & B_{12}(L) \\ B^\dagger_{21}(L) & B_{22}(L) \end{pmatrix} \begin{pmatrix} U(t) \\ V^\dagger(t) \end{pmatrix} \tag{2.13}$$

In (2.11), $U(t)$ and $V^\dagger(t)$ are uncorrelated by construction $B_{12}(0) = 0$ but $B^\dagger_{21}(0) \neq 0$ (in general). Let $\tilde{B}(\lambda)$ denote the Fourier transform of a matrix polynomial lag operator and $f_X(\lambda)$ the spectral density of $\{X(t)\}$, (2.13) implies

$$f_X(\lambda) = \tilde{B}^\dagger_{11}(\lambda) \Sigma_2 \tilde{B}^\dagger_{11}(\lambda)^* + \tilde{B}_{12}(\lambda)(T_2 - C^*\Sigma_2^{-1}C)\tilde{B}_{12}(\lambda)^*. \tag{2.14}$$

Chapter 2. An Overview of Causal Analysis

This provides the classical spectral decomposition of variance in X, together with a further decomposition of variance into that attributed to $U(t)$ and $V^\dagger(t)$. The vector $U(t)$ has a concise interpretation, most readily seen in (2.10). It is the part of $\varepsilon(t)$ that first entered the system only through its effect on $\{X(t)\}$. Proceeding as in the construction of $F_{Y\to X}$, the measure of linear feedback

$$f_{Y\to X}(\lambda) = \log(|f_X(\lambda)|/\tilde{B}_{11}^\dagger(\lambda)\Sigma_2\tilde{B}_{11}^\dagger(\lambda)^*|). \tag{2.15}$$

is suggested. It turns out to be the case [Geweke (1982), theorem 2] that

$$\frac{1}{2\pi}\int_{-\pi}^{\pi} f_{Y\to X}(\lambda)d(\lambda) \le F_{Y\to X}, \tag{2.16}$$

but $F_{Y\to X} = \frac{1}{2\pi}\int_{-\pi}^{\pi} f_{Y\to X}(\lambda)d(\lambda)$ if and only if $B_{11}^\dagger(\lambda)$ is invertible that is, $|B_{11}^\dagger(\lambda)| \ne 0$ for all $|L| \le 1$. The latter condition is not implied by our assumptions but is nearly always satisfied by point estimates of $B_{11}^\dagger(\lambda)$.

Chapter 3

Hosoya's Causal Measures

In this chapter, we will summarize the main results of the causal measures given by Hosoya (1991, 1997), Yao and Hosoya (2000). These measures are the measure of association, the measure of one-way effect, and the measure of reciprocity. Each of the measures is defined in frequencywise as well as overall. The measure of association is equal to the sum of the others. Those measures were originally introduced in Hosoya (1991) in connection with the problem of extracting from each of a pair of processes the component process which causes the other in purely one-way or feedback free manner in view of the Granger causality. The advantage of frequency-wise decomposability enables us to see how a pair of time series interacts in frequency bands of interest in the long-run or the short-run [see also Geweke (1982, 1984)]. In such cases, the concepts of "the contribution" and "the mean" of the one-way effect for a special frequency band will be used. These measures characterize the interdependent structure of two given orthogonal processes.

A measure of the predictive contribution of the process $\{Y(t)\}$ in the one-step ahead prediction of $X(t)$ is the log-ratio

$$F_{Y \to X} = \log\Big[det\{Cov(X_{-1,\cdot}(t))\}/det\{Cov(X_{-1,-1}(t))\}\Big],$$

Geweke (1982) called it the measure of the linear feedback and gave an expression of causal measure in the time domain and in the frequency domain. But his representation is not quite satisfactory and even for some autoregressive processes. In general, if $M_{Y \to X}(\lambda)$ is a measure of the strength of causality of Y to X at frequency λ, then it should takes the value zero if there is no causality at that frequency and otherwise should be positive. If $M_{Y \to X}$ is an overall measure of the strength of causality of Y to X, then an obvious desirable property is that

$$\int_{-\pi}^{\pi} M_{Y \to X}(\lambda) d\lambda = M_{Y \to X}. \tag{3.1}$$

Even there have many attempts to define such a measure, no one can achieved the necessary equality of (3.1), or at least appear not to achieve it. Hosoya's (1991) sensitive definition of causality measure is a perfection of what everyone tried to achieve.

Remark 3.1 Though terminology "measure of feedback" was usually used in the earlier works, we prefer to use "measure of association" as will be given in the following sections. "Feedback" is something that either exists between two variables or series, thus being a symmetric relation, or the existence of feedback from (say) Y to X presupposes a predictive relationship from X to Y (which one would then characterize as feeding forward). In this usage, it more closely approximates that in much of the control theory literature, an unidirectional relationship possesses no feedback. Geweke (1982) introduced the "measure of feedback" is mainly under the consideration of identifying relationships between the new concept and older, more familiar ones. As the "measure of association" is more natural to our discussions so that we prefer to use the "measure of association".

3.1 The Measure of One-way Effect

Suppose that $\{U(t), V(t), t \in \mathcal{J}\}$ is a zero mean jointly covariance stationary process where the $U(t)$ and $V(t)$ are $p_1 \times 1$ and $p_2 \times 1$ real vectors respectively ($p = p_1 + p_2$). Suppose also that the process $\{U(t), V(t)\}$ is nondeterministic and has the $p \times p$ spectral density matrix

$$f(\lambda) = \begin{bmatrix} f_{11}(\lambda) & f_{12}(\lambda) \\ f_{21}(\lambda) & f_{22}(\lambda) \end{bmatrix}, \quad -\pi < \lambda \leq \pi,$$

where $f_{11}(\lambda)$ is the $p_1 \times p_1$ spectral density of $\{U(t)\}$, $f_{12}(\lambda)$ is the $p_1 \times p_2$ cross spectral density of $\{U(t)\}$ and $\{V(t)\}$.

3.1. The Measure of One-way Effect

Assumption 3.1 The spectral density matrix $f(\lambda)$ of the process $\{U(t), V(t)\}$ satisfies

$$\int_{-\pi}^{\pi} \log det f(\lambda) d\lambda > -\infty. \tag{3.2}$$

Under the condition (3.2), $f(\lambda)$ has a factorization such that

$$f(\lambda) = \frac{1}{2\pi} \Lambda(e^{-i\lambda}) \Lambda(e^{-i\lambda})^*, \tag{3.3}$$

where $\Lambda(e^{-i\lambda})$ is the boundary value $\lim_{\mu \to 1_-} \Lambda(\mu e^{-i\lambda})$ of a $p \times p$ matrix-valued function $\Lambda(z)$ which is analytic and has no zeros inside the unit disc $\{z : |z| < 1\}$ of the complex plane. Such a factorization is said to be a canonical factorization in the sequel. Let Σ be the covariance of the one-step ahead linear prediction error of the process $\{U(t), V(t)\}$ by its own past; then $\Lambda(0)\Lambda(0)^* = \Sigma$, and we have

$$det\{\Lambda(0)\Lambda(0)^*\} = det\Sigma = (2\pi)^p \exp\{\frac{1}{2\pi} \int_{-\pi}^{\pi} \log det f(\lambda) d\lambda\}, \tag{3.4}$$

[see Rozanov (1967) pp.71-7, for example]. The relationship (3.3) is the frequency domain version of the time-domain Wold decomposition representation

$$\begin{pmatrix} U(t) \\ V(t) \end{pmatrix} = \sum_{j=0}^{\infty} \tilde{\Lambda}(j) \varepsilon(t-j),$$

where $\{\varepsilon(t)\}$ is a white-noise process with $Var\{\varepsilon(t)\} = I_p$ and the matrices $\tilde{\Lambda}(j)$ are the real-matrix coefficients in the expansion of the analytic function $\Lambda(z)$; namely $\Lambda(z) = \sum_{j=0}^{\infty} \tilde{\Lambda}(j) z^j$.

A series $\{V(t)\}$ causes another $\{U(t)\}$ in Granger's sense if the additional information $\{V(t-j), j \in \mathcal{J}^+\}$ improves the prediction of $U(t)$, whence it would be natural to measure the strength of causality by the extent the one-step ahead prediction error of $U(t)$ is reduced by adding the information $\{V(t-j), j \in \mathcal{J}^+\}$. The one-way effect component of $V(t)$ is the component which causes $\{U(t)\}$ one-sidedly but suffers no feedback from it in Granger's sense. We can extract such component from $V(t)$ as the linear regression residual obtained by regressing $V(t)$ on $\mathcal{H}\{U(t), V(t-1)\}$, and the residual is denoted by $V_{0,-1}(t)$ (see Figure 3.1). It turns out that $\{V_{0,-1}(t)\}$ is a white noise process with covariance matrix $\Sigma_{22} - \Sigma_{21}\Sigma_{11}^{-1}\Sigma_{12}$ and that $\{V(t)\}$ does not cause $\{V_{0,-1}(t)\}$ in Granger's sense [see Hosoya (1991)]. Although we have no way of measuring directly how the

Chapter 3. Hosoya's Causal Measures

addition of the series $\{V(t)\}$ improves the one-step ahead prediction of $\{U(t)\}$, the series $\{V_{0,-1}(t)\}$ enables us to do so.

Since $\{U(t)\}$ does not cause $\{V_{0,-1}(t)\}$ and $U(t)$ is orthogonal to $V_{0,-1}(t)$, the $U(t)$ has the Sims representation

$$U(t) = \sum_{j=1}^{\infty} \tilde{\Pi}(j) V_{0,-1}(t-j) + N(t), \quad t \in \mathcal{J} \tag{3.5}$$

where the $\tilde{\Pi}(j)$ are $p_1 \times p_2$ matrices and $N(t)$ is a possibly dependent stationary process which is orthogonal to the process $\{V_{0,-1}(t)\}$. It follows from (3.5) that $f_{11}(\lambda)$ the spectral density matrix of $\{U(t)\}$ is decomposed as

$$f_{11}(\lambda) = g^{(1)}(\lambda) + g^{(2)}(\lambda) \tag{3.6}$$

where

$$g^{(1)}(\lambda) = \frac{1}{2\pi} \left(\sum_{j=0}^{\infty} \tilde{\Pi}(j) e^{-ij\lambda} \right) (\Sigma_{22} - \Sigma_{21} \Sigma_{11}^{-1} \Sigma_{12}) \left(\sum_{j=0}^{\infty} \tilde{\Pi}(j) e^{-ij\lambda} \right)^*$$

and $g^{(2)}(\lambda)$ is the spectral density matrix of the process $\{N(t)\}$. Also it follows from (3.5) that the regression residual of $U(t)$ on $\mathcal{H}\{V_{0,-1}(t-1), U(t-1)\}$ is equal to the one of $N(t)$ on $\mathcal{H}\{N(t-1)\}$ so that the determinant of that covariance matrix is provided in view of (3.4) by

$$(2\pi)^{p_1} \exp\{\frac{1}{2\pi} \int_{-\pi}^{\pi} \log \det g^{(2)}(\lambda) d\lambda\}$$

whereas the corresponding quantity of the residual by regressing $U(t)$ on $\mathcal{H}\{U(t-1)\}$ is equal to

$$(2\pi)^{p_1} \exp\{\frac{1}{2\pi} \int_{-\pi}^{\pi} \log \det f_{11}(\lambda) d\lambda\}.$$

Since for each λ by (3.6),

$$\log \det f_{11}(\lambda) \leq \log \det g^{(2)}(\lambda),$$

the quantity

$$\log\{\det f_{11}(\lambda) / \det g^{(2)}(\lambda)\}$$

and the integration over $(-\pi, \pi]$ can be regarded as measuring the frequency-wise as well as overall improvement of prediction by the use of the information

3.1. The Measure of One-way Effect

$\mathcal{H}\{V_{0,-1}(t-1)\}$ respectively, equivalently as measuring the strength of causality of $\{V_{0,-1}(t)\}$ to $\{U(t)\}$.

For the purpose of obtaining an explicit analytic expression of the prediction improvement, it is convenient to translate the above rather time-domain oriented construction in terms of frequency-domain representations. In contrast to the Wold decomposition of $\{U(t), V(t)\}$ which is a decomposition into an orthogonal sum in the time domain, $\{U(t), V(t)\}$ is known to have the spectral representation

$$U(t) = \int_{-\pi}^{\pi} e^{i\lambda t} d\tilde{U}(\lambda) \quad \text{and} \quad V(t) = \int_{-\pi}^{\pi} e^{i\lambda t} d\tilde{V}(\lambda)$$

where $\tilde{U}(\lambda)$ and $\tilde{V}(\lambda)$ are (frequency-wise orthogonal) random measures such that

$$Cov\{d\tilde{U}(\lambda), d\tilde{V}(\lambda)\} = f(\lambda);$$

namely, the processes $\{U(t)\}$ and $\{V(t)\}$ are interpreted as weighted sums of harmonic oscillations with orthogonal random weight for the respective frequency. On the other hand, the prediction error formula (3.4) implies that the one-step ahead prediction error of $U(t)$ measured in terms of the determinant of the prediction error covariance matrix is the geometric mean of the $detCov\{d\tilde{U}(\lambda)\}$ over the frequency domain $-\pi < \lambda \leq \pi$. In other words, the variability of $d\tilde{U}(\lambda)$ expresses the frequency-wise contribution to the one-step ahead prediction error of $U(t)$. In the case of the joint one-step ahead prediction of $\{U(t), V(t)\}$, a similar argument applies and the variability expressed by $detCov\{d\tilde{U}(\lambda), d\tilde{V}(\lambda)\}$ indicates the contribution of the λ-frequency oscillation to the joint prediction error of $U(t)$ and $V(t)$.

Now in view of the Granger concept of causality, the questions to be asked are how much of the prediction error reduction in $U(t)$ is attributed to the other series $\{V(s), s \leq t-1\}$ when it is added for the prediction of $U(t)$ and which portion of the variability in the pair $\{d\tilde{U}(\lambda), d\tilde{V}(\lambda)\}$, which is correlated in general, is attributable to the series $\{V(t)\}$. The pairing $\{U(t), V_{0,-1}(t)\}$ instead of the original pair $\{U(t), V(t)\}$ helps us to solve these questions. In view of its construction of $V_{0,-1}(t)$, the projection residual of $U(t)$ onto $H\{V_{0,-1}(t-1)\}$ is given by

$$N(t) = \int_{-\pi}^{\pi} e^{it\lambda}\{d\tilde{U}(\lambda) - \tilde{f}_{12}(\lambda)\tilde{f}_{22}^{-1}(\lambda)d\tilde{V}_{0,-1}(\lambda)\}, \tag{3.7}$$

Chapter 3. Hosoya's Causal Measures

where the spectral density matrix of the process $\{U(t), V_{0,-1}(t)\}$ is denoted by the p_1 to p_2 partitioned matrix

$$\tilde{f}(\lambda) = \begin{bmatrix} \tilde{f}_{11}(\lambda) & \tilde{f}_{12}(\lambda) \\ \tilde{f}_{21}(\lambda) & \tilde{f}_{22}(\lambda) \end{bmatrix}$$

and

$$\tilde{f}_{11}(\lambda) = f_{11}(\lambda), \quad \tilde{f}_{22}(\lambda) = \frac{1}{2\pi}\{\Sigma_{22} - \Sigma_{21}\Sigma_{11}^{-1}\Sigma_{12}\}.$$

Since the inverse $\Lambda(e^{-i\lambda})^{-1}$ exists a.e., and then $f(\lambda)$ does not degenerate a.e., it follows the representation of density function $\tilde{f}_{21}(\lambda)$.

Lemma 3.1. *It holds $\tilde{f}_{21}(\lambda) = \tilde{f}_{12}(\lambda)^*$, and*

$$\tilde{f}_{21}(\lambda) = \{-\Sigma_{21}\Sigma_{11}^{-1}, I_{p_2}\}\Lambda(0)\Lambda(e^{-i\lambda})^{-1}f_{\cdot 1}(\lambda) \qquad a.e.,$$

where $f_{\cdot 1}(\lambda)$ is the $p \times p_1$ matrix which consists of the first p_1 columns of $f(\lambda)$ [Hosoya (1991), pp.432-3].

The relation (3.7) [see Whittle (1963)] is nothing but the frequency-domain version of (3.5). Since the one-step ahead prediction error of $U(t)$ on the basis of $\mathcal{H}\{U(t-1), V_{0,-1}(t-1)\}$ and $V_{0,-1}(s)$ ($s \leq t-1$) is the same as that of $N(t)$ on the basis of its own past, it follows that

$$det\Sigma'_{11} = (2\pi)^{p_1} \exp\Big[\frac{1}{2\pi}\int_{-\pi}^{\pi} \log det Cov\{d\tilde{U}(\lambda) \tag{3.8}$$
$$- \tilde{f}_{12}(\lambda)\tilde{f}_{22}^{-1}(\lambda)d\tilde{V}_{0,-1}(\lambda)\}d\lambda\Big],$$

where Σ'_{11} denotes the covariance matrix of the one-step ahead prediction error of $N(t)$; whereas as for the prediction of $U(t)$ by its own past values, we have the relation

$$det\Sigma_{11} = (2\pi)^{p_1} \exp\Big[\frac{1}{2\pi}\int_{-\pi}^{\pi} \log det Cov\{d\tilde{U}(\lambda)\}d\lambda\Big]. \tag{3.9}$$

The comparison of (3.8) and (3.9) implies that the prediction improvement by the additional information of $V_{0,-1}(t)$ is given by

$$M_{V \to U} = \log\{det\Sigma_{11}/det\Sigma'_{11}\} \tag{3.10}$$

and that the frequency-wise reduction of the variability from $d\tilde{U}(\lambda)$ to $d\tilde{U}'(\lambda)$ is given by

$$M_{V \to U}(\lambda) = \log\Big[det Cov\{d\tilde{U}(\lambda)\} \tag{3.11}$$
$$/det Cov\{d\tilde{U}(\lambda) - \tilde{f}_{12}(\lambda)\tilde{f}_{22}^{-1}(\lambda)d\tilde{V}_{0,-1}(\lambda)\}\Big].$$

3.1. The Measure of One-way Effect

It turns out that $\{V(t)\}$ does not cause $\{U(t)\}$ in the Granger sense if and only if $M_{V\to U} = 0$ [see Hosoya (1991), p.432]. Consequently, in conformity with Granger's causality concept, we might call $M_{V\to U}$ the overall measure of one-way effect (OMO) from V to U and $M_{V\to U}(\lambda)$ the frequency-wise measure of one-way effect (FMO). It is obvious that $M_{V\to U}(\lambda)$ in (3.11) can also be expressed by the function of f and $\tilde{f}$, this gives

Theorm 3.1   *The one-way effect of V to U in the frequency domain and in the time domain are respectively given by*

$$M_{V\to U}(\lambda) = \log\Big[det f_{11}(\lambda)/det\{f_{11}(\lambda) - \tilde{f}_{12}(\lambda)\tilde{f}_{22}^{-1}(\lambda)\tilde{f}_{21}(\lambda)\}\Big], \tag{3.12}$$

and

$$M_{V\to U} = \frac{1}{2\pi}\int_{-\pi}^{\pi} M_{V\to U}(\lambda)d\lambda. \tag{3.13}$$

Example 3.1   Consider a bivariate process $\{u(t), v(t); t \in \mathcal{J}^+\}$ which is generated by

$$\begin{cases} u(t) = \epsilon(t) - \epsilon(t-1) + a\eta(t-1) \\ v(t) = \eta(t) + b\eta(t-1) \end{cases} \quad b \le 1$$

where $\{\epsilon(t), \eta(t)\} \sim i.i.d.N(0, I_2)$. Set

$$\Lambda(z) = \begin{pmatrix} 1-z & az \\ 0 & 1+bz \end{pmatrix}$$

Then a spectral density matrix of the process $\{u(t), v(t)\}$ can be given by

$$f(\lambda) = \frac{1}{2\pi}\Lambda(e^{-i\lambda})\Lambda(e^{-i\lambda})^*$$

In this case, $\{v_{0,-1}(t)\}$ is equivalent to $\{\eta(t)\}$. The process $\{u(t), v_{0,-1}(t)\}$ has a spectral density $\tilde{f}(\lambda)$ which can be given by

$$\tilde{f}(\lambda) = \frac{1}{2\pi}\begin{pmatrix} |1-e^{-i\lambda}|^2 + a^2 & ae^{-i\lambda} \\ ae^{i\lambda} & 1 \end{pmatrix}.$$

According to (3.12), the one-way effect causal measure of $\{v(t)\}$ to $\{u(t)\}$ is

$$M_{v\to u}(\lambda) = \log\frac{|1-e^{-i\lambda}| + a^2}{|1-e^{-i\lambda}|^2}.$$

Therefore $\{v(t)\}$ does not cause $\{u(t)\}$ is and only if $a = 0$.

Chapter 3. Hosoya's Causal Measures

There is also anther way that can give some intuitive exposition of those measures. It is known that any stationary process, such as $\{U(t)\}$, can be regarded as a sum of the sine and cosine curves of various frequencies with orthogonal random weights whose covariance at frequency λ is proportional to the spectral density matrix $f_{11}(\lambda)$. The one-step ahead prediction error of $\{U(t)\}$ is denoted as $U_{-1\cdot}(t)$ (based on the $\{U(t-j); j \in \mathcal{J}^+\}$) and has the property that the determinant of the covariance $Cov\{U_{-1\cdot}(t)\}$ is representable as the geometric mean of $det f_{11}(\lambda)$. In view of this property, $det f_{11}(\lambda)$ can be considered as a measure of the contribution of the frequency (λ) component to the total one-step ahead prediction error. $U'_{-1,-1}(t)$ denotes the residuals of the projection of $U(t)$ on to $\mathcal{H}\{U(t-1), V_{0,-1}(t-1)\}$ (see Figure 3.2 for the graphic display of the prediction error reduction). Then the overall measure of one-way effect from $V(t)$ to $U(t)$ can also be defined by

$$M_{V \to U} = \log\Big[det Cov\{U_{-1\cdot}(t)\}/det Cov\{U'_{-1,-1}(t)\}\Big],$$

where the covariance matrix of $Cov\{U_{-1\cdot}(t)\}$ and $Cov\{U'_{-1,-1}(t)\}$ have the following decomposability property in frequency domain:

$$Cov\{U_{-1,\cdot}(t)\} = (2\pi)^p \exp\Big[\frac{1}{2\pi}\int_{-\pi}^{\pi} \log det\{f_{11}(\lambda)\}d(\lambda)\Big],$$

$$Cov\{U'_{-1,-1}(t)\} = (2\pi)^p \exp\Big[\frac{1}{2\pi}\int_{-\pi}^{\pi} \log det\{f_{11}(\lambda) - \tilde{f}_{12}(\lambda)\tilde{f}_{22}^{-1}(\lambda)\tilde{f}_{21}(\lambda)\}d(\lambda)\Big].$$

The one-way effect $M_{U \to V}$ can be defined similarly.

3.2 Causal Measures for Non-stationary Processes

We will first summarize a probability-theoretic framework which extended all the causal measures presented by Hosoya (1991) to a wide class of nonstationary processes [Hosoya (1997)]. At the end of this section, some concepts related to the analysis of long-run and short-run causality are shown [see Yao and Hosoya (2000)]. It can be seen that the key to extending the above results to some nonstationary processes is to provide a device to bridge the gap between stationary and nonstationary processes.

3.2. Causal Measures for Non-stationary Processes

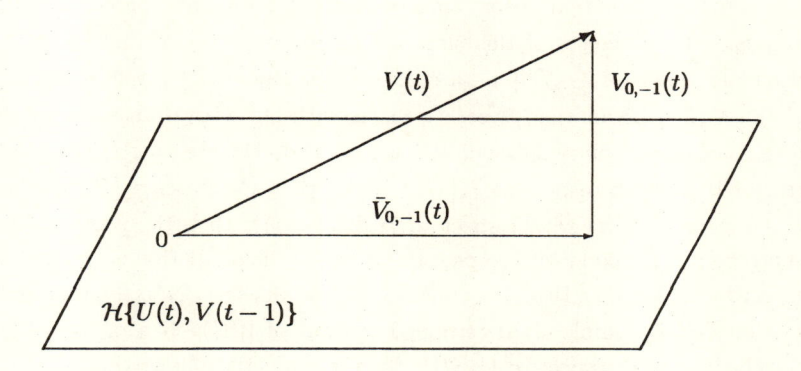

Figure 3.1 The One-way Effect Process $\{V_{0,-1}(t)\}$

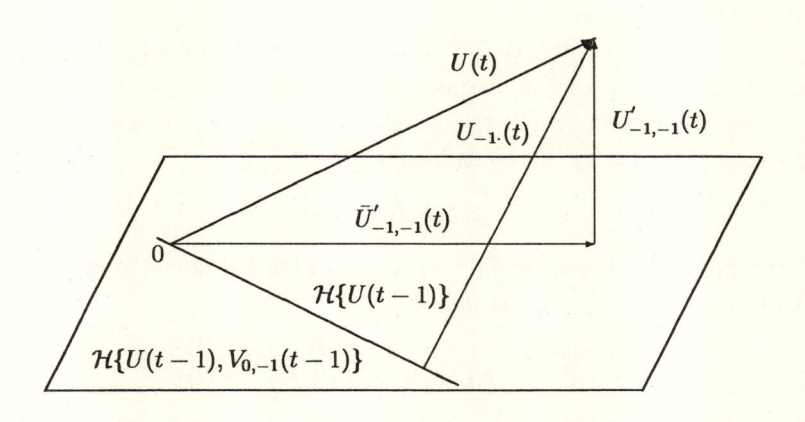

Figure 3.2 Comparison of the Prediction Errors $U'_{-1,-1}(t)$ and $U_{-1\cdot}(t)$

Chapter 3. Hosoya's Causal Measures

Reproducible processes: There is a class of possibly nonstationary processes to which the prediction theory of second-order stationary processes naturally extends. The processes of this class are termed reproducible processes. To be formal, let $\{W(t), t \in \mathcal{J}^+\}$ be a second-order stationary p-vector process and $\{Z(t), t \in \mathcal{J}^+\}$ be another p-vector process with finite covariance matrix defined on the same probability space as $W(t)$ is defined. Denote by $\varepsilon(t)$ the prediction error of $W(t)$ with respect to $\mathcal{H}\{W(t-1)\}$, then the process $\{Z(t)\}$ is said to be the error of $W(t)$ with respect to $\mathcal{H}\{W(t-1)\}$, then the process $\{Z(t)\}$ is said to be reproducible with respect to $\{W(t)\}$ if the prediction error of $Z(t)$ with respect to $\mathcal{H}\{Z(t-1), W(0)\}$ is equal to $\varepsilon(t)$ for all $t \geq 1$. Namely, the prediction error of $Z(t)$ is completely determined by that of $W(t)$. If a process $\{Z(t)\}$ is reproducible with respect to $\{W(t)\}$, then it evidently follows that

$$\mathcal{H}\{Z(t), W(0)\} = \mathcal{H}\{W(t-1)\}. \tag{3.14}$$

There are two cases of reproducible nonstationary processes which are important in application to econometric analyses. One is a class of second-order time-dependent linear processes and the other is nonstationary autoregressive processes with dependent shocks.

Example 3.2 Let $A(L, t) = \sum_{j=0}^{s} A(j, t) L^j$ be a finite-order time-dependent linear filter, $A(j, t)$ is $p \times p$ matrices and $A(0, t) = I_p$ for all t. Given a second-order stationary process $\{W(t)\}$, a class of second-order time-dependent linear processes $\{Z(t), t \geq 1\}$ can be represented by

$$A(L, t) Z(t) = W(t).$$

If we suppose that the linear filter $A(L, t)$ has a block diagonal form, then $Z(t) = (X(t)^*, Y(t)^*)^*$ has the representation

$$\begin{pmatrix} A_{11}(L, t) & 0 \\ 0 & A_{22}(L, t) \end{pmatrix} \begin{pmatrix} X(t) \\ Y(t) \end{pmatrix} = \begin{pmatrix} U(t) \\ V(t) \end{pmatrix},$$

where $A_{jj}(L, t)$ is a $p_j \times p_j$ matrix, $j = 1, 2$. It is clear that the later is a nonstationary autoregressive processes with dependent shocks. Both of the two processes are seen to be reproducible with respect to $\{W(t)\}$.

The Granger causality is defined for a pair of reproducible processes as follows. Suppose that the processes $\{X(t)\}$ and $\{Y(t)\}$ are reproducible with respect to

3.2. Causal Measures for Non-stationary Processes

$\{U(t)\}$ and $\{V(t)\}$ respectively. If the prediction error of $X(t)$ with respect to $\mathcal{H}\{U(t-1), V(t-1)\}$ is equal to the one with respect to $\mathcal{H}\{U(t-1)\}$, then $\{Y(t)\}$ is said not to cause $\{X(t)\}$. In the following discussions we will show that if $\{Y(t)\}$ does not cause $\{X(t)\}$ if and only if $\{V(t)\}$ does not cause $\{U(t)\}$. This illustrates that the situation where the causal relation in Granger's sense between two nonstationary processes $\{X(t)\}$ and $\{Y(t)\}$ is determined by the corresponding relation between the generating processes $\{U(t)\}$ and $\{V(t)\}$. The question then is whether frequency-domain relations of second-order stationary processes are extendable to reproducible nonstationary processes.

In order to extend causal analysis of nondeterministic stationary time-series to nonstationary processes, consider the possibly nonstationary process $\{X(t), Y(t)\}$ which is generated by

$$A(L) \begin{bmatrix} X(t) \\ Y(t) \end{bmatrix} = \begin{bmatrix} U(t) \\ V(t) \end{bmatrix}, \quad (t \in \mathcal{J}^+) \tag{3.15}$$

where $\{U(t), V(t), t \in \mathcal{J}^+\}$ is the stationary process defined as before, and the lag polynomial matrix $A(L)$ is a $p \times p$ matrix such that

$$A(L) = \begin{bmatrix} A_{11}(L) & 0 \\ 0 & A_{22}(L) \end{bmatrix} = \begin{bmatrix} \sum_{j=0}^{l} A_{11,j} L^j & 0 \\ 0 & \sum_{j=0}^{l} A_{22,j} L^j \end{bmatrix}$$

for some positive l where $A_{11,0} = I_{p_1}$ and $A_{22,0} = I_{p_2}$. Suppose in the sequel that $X(t)$ and $Y(t)$ for $t \leq 0$ are random vectors which belong to $\mathcal{H}\{U(t), t \leq 0\}$ and $\mathcal{H}\{V(t), t \leq 0\}$ respectively. The process given by (3.15) has the characteristic that the one-step ahead prediction and the residual of $X(t)$ based on $\mathcal{H}\{X(t-1)\} \oplus \mathcal{H}\{U(0)\}$ and $Y(t), t \geq 1$, based on $\mathcal{H}\{Y(t-1)\} \oplus \mathcal{H}\{V(0)\}$ are the same as those of $U(t)$ and $V(t)$ based on $\mathcal{H}\{U(t-1)\}$ and $\mathcal{H}\{V(t-1)\}$ respectively. Similarly, the joint prediction of $\{X(t), Y(t)\}$ based on $\mathcal{H}\{X(t-1), Y(t-1)\} \oplus \mathcal{H}\{U(0), V(0)\}$ is the same as the prediction of $\{U(t), V(t)\}$ based on $\mathcal{H}\{U(t-1), V(t-1)\}$. Therefore the predictional properties of the process $\{X(t), Y(t)\}$ for $t \geq 1$ are entirely determined by those of the generating stationary process $\{U(t), V(t)\}$. Since the one-way effect structure of $\{X(t), Y(t)\}$ is determined only by its predictional properties, it follows that it is given by the corresponding structure of $\{U(t), V(t)\}$. Namely, the *OMO* and the *FMO* between $\{X(t)\}$ and $\{Y(t)\}$ can be equated with the corresponding measures between the generating

Chapter 3. Hosoya's Causal Measures

processes $\{U(t)\}$ and $\{V(t)\}$. This is the basic idea for the extension of the definitions of OMO and FMO to nonstationary processes.

It should be noted, however, that the relationship (3.15) is not very well defined. Suppose that $B(L)$ is another block diagonal matrix given by

$$B(L) = \begin{bmatrix} B_{11}(L) & 0 \\ 0 & B_{22}(L) \end{bmatrix},$$

where $B_{11}(L)$ and $B_{22}(L)$ are lag polynomials such that $B_{11,0} = I_{p_1}$ and $B_{22,0} = I_{p_2}$. The left multiplication of $B(L)$ to each member of the equation (3.15) produces a different representation of the process $\{X(t), Y(t)\}$. Unless $B(L) = I_p$, the resulting generating process $\{B_{11}(L)U(t), B_{22}(L)V(t)\}$ might possibly possess a spectral structure different from that of $\{U(t), V(t)\}$. In order to retain invariance of the one-way effect structure under such a multiplication, a certain restriction on the generating mechanism (3.15) is required. Let $f_{11}(\lambda) = \Lambda^{(1)}(e^{-i\lambda})\Lambda^{(1)}(e^{-i\lambda})^*$ and $f_{22}(\lambda) = \Lambda^{(2)}(e^{-i\lambda})\Lambda^{(2)}(e^{-i\lambda})^*$ be canonical factorizations respectively.

Assumption 3.2 The process (3.15) satisfies either
(i) the zeroes of $det A_{11}(z)$ and $det A_{22}(z)$ are all on or outside of the unit disc; or
(ii) There are no common zeroes between $det A_{11}(z)$ and $det\Lambda^{(1)}(z)$ and between $det A_{22}(z)$ and $det\Lambda^{(2)}(z)$.

Remark 3.2 The assumption (i) is convenient to deal with such unit-root type processes as cointegration processes, where nonstationary is generated by a unit-root common trend. Since, then, $B(L)$ is limited to such lag polynomials for which the zeroes of $det B_{11}(z)$ and $det B_{22}(z)$ are on or outside the unit disc, the one-way effect structure between $B_{11}(L)U(t)$ and $B_{22}(L)V(t)$ remains invariant, thanks to the relations that

$$\int_{-\pi}^{\pi} \log det B_{ii}(e^{-i\lambda})B_{ii}(e^{-i\lambda})^* d\lambda = 0, \quad i = 1, 2,$$

which follows from a more basic relationship in calculus that for real r such that $|r| \leq 1$,

$$\int_{-\pi}^{\pi} \log |1 - 2r\cos\lambda + r^2| d\lambda = 0.$$

3.2. Causal Measures for Non-stationary Processes

If some zeroes of $det A(z)$ is allowed to be inside the unit circle so that the process has a greater-than-unity root, this invariance property does not hold any longer. To deal with such a circumstance, the assumption (ii) would be useful in order to identify the generating process.

The preceding consideration leads us to the following extended definitions of the Granger non-causality and of the measures OMO and FMO. Suppose the process $\{X(t), Y(t), t \in \mathcal{J}^+\}$ generated by (3.15) satisfies Assumption 3.2.

Definition 3.1 $\{Y(t)\}$ is said not to cause $\{X(t)\}$ if and only if the prediction error covariance matrices of $X(t)$ based on $\mathcal{H}\{U(s), V(s), s \leq t-1\}$ and based on $\mathcal{H}\{U(s), s \leq t-1\}$ are identical.

Note that we have

$$\mathcal{H}\{U(t-1), V(t-1)\} = \mathcal{H}\{X(t-1), Y(t-1); U(0), V(0)\}$$

and

$$\mathcal{H}\{U(t-1)\} = \mathcal{H}\{X(t-1); U(0)\},$$

then the next theorem is an obobvious consequence of this extended definition

Theorem 3.2 $\{Y(t)\}$ does not cause $\{X(t)\}$ if and only if $\{V(t)\}$ does not cause $\{U(t)\}$.

Following this theorem we can have next definition.

Definition 3.2 The one-way effect causal measure of Y to X at frequency λ, $M_{Y \to X}(\lambda)$ and the one-way effect overall measure $M_{Y \to X}$ are defined by

$$M_{Y \to X}(\lambda) \equiv M_{V \to U}(\lambda)$$

and

$$M_{Y \to X} \equiv M_{V \to U}$$

respectively.

The Long-run and Short-run Relations

A variety of causal measures can be derived on the basis of the OMO and the FMO between $\{X(t)\}$ and $\{Y(t)\}$ for the purposes of the long-run or short-run characterization of causal relation. In case $M_{Y \to X} \neq 0$, for example, the

35

contribution of long-run effect in the overall one-way effect is given by

$$D_{Y \to X}(\varepsilon|\theta, \psi) = \frac{1}{\pi} \int_0^\varepsilon M_{Y \to X}(\lambda|\theta, \psi) d\lambda / M_{Y \to X}, \qquad (3.16)$$

for a certain low frequency band $(0, \varepsilon]$, or one might be rather interested in the contribution of the local one-way effect for a given period band $[t_1, t_2] (2 \leq t_1 < t_2)$

$$D_{Y \to X}(t_1, t_2|\theta, \psi) = \frac{1}{\pi} \int_{2\pi/t_2}^{2\pi/t_1} M_{Y \to X}(\lambda|\theta, \psi) d\lambda / M_{Y \to X}, \qquad (3.17)$$

where period implies the time-length of a cycle and we used the relation $T = 2\pi/\lambda$ between time period T and frequency λ ($\lambda > 0$).

The long-run effect may be measured in another way, by the mean FMO which is given by

$$\bar{D}_{Y \to X}(\varepsilon|\theta, \psi) = \frac{1}{\varepsilon} \int_0^\varepsilon M_{Y \to X}(\lambda|\theta, \psi) d\lambda, \qquad (3.18)$$

where ε is a small positive number, or its limit as $\varepsilon \to 0$. The local one-way effect, or the one-way effect in a period band $[t_1, t_2]$ may be defined by

$$\bar{D}_{Y \to X}(t_1, t_2|\theta, \psi) = \frac{t_1 t_2}{2\pi(t_2 - t_1)} \int_{2\pi/t_2}^{2\pi/t_1} M_{Y \to X}(\lambda|\theta, \psi) d\lambda. \qquad (3.19)$$

Note that the one-way effect causal definitions, $D_{Y \to X}(\varepsilon|\theta, \psi)$, $D_{Y \to X}(t_1, t_2|\theta, \psi)$, $\bar{D}_{Y \to X}(\varepsilon|\theta, \psi)$ and $\bar{D}_{Y \to X}(t_1, t_2|\theta, \psi)$ are smooth functions of (θ, ψ). In any case, in order to interpret those quantities on the basis of empirical data, statistical test is needed.

Remark 3.3 The definitions of the one-way effect causal measures expressed in (3.16) to (3.19) used the property of $M_{Y \to X}(\lambda) = M_{Y \to X}(-\lambda)$. In fact we also have

$$M_{Y \to X} = \frac{1}{\pi} \int_0^\pi M_{Y \to X}(\lambda) d\lambda. \qquad (3.20)$$

3.3 The Measures of Association and Reciprocity

This section shows the measures of association and of reciprocity in addition to the measure of one-way effect discussed in Section 3.1 so as to characterize the

3.3. The Measures of Association and Reciprocity

interdependency of the processes $\{U(t)\}$ and $\{V(t)\}$, and also shows that the measure of association is decomposed into the measure of one-way effect and the measure of reciprocity. The relationships of some other causal measures are also showed in this section.

In view of the notations introduced as above, based on the one-way effect processes $\{U_{-1,0}(t)\}$ and $\{V_{0,-1}(t)\}$, the processes $\{U(t)\}$ and $\{V(t)\}$ can be decomposed into

$$U(t) = U'_{\cdot,\infty}(t) + \bar{U}'_{\cdot,\infty}(t),$$
$$V(t) = V'_{\infty,\cdot}(t) + \bar{V}'_{\infty,\cdot}(t),$$

where $\bar{U}'_{\cdot,\infty}(t)$ and $U'_{\cdot,\infty}(t)$ are the projection of $U(t)$ onto $\mathcal{H}\{V_{0,-1}(\infty)\}$ and its residual, $\bar{V}'_{\infty,\cdot}(t)$ and $V'_{\infty,\cdot}(t)$ are the projection of $V(t)$ onto $\mathcal{H}\{U_{-1,0}(\infty)\}$ and its residual. Set a joint spectral density of $\{U'_{\cdot,\infty}(t), V'_{\infty,\cdot}(t)\}$ as

$$f'(\lambda) = \begin{pmatrix} f'_{11}(\lambda) & f'_{12}(\lambda) \\ f'_{21}(\lambda) & f'_{22}(\lambda) \end{pmatrix}. \tag{3.21}$$

Explicit evaluation of the measures of association and reciprocity at each frequency λ requires a representation of $f'(\lambda)$.

Denote $\tilde{g}_{12}(\lambda) = (I_{p_1}, -\Sigma_{12}\Sigma_{22}^{-1})\Lambda(0)\Lambda(e^{-i\lambda})^{-1}f_{\cdot 2}^*(\lambda)$ and $\tilde{g}_{21}(\lambda) = \tilde{g}_{12}^*(\lambda)$, where $f_{\cdot 2}(\lambda)$ is the $p \times p_2$ matrix which consists of the last p_2 columns of $f(\lambda)$. In view of the discussion in section 3.1, we can get the following corollary.

Corollary 3.2 *The spectral density matrix of* $\{U'_{\cdot,\infty}(t)\}$ *can be given by*

$$f'_{11}(\lambda) = f_{11}(\lambda) - \tilde{f}_{12}(\lambda)\tilde{f}_{22}^{-1}\tilde{f}_{21}(\lambda),$$

and the spectral density matrix of $\{V'_{\infty,\cdot}(t)\}$ *can be given by*

$$f'_{22}(\lambda) = f_{22}(\lambda) - \tilde{g}_{21}(\lambda)\tilde{f}_{11}^{-1}\tilde{g}_{12}(\lambda).$$

$f'_{21}(\lambda) = f'_{12}(\lambda)^*$, *and* $f'_{12}(\lambda)$ *is given as,*

$$\begin{aligned} f'_{12}(\lambda) &= f_{12}(\lambda) - 2\pi\tilde{h}(\lambda)\tilde{\Sigma}_{11}^{-1}\tilde{g}_{12}(\lambda) - 2\pi\tilde{f}_{12}(\lambda)\tilde{\Sigma}_{22}^{-1}\tilde{k}(\lambda) \\ &\quad + 2\pi\tilde{f}_{12}(\lambda)\tilde{\Sigma}_{22}^{-1}(\Sigma_{21}\Sigma_{11} - \Sigma_{21}\Sigma_{11}^{-1}\Sigma_{12}\Sigma_{22}^{-1})\tilde{\Sigma}_{11}^{-1}\tilde{g}_{12}(\lambda) \qquad a.e., \end{aligned}$$

where

$$\tilde{h}(\lambda) = f_{\cdot 1}^*(\lambda)(\Lambda(e^{-i\lambda})^*)^{-1}\Lambda(0)^*(-\Sigma_{12}\Sigma_{22}^{-1}, I_{p_2})^*,$$

Chapter 3. Hosoya's Causal Measures

$$\tilde{k}(\lambda) = (I_{p_1}, -\Sigma_{12}\Sigma_{22}^{-1})\Lambda(0)\Lambda(e^{-i\lambda})^{-1}f_{\cdot 2}(\lambda).$$

Now we can get the next theorem.

Theorem 3.3 *Define $M_{U,V}(\lambda)$ the measure of association at frequency λ of the processes $\{U(t)\}$ and $\{V(t)\}$ by*

$$M_{U,V}(\lambda) = \log[det f_{11}(\lambda) det f_{22}(\lambda)/det f'(\lambda)], \qquad (3.22)$$

and define $M_{U\cdot V}(\lambda)$ the measure of reciprocity at frequency λ by

$$M_{U\cdot V}(\lambda) = \log[det f'_{11}(\lambda) det f'_{22}(\lambda)/det f'(\lambda)]. \qquad (3.23)$$

It evidently follows from non-negative definiteness of $f_{11}(\lambda) - f'_{11}(\lambda)$ and $f_{22}(\lambda) - f'_{22}(\lambda)$ that $M_{U,V}(\lambda) \geq 0$. It is clear that $M_{U\cdot V}(\lambda) \geq 0$. Furthermore the corresponding overall measures $M_{U,V}$ and $M_{U\cdot V}$ can be defined respectively by

$$M_{U,V} = \frac{1}{2\pi}\int_{-\pi}^{\pi} M_{U,V}(\lambda)d\lambda,$$

$$M_{U\cdot V} = \frac{1}{2\pi}\int_{-\pi}^{\pi} M_{U\cdot V}(\lambda)d\lambda.$$

Between those measures and the measures of one-way effect, there exists the following relationship.

$$M_{U,V}(\lambda) = M_{U\to V}(\lambda) + M_{U\cdot V}(\lambda) + M_{V\to U}(\lambda) \quad a.e., \qquad (3.24)$$

and in particular

$$M_{U,V} = M_{U\to V} + M_{U\cdot V} + M_{V\to U}. \qquad (3.25)$$

As far as the overall measures of association, one-way effect and reciprocity are concerned, they are defined based only on the one-step ahead prediction error of the processes $\mathcal{H}\{U(t), V(t)\}, \mathcal{H}\{U'_{\cdot,\infty}(t), V'_{\infty,\cdot}(t)\}$ or of their component processes. And also the processes $\{U_{-1,0}(t)\}$ and $\{V_{0,-1}(t)\}$ are defined by means of the projection. Therefore in order to work only with these concepts, the assumption of stationary can be dispensed with. In particular, the decomposition

3.3. The Measures of Association and Reciprocity

$M_{V,U} = M_{U \to V} + M_{U \cdot V} + M_{V \to U}$ is still valid for non-stationary second-order processes, and also valid for the proposition that the log-ratio of $detCov\{U_{-1,\cdot}(t)\}$ to $detCov\{U'_{-1,-1}(t)\}$, and it is equal to the log-ratio of the determinants of the one-step ahead prediction errors of $\{U(t)\}$ and $\{U'_{\cdot,\infty}(t)\}$.

As a measure characterizing the interdependency, Gel'fand and Yaglom (1959) introduced the measure of information $\tilde{M}_{U,V}$ which is defined as

$$\begin{aligned}\tilde{M}_{U,V}(\lambda) &= \log[detCov\{U_{-1,\cdot}(t)\}det\{V_{\cdot,-1}(t)\} \\ &\quad /detCov\{U_{-1,-1}(t), V_{-1,-1}(t)\}] \\ &= \log[det(f_{11}(\lambda)det(f_{22}(\lambda)/detf(\lambda)]. \end{aligned} \quad (3.26)$$

Geweke called $\tilde{M}_{U \cdot V} = \log[det\Sigma_{11} det\Sigma_{22}/det\Sigma]$ the measure of instantaneous feedback. It is easy to get this expression from (2.8). The measures of association and reciprocity coincide with those measures under certain conditions. If $\mathcal{H}\{U'_{\cdot,\infty}(t), V'_{\infty,\cdot}(t)\} = \mathcal{H}\{U(t), V(t)\}$, then

$$M_{U,V} = \tilde{M}_{U,V}.$$

If $\mathcal{H}\{U'_{\cdot,\infty}(t) = \mathcal{H}\{U_{-1,-1}(t)\}$ and $V'_{\infty,\cdot}(t)\} = \mathcal{H}\{V_{-1,-1}(t)\}$, then

$$M_{U,V} = \tilde{M}_{U,V},$$

$$M_{U \cdot V} = \tilde{M}_{U \cdot V}.$$

In general the measure of association $M_{U,V}$ is not equal to the Gel'fand-Yaglom (1959) measure $\tilde{M}_{U,V}$. Hosoya (1991) also gives an example where $M_{U,V} \neq \tilde{M}_{U,V}$.

In a study of linear feedback relationships in the frequency domain, Akaike (1968) introduced the concept of RPC (relative power contribution), by means of which he measured the frequency-wise contribution of a component noise process to an observation series in a multivariate autoregressive process [see Pierce (1979) for other proposals of measurement of interdependency]. Dealing with a somewhat different question, his measure in itself does not seem to be suited to the direct measurement of the effect of one process on the other in the frequency domain. However, Akaike (1968)'s notion of RPC can be used in an extended form for the purpose of the representation of $M_{V \to U}(\lambda)$. Let $g_{11}(\lambda)$ be a spectral density of the process $\{U'_{-1,-1}(t)\}$, namely

$$g_{11}(\lambda) = f_{11}(\lambda) - f'_{11}(\lambda) \quad \text{a.e.,}$$

Chapter 3. Hosoya's Causal Measures

and let $r_1(\lambda), \cdots, r_p(\lambda)$ be the eigenvalues of the matrix $g_{11}(\lambda) f_{11}(\lambda)^{-1}$ such that $r_1(\lambda) \geq \cdots \geq r_p(\lambda)$. It is easy to see that the $r_j(\lambda)$'s are all real, $r_1(\lambda) \leq 1$ and $r_p(\lambda) \geq 0$ a.e.. Define $RPC_{V \to U}(\lambda)$ by the diagonal matrix with $r_j(\lambda)$ in the (j,j) and call it the relative power one-way contribution of $\{V(t)\}$ to $\{U(t)\}$. Since

$$M_{V \to U}(\lambda) = \log[det(f_{11}(\lambda)/det(f'_{11}(\lambda)],$$

it follows that

$$M_{V \to U}(\lambda) = \log det[I_p - RPC_{V \to U}(\lambda)].$$

Chapter 4

Cointegration and Statistical Tests

The recent surge of interest in cointegration analysis has been of both a theoretical and an applied nature, and the diffusion of cointegration techniques has been very rapid. An important factor contributing to this diffusion is that cointegration provided a formal link between the use of error-correction models and vector autoregressive models of dynamic economic relationships. The possibility of interpreting cointegration vectors as economic long-run relations is the main reason that the VAR model has been widely used in the empirical analysis of economic data. Cointegration analysis is now a standard tool for applied econometricians. A commonly used procedure is to test the rank of a long-run matrix using the ML procedure. An empirical exercise should never just test for cointegration but, for extra gain in interpretation, should always be followed by estimation of a full error-correction model.

4.1 Integration and Cointegration

Many time series are not stationary, and the type of non-stationary time series that can be removed by differencing are often considered. The definition of cointegration is related to the concept of integration. A linear process is defined by

$$U(t) = \sum_{i=0}^{\infty} c_i \varepsilon(t-i), \ t \in T^+,$$

Chapter 4. Cointegration and Statistical Tests

where $\varepsilon(t)$ is white noise, $\sum_{i=0}^{\infty}|c_i| < \infty$ and the roots of polynomial equation $c(z) = \sum_{i=0}^{\infty} c_i z^i = 0$ are out side unit circle. The linear process $U(t) = \sum_{i=0}^{\infty} c_i \varepsilon(t-i)$, $t \in \mathcal{T}^+$ is called integrated of order zero ($I(0)$) if $\sum_{i=0}^{\infty} c_i \varepsilon(t-i) \neq 0$, and it is usually denoted by

$$U(t) \sim I(0).$$

It is clear that white noise process $\{\varepsilon(t)\}$ is integrated of order 0. In general, for a positive integer d, a nonstationary stochastic process $\{X(t)\}$ is called integrated of order d if

$$\Delta^d(X(t) - E(X(t))) \sim I(0),$$

where $E(X(t))$ is the expectation of the process $\{X(t)\}$. We can see for any constant μ, if $X(t) \sim I(d)$, then $\mu + X(t) \sim I(d)$. Note that the concept of $I(0)$ is defined without allowing deterministic terms like a mean or a trend, and also that there are no restrictions on the levels of an integrated process, only the difference. In the following studies we mainly discuss the processes of $I(0)$ and $I(1)$.

Based on the concepts of integration, there comes the definition of cointegration. Let p-dimensional process $\{X(t)\}$ be integrated of order 1; we call $\{X(t)\}$ cointegrated with non-zero cointegrating p-dimensional vector b if $b^* X(t)$ is integrated of order 0, i.e., $b^* X(t)$ can be made stationary by a suitable choice of its initial distribution. The cointegration rank r is the number of linearly independent cointegrating vectors $b_1, \cdots, b_r$, and the space spanned by the cointegrating relations is the cointegrating space. For the $p \times r$ matrix $\beta = (b_1, \cdots, b_r)$ (the long-run equilibrium relationships, $rank \beta = r$), the r-dimensional vector $\beta^* X(t)$ is stationary, i.e., $\beta^* X(t) \sim I(0)$. Here we used the concept of the integrated r-dimensional process. A r-dimensional process $Y(t) = (y_1(t), \cdots, y_r(t))^*$ is integrated of order d means $y_i \sim I(d_i)$, $i = 1, \cdots, r$, and $d = \max\{d_i; i = 1, \cdots, r\}$.

Several methods to estimate cointegrating vectors have been proposed in the literature since Granger (1983) introduced the idea of cointegration. Chronologically they are: ordinary least squares (OLS) by Engle and Granger (1987), nonlinear least squares (NLS) by Stock (1987), principal components by Stock and Watson (1988), canonical correlations by Bossaerts (1988), maximum likelihood in a fully specified error correction model (MLECM) by Johansen (1988).

4.1. Integration and Cointegration

The asymptotic distribution of the Gaussian MLE in a vector error correction model was also derived independently [to Johansen (1988)] by Ahn and Reinsel (1990). Engle and Granger (1987) is an seminal paper on cointegration. Stock and Watson (1988) is a useful overview. As for the other methods to estimate cointegrating vectors, see instrumental variables by Hansen and Phillips (1990), and spectral regression by Phillips (1990), three-step estimator by Engle and Yoo (1989) and the other a single-equation error correction model with leads and lags proposed by Phillips and Loretan (1991), Saikkonen (1991). All of these estimators are asymptotically equivalent to MLECM.

Gonzalo (1994) compared the first five representative methods for estimating cointegrating vectors. It is pointed that although all of them are superconsistent, an empirical example shows that the estimates can vary significantly. The paper examines the asymptotic distribution of the estimators resulting from these methods, and shows that MLECM (Johansen's approach) has clearly better properties than the other estimators. Although the above properties are based on asymptotic theory, the paper shows, via a Monte Carlo study, that this conclusion is still valid for finite samples. Since the estimators resulting from the above methods are superconsistent (the rate of convergence is T instead of $T^{1/2}$), it is assumed that there should not be a big difference among their estimates with real data if the number of observations is not too small. This is true even when the errors are non-Gaussian or when the dynamics are unknown. The estimates of the cointegrated vector may vary significantly depending on the method which was used, and also that in the methods based on dynamic regressions we get different estimates depending on the number of lags. We usually overparameterize by including additional lags in the ECM.

Concerning the general investigation of long-run and short-run structures, Johansen and Juselius (1994) have pointed out that when the empirical model is identified with data that are nonstationary in levels the identification of the long-run structure, i.e., the identification of the cointegration, as well as the identification of the short-run structure, i.e., the equations should be identified. The identification of the equations and the cointegration relations is achieved by linear restrictions on the parameters, and a criterion for a statistical model to be identified is given. They also defined the empirical identification of an estimated

Chapter 4. Cointegration and Statistical Tests

structure and illustrated the concepts with an empirical analysis of the ISLM model using Australian monetary data.

Bewley and Orden (1994) developed a system approach and compared the canonical estimators of Box-Tiao (1977) and Johansen (1988). Two variants of the Box-Tiao canonical estimator were developed, and associated tests for the number of cointegrating vectors were introduced. A simulation study indicates that, while both Box-Tiao estimators have empirical distributions with fatter tails than normal, there is evidence that the incidence of extreme values is even greater with Johansen's ML procedure. McAleer, Mckenzie and Pesaran (1994) reviewed and extended cointegration analysis with respect to direct tests of some of the implications of the rational expectations hypothesis in the presence of stationary and non-stationary variables. Alternative linear and non-linear methods for converting qualitative survey responses into quantitative expectations series are examined for use in the orthogonality test. The testing of orthogonality and the issue of generated regressors for models estimated by two-step methods are re-evaluated when the variable to be explained is stationary.

The method we are looking for should have the following characteristics:

1. Incorporate all prior knowledge about the presence of unit roots; this eliminates the median bias, the nonsymmetry, part of the nuisance parameter dependencies, and increases efficiency.

2. Full system estimation; this eliminates the simultaneous equation bias and increases efficiency.

3. Flexible enough to capture the dynamics of the system.

Of the five methods (OLS, NLS, MLECM, principal components, and canonical correlations) only the MLECM satisfies these requirements. As it is shown in Phillips (1991) and Gonzalo (1994), this approach ensures that coefficient estimates are symmetrically distributed and median unbiased, and that hypothesis tests may be conducted by using standard asymptotic χ^2 tests. None of the other methods analyzed offer all of these properties.

The theory developed in the above mentioned studies is valid for first-order nonstationary processes, but empirical experience with the analysis of nominal variables pointed to the importance of allowing for second-order nonstationarity. Johansen (1992) described the mathematical treatment for I(2) processes, giving a brief survey of the I(2) model and the properties of the process and suggesting a two stage procedure whereby the statistical analysis of the I(2) model can be performed by repeated application of reduced-rank analysis. Since a detailed description of the analysis of the likelihood function would be rather tedious, the following sections will mainly focus the technical details of the MLECM in levels of the general VAR model for first-order nonstationary time series. These results will be used in Chapters 5 and 6.

4.2 VAR Model and Error Correction Form

The VAR model is a simple and very useful econometric model for analyzing the stochastic variation of economic time series. We will first discuss the general VAR model for a p-dimensional vector process with Gaussian errors given by

$$Z(t) = \sum_{i=1}^{a-1} \Pi_i Z(t-i) + \mu + \Phi P(t) + \varepsilon(t), \qquad (4.1)$$

where $\{\varepsilon(t)\}$ is Gaussian white noise process with mean 0 and non-degenerate covariance matrix Σ, d-dimensional deterministic terms $P(t)$ can be a linear term, seasonal dummies or other deterministic variables [see the following (5.2)]; the initial values $Z(-a+1), \cdots, Z(0)$ are kept fixed, μ is the intercept of p-vector. For quarterly observations of $\{Z(t)\}$ and $P(t)$ the centered seasonal dummies, model (4.1) gives Tp observations and $p + 3p + ap^2 + p(p+1)/2$ parameters. The properties of $Z(t)$ depend on the stochastic properties of $\varepsilon(t)$, the choice of the parameters and the initial values of the process.

Using difference operator Δ, it is convenient to rewrite model (4.1) as a first difference form

$$\Delta Z(t) = \Pi Z(t-1) + \sum_{i=1}^{a-1} \Gamma_i \Delta Z(t-i) + \mu + \Phi P(t) + \varepsilon(t), \qquad (4.2)$$

where

$$\Pi = -I + \sum_{i=1}^{a} \Pi_i \quad \text{and} \quad \Gamma_i = -\sum_{j=i+1}^{a} \Pi_j, \quad i = 1, \cdots, a-1.$$

Chapter 4. Cointegration and Statistical Tests

By the transformation of

$$\Pi_1 = I + \Gamma_a + \Pi, \qquad \Pi_a = -\Gamma_{a-1},$$

$$\Pi_j = \Gamma_j - \Gamma_{j-1} \quad (j = 2, \cdots, a-1),$$

model (4.1) can also be derived from model (4.2).

The dynamic features of the process are conveniently described at the root of the characteristic polynomial

$$A(z) = (1-z)I_p - \Pi z - \sum_{i=1}^{a-1}(1-z)\Pi_i z^i.$$

The parameters of the model should be chosen such that the roots are on or outside the unit disc. Parameterization is convenient since the hypothesis of cointegration now becomes a hypothesis on matrix Π alone, leaving the other parameters unrestricted. In an empirical analysis, the assumption that the roots should be on or outside the unit circle is often left out, since it is difficult to handle the condition analytically. Fortunately, as it happens often, the estimates of the roots have the proper position; however, if they do not, it is important to obtain this information. At this point, it is necessary to find out whether the coefficient matrix Π contains information about long-run relationships between the variables in the data vector. There are three possible cases:

1. Rank $\Pi = p$, i.e. the matrix Π has full rank, indicating that the vector process is stationary.

2. Rank $\Pi = 0$, i.e. the matrix Π is the null matrix and (4.2) corresponds to a difference vector time series model.

3. Rank $\Pi = r < p$ implying that there are $p \times r$ matrices α and β such that $\Pi = \alpha\beta^*$.

The cointegration vector β have the property that $\beta^* Z(t)$ is stationary even though $Z(t)$ itself may be non-stationary. In this case (4.2) can be interpreted as an error correction model (ECM) corresponding to model (4.1) [see Engle and Granger (1987), Johansen (1988)]. The hypothesis of r cointegration vectors is

$$H_2: \ \Pi = \alpha\beta^*, \tag{4.3}$$

4.2. VAR Model and Error Correction Form

where α and β are $p \times r$ matrices ($r \leq p$).

The $I(1)$ model $H_2(r)$ can be formulated as the condition that the rank of Π is less than or equal to r. This formulation shows that $I(1)$ models from a nested sequence of models

$$H_2(0) \subset \cdots \subset H_2(r) \subset \cdots \subset H_2(p),$$

where $H_2(p)$ is the unrestricted VAR model or the $I(0)$ model, and $H_2(0)$ corresponds to the unrestriction $\Pi = 0$ which is just the VAR model for the process in differences.

If Π is restricted as in H_2 and $\mu \neq 0$, the nonstationary process $Z(t)$ has linear trends with coefficients which are functions of $\alpha_\perp^* \mu$, where $\alpha_\perp^*$ is a $p \times (p-r)$ matrix of vectors chosen orthogonal to α. Thus the hypothesis $\mu = \alpha \beta_0^*$ or alternatively $\alpha_\perp^* \mu = 0$, is the hypothesis about the absence of a linear trend in the process. Note that when $\mu = \alpha \beta^*$ we can write

$$\alpha \beta^* Z(t-1) + \mu = \alpha \beta^* Z(t-1) + \alpha \beta_0^* = \alpha (\beta^+)^* Z^+(t-1),$$

where $(\beta^+)^* = (\beta^*, \beta_0^*)^*$ and $Z^+(t-1) = (Z(t-1), 1)^*$. Since the asymptotic distributions of the test statistics and estimators depend on which assumption is maintained, it is important to choose the appropriate model formulation.

We now consider the maximum likelihood estimation of the parameters in the unrestricted model (4.2). We first introduce the notation $Z_0(t) = \Delta Z(t)$, $Z_1(t) = Z(t-1)$, and $Z_2(t)$ denotes the stacked variables $\Delta Z(t-1), \cdots, \Delta Z(t-k+1), P(t)$ and 1, Γ is the matrix of parameters corresponding to $Z_2(t)$, i.e. the matrix consisting of $\Gamma_1, \cdots, \Gamma_{k-1}, \Phi$, and μ. Then model (4.2) can be expressed by

$$Z_0(t) = \Pi Z_1(t) + \Gamma Z_2(t) + \varepsilon(t), \qquad (t = 1, \cdots, T). \tag{4.4}$$

For a fixed value of Π, maximum likelihood estimation consists of a regression of $Z_0(t)$ on $Z_2(t)$ giving the normal equation

$$\sum_{t=1}^T Z_0(t) Z_2(t)^* = \Gamma \sum_{t=1}^T Z_2(t) Z_2(t)^* + \Pi \sum_{t=1}^T Z_1(t) Z_2(t)^*.$$

The product moment matrices are denoted:

$$M_{ij} = T^{-1} \sum_{t=1}^T Z_i(t) Z_j(t)^*, \quad (i, j = 0, 1, 2), \tag{4.5}$$

Chapter 4. Cointegration and Statistical Tests

and then we have:
$$M_{02} = \Gamma M_{22} + \Pi M_{12}, \tag{4.6}$$
or
$$\Gamma = M_{02} M_{22}^{-1} - \Pi M_{12} M_{22}^{-1}. \tag{4.7}$$

This leads to the definition of the residuals
$$R_0(t) = Z_0(t) - M_{02} M_{22}^{-1} Z_2(t),$$
$$R_1(t) = Z_1(t) - M_{12} M_{22}^{-1} Z_2(t),$$

i.e., the residuals we would obtain by regressing $\Delta Z(t)$ and $Z(t-1)$, respectively, on $\Delta Z(t-1), \cdots, \Delta Z(t-a+1), P(t)$ and 1.

The concentrated likelihood function becomes:
$$|\Sigma|^{T/2} \exp\Big\{\sum_{t=1}^{T}(R_0(t) - \Pi R_1(t))^* \Sigma^{-1}(R_0(t) - \Pi R_1(t))/2\Big\}.$$

By introducing the notation
$$S_{ij} = T^{-1} \sum_{t=1}^{T} R_i(t) R_j(t)^* = M_{ij} - M_{i2} M_{22}^{-1}, \quad (i,j = 0, 1), \tag{4.8}$$

we express the estimates under the model (4.2) by the ordinary least squares
$$\hat{\Pi} = T^{-1} \sum_{t=1}^{T} S_{01} S_{11}^{-1} \tag{4.9}$$
and
$$\hat{\Sigma} = S_{00} - S_{01} S_{11}^{-1} S_{10}, \tag{4.10}$$

The estimate of Π inserted into (4.7) gives the estimate of Γ.

4.3 Statistical Analysis of Cointegrated Vectors

The derivation of the estimators of α and β under the hypothesis $\Pi = \alpha\beta^*$ is giving as follows. For fixed β, it is easy to estimate α and Σ by regressing $R_0(t)$ on $\beta^* R_1(t)$ to obtain
$$\hat{\alpha}(\beta) = S_{01} \beta (\beta^* S_{11}^{-1} \beta)^{-1}, \tag{4.11}$$

4.3. Statistical Analysis of Cointegrated Vectors

$$\hat{\Sigma}(\beta) = S_{00} - S_{01}\beta(\beta^* S_{11}^{-1}\beta)^{-1}\beta^* S_{10}$$
$$= S_{00} - \hat{\alpha}(\beta)(\beta^* S_{11}^{-1}\beta)^{-1}\hat{\alpha}(\beta) \quad (4.12)$$

and

$$L_{\max}^{T/2}(\beta) = |\hat{\Sigma}(\beta)| = |S_{00} - S_{01}\beta(\beta^* S_{11}^{-1}\beta)^{-1}\beta^* S_{10}|.$$

As shown in Johansen (1988) and Tso (1981), one proceeds to estimate β by applying the identity

$$|S_{00} - S_{01}\beta(\beta^* S_{11}^{-1}\beta)^{-1}\beta^* S_{10}|$$
$$= |S_{00}||(\beta^* S_{11}\beta) - \beta^* S_{10}S_{00}^{-1}S_{01}\beta|/|\beta^* S_{11}\beta|$$
$$= |S_{00}||(\beta^*(S_{11} - S_{10}S_{00}^{-1}S_{01})\beta|/|\beta^* S_{11}\beta|. \quad (4.13)$$

This is minimized by solving the equation $|\lambda S_{11} - S_{10}S_{00}^{-1}S_{10}| = 0$.

Denote model (4.1) as H_1, under the hypothesis $\Pi = \alpha\beta^*$, the ML estimator of β is found by the following procedure.

(1) First solve the equation

$$|\lambda S_{11} - S_{10}S_{00}^{-1}S_{10}| = 0, \quad (4.14)$$

giving the eigenvalues $\hat{\lambda}_1 > \cdots > \hat{\lambda}_p$ and eigenvectors $\hat{V} = (\hat{v}_1, \cdots, \hat{v}_p)$ normalized such that $\hat{V}^* S_{11} \hat{V} = I$.

(2) The choice of β is

$$\hat{\beta} = (\hat{v}_1, \cdots, \hat{v}_r) \quad (4.15)$$

which gives

$$L_{\max}^{T/2}(H_2) = |S_{00}|\Pi_{i=1}^{r}(1 - \hat{\lambda}_i). \quad (4.16)$$

The estimates of the other parameters are found by inserting $\hat{\beta}$ into the above equations. Since H_1 is a special case of H_2 for the choice $r = p$, the likelihood ratio test statistic for the hypothesis H_2 in H_1 is:

$$\tau_{trace}(r) = -T\log \sum_{i=r+1}^{p}(1 - \hat{\lambda}_i). \quad (4.17)$$

Similarly the likelihood ratio test statistic for testing $H_2(r)$ in $H_2(r+1)$ is given by

$$\tau_{\lambda-\max}(r) = -T\log(1 - \hat{\lambda}_{r+1}). \quad (4.18)$$

Chapter 4. Cointegration and Statistical Tests

Testing the rank of the system corresponds to determining how many of the (true) eigenvalues, $\hat{\lambda}_1, \cdots, \hat{\lambda}_p$, are non-zero. If the (true) rank is r then exactly r of the p eigenvalues are non-zero.

The eigenvalue $\hat{\lambda}_i$ corresponds to the squared canonical correlations between the level residuals and the difference residuals, as defined above. The eigenvectors $\hat{v}_i$ determine the linear combinations $\hat{v}_i Z(t)$, $i = 1, \cdots, r$, which are most correlated with the process $\Delta Z(t)$ conditional on $\Delta Z(t-i), i = 1, \cdots, k-1$. Thus, the magnitude of $\hat{\lambda}_i$ is a measure of how strongly the cointegration relation $\hat{v}_i Z(t)$ is correlated with the stationary part of the process. The last $(p-r)$ combinations $\hat{v}_i Z(t)$ $(i = r+1, \cdots, p)$ give the directions in which the process is found to be nonstationary. Theoretically, these latter combinations are uncorrelated with the stationary part of the process, and, consequently, the population value of $\hat{\lambda}_i$ is 0 for $i = r+1, \cdots, p$. The statistical problem is to discriminate between nonzero and zero eigenvalues and the ML solution is given by the likelihood-ratio test procedure. To each vector $\hat{v}_i$ $(i = 1, \cdots, r)$, there is a corresponding vector α_i of dimension $p \times 1$ for which at least one element is nonzero. The elements of α_i can be interpreted as the weights with which the cointegration relation $\hat{v}_i Z(t)$ enters each of the equations in the system.

Note that in terms of stationarity only the space spanned by α and β is uniquely defined as the column space and row space of Π. The individual parameters α_{ij} and β_{ij} can be chosen arbitrarily relative to a non-singular $(r \times r)$ matrix ξ, $\alpha \xi$ and $\beta \xi^{-1}$, since this transformation will result in the same matrix Π and hence determine the same probability distribution for the vector $Z(t)$ [Johansen and Juselius (1990)]. To facilitate the interpretation of the estimated vectors when $r > 1$, it is often necessary to impose more structure on the cointegration space. A variety of linear tests for structural hypotheses is discussed in Johansen and Juselius (1992).

Under the hypothesis

$$H_2^+ : \ \Pi = \alpha \beta^* \quad \text{and} \quad \mu = \alpha \beta_0^*,$$

define $Z_{0t}^+ = Z_{0t} = \Delta Z_t$, let Z_{st}^+ be the stacked variables $\Delta Z_{t-1}, \cdots, \Delta Z_{t-a+1}, P_t$, whereas $Z_{1t}^{+*} = Z_{t-1}^{+*} = (Z_{t-1}^*, 1)$. Further, we define Γ^+ as the matrix of the relevant parameters $\Gamma_1, \cdots, \Gamma_{a-1}, \Phi$. The M_{ij}^+ and S_{ij}^+ defined similarly.

4.3. Statistical Analysis of Cointegrated Vectors

For a more general VAR representation expressed in the first order differences and lagged levels

$$\Delta Z(t) = \alpha\beta^* Z(t-1) + \sum_{i=1}^{a-1} \Gamma_i \Delta Z(t-i) + \mu_0 + \mu_1 t + \Phi P(t) + \varepsilon(t), \qquad (4.19)$$

where μ_0 is the intercept and μ_1 is the trend coefficient. $\varepsilon(t)$ is i.i.d. $N_p(0, \Sigma)$. For $\alpha_\perp$ a $p \times (p-r)$ matrix orthogonal to α, define

$$\beta_0 = (\alpha^*\alpha)^{-1}\alpha\mu_0 \quad \text{and} \quad \gamma_0 = (\alpha_\perp^*\alpha_\perp)^{-1}\alpha_\perp^*\mu_0,$$

$$\beta_1 = (\alpha^*\alpha)^{-1}\alpha\mu_1 \quad \text{and} \quad \gamma_1 = (\alpha_\perp^*\alpha_\perp)^{-1}\alpha_\perp^*\mu_1,$$

the projections of the deterministic parts of the model on the α-space and $\alpha_\perp$-space. Restrictions on the parameters β_0, γ_0 ($r \times 1$ matrix) and β_1, γ_1 (($p-r$) $\times 1$ matrix) are important in distinguishing the correct asymptotic distribution of the test statistics used in determining the rank of $\alpha\beta^*$.

In Johansen (1988, 1991), the asymptotic distribution of the two cointegration rank test statistics $\tau_{trace}(r)$ and $\tau_{\lambda-\max}(r)$ were derived. The asymptotic distribution of each test statistic is not invariant under different combinations of zero restrictions on $\beta_0, \gamma_0, \beta_1$ and γ_1 in the data generating process. The distribution of the test statistics, which is a nonstandard multivariate Dickey-Fuller type, is given by an expression involving stochastic integrals of Brownian motions (including certain deterministic components) of the following form:

$$\int dBF^* \left[\int FF^* du \right]^{-1} \int F dB^*, \qquad (4.20)$$

where B is a vector Brownian motion, and F is a function of B and includes certain deterministic components differently for different null hypothesis. Some of the tabulated results by simulations for the asymptotic case can be seen in Johansen (1988), Johansen and Juselius (1990). They discussed a model different to model (4.2). There they used $\Pi Z(t-a)$ in the right hand side of the equation in stead of $\Pi Z(t-1)$ which we used here.

The test tables have been conducted by Osterwald-Lenum (1992) with a calculation from numerical simulated distributions. The empirical distribution of the largest eigenvalue and the trace of (4.20) was estimated from 6,000 replications of

Chapter 4. Cointegration and Statistical Tests

a discrete time approximation to (4.20) substituting a Gaussian 400 step random walk for the Brownian motion.

In the case of there is no or little prior information about r, we might estimate r as follows: Denote by $\tau(i|1-\alpha)$ the $(1-\alpha)$ quantile of $\tau(i)$ and by $\hat{\tau}(i)$ be the observation of $\tau(i)$. If $\hat{\tau}(0) < \tau(0|1-\alpha)$, we choose $\hat{r} = 0$. For $r = 1, \cdots, p-1$, let $\hat{r}$ be the first r such that

$$\hat{\tau}(r-1) > \tau(r-1|1-\alpha), \text{ and } \hat{\tau}(r) < \tau(r|1-\alpha),$$

and if there is no such r, then set $\hat{r} = p$. This procedure defines an estimator $\hat{r}$ which takes on the values $0, 1, \cdots, p$ and which converges in probability to the true value, if α tends to 0 with appropriate speed as the sample size tends to infinity [see Hosoya(1989) pp.442-3]. A variety of aspects of the identification problem are discussed by Johansen (1995), but we choose in our analysis the least restrictive model specification.

The last section this chapter contains a brief discussion of the asymptotic properties of the estimators which will be used in the following Wald test of the causal measures based on a cointegrated process. Details of the very complex expression and proof of the asymptotic properties of the estimators can be found in Stock (1987) and Johansen (1991 or 1995).

Denote τ the linear trend of the process $Z(t)$, take $p \times (p-r-1)$-dimensional vector γ which is orthogonal to τ and linearly independent of β,

$$C = \beta_\perp (\alpha_\perp^* \Gamma \beta_\perp)^{-1} \alpha_\perp^*,$$

and also

$$G = \begin{pmatrix} \bar{\gamma}^* C(W(u) - \bar{W}) \\ u - \frac{1}{2} \end{pmatrix} \equiv \begin{pmatrix} G_1 \\ G_2 \end{pmatrix},$$

where $\bar{\gamma} = \gamma(\gamma^*\gamma)^{-1}$.

Let $\hat{\beta}$ and also then β be normalized by such a c that $c^*\hat{\beta} = c^*\beta = I_p$, then the limit distribution of $T(\hat{\beta} - \beta)$ is

$$(I_p - \beta c^*)\bar{\gamma}[\int_0^1 G_{1.2} G_{1.2}^* du]^{-1} \int_0^1 G_{1.2} dV_\alpha^*,$$

so that

$$\hat{\beta} - \beta \in O(T^{-1}) \tag{4.21}$$

4.3. Statistical Analysis of Cointegrated Vectors

and

$$G_{1.2}(u) = G_1(u) - \int_0^1 G_1 G_2^* du \int_0^1 G_2 G_2^* du]^{-1} G_2(u),$$
$$V_\alpha = (\alpha^* \Sigma^{-1} \alpha)^{-1} \alpha^* \Sigma^{-1} W.$$

Define the variable

$$\mathcal{Y}(t) = (\Delta Z^*(t-1), \cdots, \Delta Z^*(t-a+1), Z^*(t-1)\beta, P^*(t))^*$$

and

$$\Omega = \lim_{T \to \infty} T^{-1} \sum_{t=1}^{T} (\mathcal{Y}(t) - \bar{\mathcal{Y}})(\mathcal{Y}(t) - \bar{\mathcal{Y}})^*.$$

Let ϑ denote all the parameters, then under the assumption of $\Pi = \alpha\beta(\vartheta)^*$, the asymptotic distribution of

$$T^{1/2}[(\tilde{\Gamma}_1, \cdots, \tilde{\Gamma}_{k-1}, \tilde{\Phi}, \tilde{\mu}) - (\Gamma_1, \cdots, \Gamma_{k-1}, \Phi, \mu)]$$

is Gaussian with mean zero and variance matrix

$$\Sigma \otimes \begin{pmatrix} \Omega^{-1} & 0 \\ 0 & 2\Sigma \end{pmatrix}.$$

This follows

$$(\tilde{\Gamma}_1, \cdots, \tilde{\Gamma}_{k-1}, \tilde{\Phi}, \tilde{\mu}) - (\Gamma_1, \cdots, \Gamma_{k-1}, \Phi, \mu) \in O(T^{-1/2}). \tag{4.22}$$

In the presence of structural breaks in deterministic terms, the statistical analysis basically remains the same; however, the asymptotic distribution of the test for the cointegration rank now depends on the time of the break. Johansen and Nielsen (1994) discussed only those special cases where nuisance parameters are not present in the limiting distribution. The asymptotic distribution can be simulated using DisCo version 1.4.

As regards the literature dealing with the cointegrated VAR model with trend breaks, even we will not make detail discussion of the very important topic, the work of Kunitomo (1996) and Hosoya and Takimoto (2000) is noteworthy. Kunitomo (1996) aimed at presenting a unified test theory for unit-root processes by means of a formal analogy between testing in multivariate regression models

Chapter 4. Cointegration and Statistical Tests

and that in unit-root or cointegrated VAR models. On the other hand, Hosoya and Takimoto (2000) presented a limiting distribution of the likelihood ratio test for the cointegration rank and a numerical computation method for the p-value evaluation by means of the Monte Carlo simulation of stochastic integrals. In their models, the distribution of the LR statistic depends upon the location of breaks and the nuisance-parameter estimate, and it is not feasible to list the tables of percentiles of the test statistics as in Osterwald-Lenum (1992).

Chapter 5

Causal Analysis of Cointegrated Processes

Granger and Lin (1995) using the definition presented by Hosoya (1991), have heuristically derived an extended measure for a bivariate cointegrated AR process. They pointed out that causation at low frequencies between a pair of cointegrated series depends quite simply on a few coefficients from the error-correction model, allowing easy interpretation of these terms. Hosoya (1997) gave an extension of the causal measures which Hosoya (1991) introduced for the purpose of quantitative characterization in the frequency domain of interactions between stationary processes, to possibly nonstationary processes including cointegrated time-series. Statistical estimation of those measures requires estimation of frequency response function for multivariate processes. Based on a cointegrated ARMA model, the frequency response function can be estimated by means of the ML estimation of the parameters in the model.

Toda and Phillips (1993) provided a Wald tests for Granger causality in levels of VAR and Johansen-type error correction model (ECM). The theory allows for stochastic and deterministic trends as well as arbitrary degrees of cointegration. For VAR models, Toda and Phillips (1994) extended their earlier work on trivariate systems. They recommend some operational procedures for conducting Granger causality tests that are based on the Gaussian ML estimation of ECM. These procedures are applicable in the important practical case of testing the causal effects of one variable on another group of variables, and vice-versa. Three

Chapter 5. Causal Analysis of Cointegrated Processes

sequential causality tests in ECM are compared with conventional causality tests based on VAR in levels and in differences. In such models, the results for inference are found not to be encouraging. Explicit information on the number of unit roots in the system and the rank of a certain sub-matrix in the cointegration space is needed to determine the appropriate limit theory in advance. Pretesting these conditions involves major complications in levels of the VAR model. Even if the information were to be available, the limit theory would frequently involve both nuisance parameters and nonstandard limit distributions, a situation in which there is no satisfactory statistical basis for mounting the tests. Toda and Phillips explained that Granger causality tests in ECM suffer from nuisance parameter dependencies asymptotically and, in some cases, non-standard limit theory. In spite of these difficulties, the Johansen-type ECM offers a sound basis for empirical testing of the rank of the cointegration space and the rank of key sub-matrices that influence the asymptotics.

In view of the discussions in Chapter 3, a developing theory of statistical estimation and testing to deal with cointegrated time series is now available. In this chapter, we summarize the main results of causal measures by Hosoya (1997) and Yao and Hosoya (2000) concerning cointegrated processes.

5.1 Causal Measures for Cointegrated ARMA Processes

Consider the p-dimensional process $Z(t) = \{X(t)^*, Y(t)^*\}^*$ represented by a finite order vector ARMA model

$$Z(t) = \sum_{j=1}^{a} A_j Z(t-j) + \sum_{k=0}^{b} B_k \varepsilon(t-k) \qquad (t \in \mathcal{J}^+), \tag{5.1}$$

where $\{\varepsilon(t)\}$ is a p-dimensional white noise process such that $E(\varepsilon(t)) = 0$ and $Cov(\varepsilon(t)) = \Sigma$, $rank\Sigma = p$, $B_0 = I_p$. The a and b are finite constant integer, A_j's and B_k's are $p \times p$ matrices such that the zeros of $det(I_p - \sum_{j=1}^{a} A_j z^j)$ and $det \sum_{k=0}^{b} B_k z^k$ are on or outside the unit circle. Set

$$A(L) = I_p - \sum_{j=1}^{a} A_j L^j \quad \text{and} \quad B(L) = \sum_{k=0}^{b} B_k L^k,$$

5.1. Causal Measures for Cointegrated ARMA Processes

then by (5.1) we have

$$A(L)Z(t) = B(L)\varepsilon(t) \qquad (t \in \mathcal{J}^+). \tag{5.2}$$

Denote by $C(L)$ the adjoint matrix of $A(L)$ so that

$$C(L)A(L) \equiv D(L),$$

where $D(L)$ is the diagonal matrix having $d(L) \equiv detA(L)$ as the common diagonal element, $d(L) = \sum_{j=0}^{d} d_j L^j$ is a lag polynomial with scalar coefficients such that $d_0 = 1$ and the zeros of $d(z)$ are either on or outside the unit circle, where d is a finite constant integer. We can also have $detC(z) = (detA(z))^{a-1}$. Since the zeros of $detA(z)$ are either on or outside the unit circle, whereas the zeros of $detC(z)$ are either on or outside the unit circle. Left-multiplying $C(L)$ to the members of the equation (5.2), we have

$$\left[\begin{array}{ccc|ccc} d(L) & & 0 & & & \\ & \ddots & & & 0 & \\ 0 & & d(L) & & & \\ \hline & & & d(L) & & 0 \\ & 0 & & & \ddots & \\ & & & 0 & & d(L) \end{array}\right] \left[\begin{array}{c} X(t) \\ \hline Y(t) \end{array}\right] = \left[\begin{array}{c} U(t) \\ \hline V(t) \end{array}\right], \tag{5.3}$$

where we set

$$W(t) = C(L)B(L)\varepsilon(t) \equiv [U(t)^*, V(t)^*]^*$$

for p_1 and p_2 vectors $U(t)$ and $V(t)$ [a similar representation in VAR model is given by Granger and Lin (1995), and a similar idea is also used in Engle and Granger (1987)]. Because the zeros of $C(z)$ and $B(z)$ are either on or outside the unit circle, there comes the following lemma.

Lemma 5.1 *The zeros of $det\{C(z)B(z)\}$ are either on or outside of the unit circle. Therefore, the covariance matrix of one-step ahead prediction error of $W(t)$ is equal to Σ.*

It follows from the above construction that $\{U(t), V(t)\}$ is a stationary MA process and that the process $\{X(t), Y(t)\}$ satisfies Assumption 3.2 (i). Therefore, in view of Definition 3.2, all the measures of one-way effect for the possibly nonstationary processes $\{X(t), Y(t)\}$ are determined by the corresponding measures of the stationary processes $\{U(t), V(t)\}$.

Chapter 5. Causal Analysis of Cointegrated Processes

Moreover, since the covariance matrix of the one-step ahead prediction error of $W(t)$ is equal to Σ and if the spectral density matrix of $\{W(t)\}$ is denoted by $f(\lambda)$, it has a canonical factorization

$$f(\lambda) = \frac{1}{2\pi}\Lambda(e^{-i\lambda})\Lambda(e^{-i\lambda})^* \qquad (5.4)$$

and

$$\Lambda(e^{-i\lambda}) = C(e^{-i\lambda})B(e^{-i\lambda})\Sigma^{1/2}, \qquad (5.5)$$

where $\Sigma^{1/2}$ is the Cholesky factor of Σ such that $\Sigma = \Sigma^{1/2}\Sigma^{1/2}$. Then the causal measures can be calculated in view of (3.13) and (3.14) by means of the spectral density $f(\lambda)$ defined by (5.4) and its factor $\Lambda(e^{-i\lambda})$.

Error correction models represent linear systems of economic variables which are in dynamically stable equilibrium in the presence of incessant incoming shocks and generate cointegrated unit-root processes [see Engle and Granger (1987)]. The following discussions show that a large part of the statistical inference on the causal measures of cointegrated economic time series can be conducted by means of a standard asymptotic theory for stationary processes.

Take the cointegrated multivariate ARMA model which is represented by

$$\Delta Z(t) = \Pi Z(t-1) + \sum_{i=1}^{a}\Gamma_i\Delta Z(t-i) + \sum_{j=0}^{b}B_j\varepsilon(t-j) \qquad (5.6)$$

with $\Pi = \alpha\beta^*$ where α and β are $p \times r$ matrices and it reduces to (5.1) by setting $A_1 = I_p + \Gamma_1 + \Pi, A_a = \Gamma_{a-1}$ and $A_i = \Gamma_i - \Gamma_{i-1}$ for $i = 2, 3, \cdots, a-1$. The frequency response function and the spectral density matrix Λ and f are determined in the form of (5.4) and (5.5), but here $C(e^{-i\lambda})$ is the adjoint matrix of the complex-valued polynomial matrix

$$\mathcal{A}(e^{-i\lambda}) = I_p - (I_p + \Pi)e^{-i\lambda} - \sum_{j=1}^{a-1}\Gamma(j)(e^{-ij\lambda} - e^{-i(j+1)\lambda}). \qquad (5.7)$$

In view of the definition of the causal measures, measure-related quantities are all functionals of $\Lambda(e^{-i\lambda})$ and $f(e^{-i\lambda})$, or the fuctions of $\alpha, \beta, \Gamma_i, B_j, \Sigma$. The overall measure of the one-way effect from vector $Y(t)$ to vector $X(t)$ (the vector may be degenerative of one dimension variable), $M_{Y\to X}(\alpha, \beta, \Gamma_i, B_j, \Sigma)$, is given

5.1. Causal Measures for Cointegrated ARMA Processes

by

$$M_{Y \to X}(\alpha, \beta, \Gamma_i, B_j, \Sigma) = \frac{1}{2\pi} \int_{-\pi}^{\pi} M_{Y \to X}(\lambda | \alpha, \beta, \Gamma_i, B_j, \Sigma) d\lambda, \qquad (5.8)$$

where $M_{Y \to X}(\lambda | \alpha, \beta, \Gamma_i, B_j, \Sigma)$ is the measure of one-way effect from vector $Y(t)$ to vector $X(t)$ at frequency λ, evaluated according to the foregoing arguments.

The parameters $\alpha, \beta, \Gamma_i, B_j, \Sigma$ are estimated by the Johansen's ML method [see Chapter 4, or Johansen (1988, 1991)] for the AR case of I(1) process. There is another method called quasi maximum likelihood method [see Hosoya and Taniguchi (1982, 93) for the quasi maximum likelihood estimation which applies to general stationary linear processes].

If we consider the cointegrated multivariate ARMA model with unrestricted constant term and deterministic dummies, the model may be represented by

$$\Delta Z(t) = \Pi Z(t-1) + \sum_{i=1}^{a} \Gamma_i \Delta Z(t-i) + \mu + \Phi P(t) + \sum_{j=0}^{b} B_j \varepsilon(t-j) \qquad (5.9)$$

where μ is the constant p-dimensional vector, $P(t)$ is a (s_d-1)-vector of dummies. The other parameters are defined as (5.2).

In this case, after identifying model (5.9) with Johansen's likelihood-ratio method, we used $\mathcal{A}(L)$ as defined in (5.7) to construct the cofactor matrix $C(L)$. It is clear that now the information of constant and dummy variables is not used for the construction of the frequency response function of the process (in fact, the effects of the constant and dummy variables are taken into account in the estimation of the whole parameters). It is important to note here that the Granger causality is defined only between non-deterministic time series and that there is no one-way effect between such deterministic components as the dummy variables and the intercept that appear in model (5.9); a deterministic component can be predicted exactly by its past values, and there is no improvement in prediction if information of another series is added [see Hosoya (1977) for a formal proof for non-causality between deterministic processes]. The same idea can also be used in the analyses of the investigation of causal relations based on the multivariate ARMA model using only constant intercept or dummy variables. As for the discussion of causal relationships in levels of the VAR model, we only need to institute $B_0 = I_p$ to the $B(L)$ defined for (5.1), i.e., for the case $b = 0$.

Chapter 5. Causal Analysis of Cointegrated Processes

5.2 Wald Tests of the One-way Effect

This section evaluates the use of the Wald test for testing hypotheses on the measures of the one-way effect based on the ECM given by (5.10) below. We provide the computational procedure and also apply the test statistics to the construction of confidence sets of those measures.

Let $\{Z(t)\} = \{X(t)^*, Y(t)^*\}^*$ be generated by a cointegrated p-vector AR model which is represented in the error-correction form

$$\Delta Z(t) = \alpha \beta^* Z(t-1) + \sum_{j=1}^{a-1} \Gamma(j) \Delta Z(t-j) + \mu + \Phi P(t) + \varepsilon(t), \qquad (5.10)$$

where α and β are $p \times r$ matrices ($r \leq p$), and μ is a constant p-vector. Also in (5.10), $P(t)$ is $(s_d - 1)$-vector of centered seasonal dummy variables, where s_d is the seasonal period so that for quarterly data, $s_d = 4$; suppose also that $\{\varepsilon(t)\}$ is a Gaussian white noise process with mean 0 and with positive definite non-degenerate variance-covariance matrix Σ. Let θ be a $(r \cdot p) \times 1$ vector consisting of the elements of β such $\theta = vec\beta^*$. Denoting $n_\psi = p \cdot (r + p \cdot (a-1)) + p \cdot (p+1)/2$, let ψ be the $n_\psi \times 1$ vector which consists of the elements of α and $\Gamma(j)$ ($j = 1, \cdots, a-1$) and the elements in the lower triangular part of Σ; namely $\psi = vec(vec(\alpha, \Gamma)^*, v(\Sigma))$, where $\Gamma = \{\Gamma(1), \cdots, \Gamma(a-1)\}$ and $v(\Sigma)$ denotes the $(p \cdot (p+1)/2) \times 1$ vector.

The spectral density matrix f and its canonical factor Λ derived for the joint process $\{Z(t)\}$ by the relation (5.4) and (5.5) are given respectively by

$$f(\lambda|\theta, \psi) = \frac{1}{2\pi} \Lambda(e^{-i\lambda}|\theta, \psi) \Lambda(e^{-i\lambda}|\theta, \psi)^*, \qquad (5.11)$$

and

$$\Lambda(e^{-i\lambda}|\theta, \psi) = C(e^{-i\lambda}|\theta, \psi) \Sigma^{1/2}, \qquad (5.12)$$

where $C(e^{-i\lambda}|\theta, \psi)$ is the adjoint matrix of the complex-valued polynomial matrix based on model (5.10)

$$I_p - e^{-i\lambda}(I_p + \alpha\beta^*) - \sum_{j=1}^{a-1} \Gamma(j)(e^{-ij\lambda} - e^{-i(j+1)\lambda}).$$

Here, we used the key idea that the Granger causality is defined only between non-deterministic time series and that there is no one-way effect between such

5.2. Wald Tests of the One-way Effect

deterministic components as the dummy variables and the intercept which appear in model (5.10).

By means of those f and Λ, we define $M_{Y \to X}(\lambda|\theta,\psi)$ the *FMO* from $\{Y(t)\}$ to $\{X(t)\}$. In view of (3.12) and the definition of the *OMO*, for the parameters (θ,ψ), we have the following overall measure of one-way effect

$$G(\theta,\psi) = \frac{1}{2\pi} \int_{-\pi}^{\pi} M_{Y \to X}(\lambda|\theta,\psi) d\lambda. \qquad (5.13)$$

Note that in these instances, the *OMO* denoted by $G(\theta,\psi)$ is differentiable function with respect to (θ,ψ).

The results in section 4.3 [for details see Johansen (1988, 1991)] showed that, if (θ,ψ) is the true value and $(\hat{\theta},\hat{\psi})$ is the ML estimate, $T(\hat{\theta} - \theta)$ tends to have a mixed multivariate normal distribution and $\sqrt{T}(\hat{\psi}-\psi)$ tends to have a multivariate normal distribution as $T \to \infty$, whence $G(\hat{\theta},\hat{\psi})$ is a $\sqrt{T}$ consistent estimate of $G(\theta,\psi)$. By the stochastic expansion, we have

$$\sqrt{T}\{G(\hat{\theta},\hat{\psi}) - G(\theta,\psi)\} = (D_\psi G)^* \sqrt{T}(\hat{\psi} - \psi) + o_p(1),$$

where $D_\psi G$ is a n_ψ-dimensional vector of the gradient of $G(\theta,\psi)$. It follows that $\sqrt{T}\{G(\hat{\theta},\hat{\psi}) - G(\theta,\psi)\}$ is asymptotically normally distributed with mean 0 and variance

$$H(\theta,\psi) = D_\psi G(\theta,\psi)^* \Psi(\theta,\psi) D_\psi G(\theta,\psi), \qquad (5.14)$$

where $\Psi(\theta,\psi)$ is the asymptotic variance-covariance matrix of $\sqrt{T}(\hat{\psi} - \psi)$. Note that the first-order asymptotic distribution of $G(\hat{\theta},\hat{\psi})$ is completely determined by $\hat{\psi}$ and the nonstandard limiting distribution of $\hat{\theta}$ is not involved, the sampling error of $\hat{\theta}$ being negligible in comparison with that of $\hat{\psi}$. Consequently, the test for $G(\theta,\psi)$ and the confidence-set construction can be conducted based on the Wald statistic

$$W \equiv T\{G(\hat{\theta},\hat{\psi}) - G(\theta,\psi)\}^2 / H(\hat{\theta},\hat{\psi}), \qquad (5.15)$$

which is asymptotically distributed as χ^2 distribution with one degree of freedom if (θ,ψ) is the true value.

As regards evaluation of $D_\psi G$ at $\hat{\theta},\hat{\psi}$, the numerical differentiation is practical in view of the complexity of the exact analytic expression. Specifically, the

Chapter 5. Causal Analysis of Cointegrated Processes

gradient of $G(\theta, \psi)$

$$D_\psi G = (\frac{\partial G}{\partial \psi_1}, \cdots, \frac{\partial G}{\partial \psi_{n_\psi}})^*$$

is evaluated by

$$\frac{\partial G}{\partial \psi_i} \approx \{G(\hat{\theta}, \hat{\psi} + h_i) - G(\hat{\theta}, \hat{\psi} - h_i)\}/(2h), \tag{5.16}$$

for sufficiently small positive h where h_i is the $n_\psi \times 1$ vector with the i-th element h and all the other elements zero; namely, $h_i = (0, \cdots, h, 0, \cdots, 0)^*, i = 1, 2, \cdots, n_\psi$.

The numerical computation of $\Psi(\theta, \psi)$ in (5.14) can be conducted as follows. We set $\psi^{(1)} = vec\{\alpha, \Gamma\}$, $\psi^{(2)} = vec(\mu, \Phi)$ and $\psi^{(3)} = v(\Sigma)$, and also we set $\psi^{(12)} = vec(\psi^{(1)}, \psi^{(2)})$. Then the log-likelihood function of the parameter $\psi^{(12)}$ and $\psi^{(3)}$ based on observations $Z(1), \cdots, Z(T)$ can be given as

$$l_T(\psi^{(12)}, \psi^{(3)}|Z) = -\frac{T}{2}(p\log 2\pi + \log det\Sigma) - \frac{1}{2}tr\Sigma^{-1}V_T,$$

where

$$V_T = \sum_{t=1}^{T} V(t)V(t)^*,$$

and

$$V(t) = \Delta Z(t) - \alpha\beta^* Z(t-1) - \sum_{j=1}^{a-1} \Gamma(j)\Delta Z(t-j) - \mu - \Phi P(t).$$

Let D be the p^2 by $p(p+1)/2$ duplication matrix and let D^+ be the Moore-Penrose inverse of matrix D [see Magnus and Neudecker (1988), p49]. Denote by $\hat{\psi}^{(12)}$ and $\hat{\psi}^{(3)}$ the ML estimators of $\psi^{(12)}$ and $\psi^{(3)}$ respectively, then the asymptotic variance-covariance matrix of $\sqrt{T}\{\hat{\psi}^{(12)} - \psi^{(12)}\}$ and $\sqrt{T}(\hat{\psi}^{(3)} - \psi^{(3)})$ is equal to

$$\begin{pmatrix} \Sigma \otimes Q^{-1} & 0 \\ 0 & 2D^+(\Sigma \otimes \Sigma)D^{+*} \end{pmatrix}, \tag{5.17}$$

where $Q = \lim_{T\to\infty}(1/T)\sum_{t=1}^{T} S(t)S(t)^*$,

$$S(t) = vec(\beta^* Z(t-1), \Delta Z(t-1), \cdots, \Delta Z(t-a-1), 1_p, P(t))$$

[see Magnus and Neudecker (1988), p321]. The asymptotic covariance of $\sqrt{T}(\hat{\psi}^{(1)} - \psi^{(1)})$, which is denoted by $\Psi_{\psi^{(1)}\psi^{(1)}}$ is then constructed from $\Sigma \otimes Q^{-1}$ by eliminating the rows and columns corresponding to $\sqrt{T}(\hat{\psi}^{(2)} - \psi^{(2)})$. In fact we can

5.2. Wald Tests of the One-way Effect

write the symmetric $(p \cdot (r + p \cdot (a-1)) + p \cdot s_d)$ dimensional matrix $\Sigma \otimes Q^{-1}$ into $p \times p$ partitioned matrix in the form of

$$\begin{pmatrix} \sigma_{11}Q^{-1} & \sigma_{12}Q^{-1} & \cdots & \sigma_{1p}Q^{-1} \\ \sigma_{21}Q^{-1} & \sigma_{22}Q^{-1} & \cdots & \sigma_{2p}Q^{-1} \\ \vdots & \vdots & \ddots & \vdots \\ \sigma_{p1}Q^{-1} & \sigma_{p2}Q^{-1} & \cdots & \sigma_{pp}Q^{-1} \end{pmatrix},$$

where all of the submatrices $\sigma_{ij}Q^{-1}(i,j=1,\cdots,p)$ are $(r+p\cdot(a-1)+s_d)$ dimensional squared matrix. The covariance matrix $\Psi_{\psi^{(1)}\psi^{(1)}}$ is constructed by eliminating all the last s_d columns and the last s_d rows of the submatrices $\sigma_{ij}Q^{-1}, i,j=1,\cdots,p$.

As for the estimation of Σ and Q in (5.17), we set

$$\hat{\Sigma} = (1/T) \sum_{t=1}^{T} (\hat{V}(t)\hat{V}(t)^*), \tag{5.18}$$

$$\hat{Q} = (1/T) \sum_{t=1}^{T} \hat{S}(t)\hat{S}(t)^*, \tag{5.19}$$

where

$$\hat{V}(t) = \Delta Z(t) - \hat{\alpha}\hat{\beta}^* Z(t-1) - \sum_{j=1}^{a-1} \hat{\Gamma}(j) \Delta Z(t-j) - \hat{\mu} - \hat{\Phi} P(t),$$

and

$$\hat{S}(t) = vec(\hat{\beta}^* Z(t-1), \Delta Z(t-1), \cdots, \Delta Z(t-a-1), 1_p, P(t)).$$

In view of the consistency of $\hat{\psi}$ and $\hat{\theta}$, if $\hat{\Psi}_{\psi^{(1)}\psi^{(1)}}$ denotes the variance-covariance matrix of $\sqrt{T}(\hat{\psi}^{(1)} - \psi^{(1)})$ evaluated at $(\hat{\theta}, \hat{\psi})$, then

$$\Psi(\theta,\psi) = \begin{pmatrix} \hat{\Psi}_{\psi^{(1)}\psi^{(1)}} & 0 \\ 0 & 2D^+(\hat{\Sigma} \otimes \hat{\Sigma})D^{+*} \end{pmatrix} + o_p(1). \tag{5.20}$$

Therefore we can use the first right-hand side member of (5.20) as a consistent estimate of $\Psi(\theta, \psi)$.

By (5.14) and (5.20), we then get a variance estimate $\hat{H} = H(\hat{\theta}, \hat{\psi})$. Denote G_{01} the given scalar, for the purpose of testing the null hypothesis $G(\theta, \psi) = G_{01}$, we evaluate the test statistic W defined by (5.15). In order to test no-causality

Chapter 5. Causal Analysis of Cointegrated Processes

in Granger's sense, we set the null hypothesis as $G_{01} = 0$ and the test statistic is given by
$$W = T\{G(\hat{\theta}, \hat{\psi})\}^2 / H(\hat{\theta}, \hat{\psi}). \qquad (5.21)$$
If $W \geq \chi_\alpha^2(1)$, for $\chi_\alpha^2(1)$ the upper α quantile of the χ^2 distribution with one degree of freedom, we may reject the null hypothesis of non-causality from Y to X. On the other hand, in view of (5.15), the $(1 - \alpha)$ confidence interval of the causal measure $G(\theta, \psi)$ is provided by
$$(\ G(\hat{\theta}, \hat{\psi}) - H_\alpha,\ G(\hat{\theta}, \hat{\psi}) + H_\alpha\ ), \qquad (5.22)$$
where $H_\alpha = \sqrt{(1/T) H(\hat{\theta}, \hat{\psi}) \chi_\alpha^2(1)}$.

Based on the model (5.11), various other measures can be constructed. For instance, in case $p \geq 3$, we might divide $Z(t)$ into three vectors $Z^1(t), Z^2(t)$ and $Z^3(t)$ such that
$$Z(t) = (Z^1(t)^*, Z^2(t)^*, Z^3(t)^*)^*$$
and investigate the pair of the vector *OMO*,
$$G(\theta, \psi) = \begin{pmatrix} M_{(Z^1, Z^2) \to Z^3}(\theta, \psi) \\ M_{(Z^2, Z^3) \to Z^1}(\theta, \psi) \end{pmatrix}.$$
Or one might be interested in the pair of a long-run and a short-run mean effect
$$G(\theta, \psi) = \begin{pmatrix} \frac{1}{2\lambda_0} \int_{|\lambda| < \lambda_0} M_{Y \to X}(\lambda | \theta, \psi) d\lambda \\ \frac{1}{2(\pi - \lambda_0)} \int_{|\lambda| \geq \lambda_0} M_{Y \to X}(\lambda | \theta, \psi) d\lambda) \end{pmatrix},$$
where $0 < \lambda_0 \ll \pi$. In order to deal with these cases, let $G_i(\theta, \psi), i = 1, \cdots, m$, be different kinds of measures and let $G(\theta, \psi)$ be a m-vector so that
$$G(\theta, \psi) = (G_1(\theta, \psi), \ldots, G_m(\theta, \psi))^*,$$
then the preceding arguments are extended to this vector-valued $G(\theta, \psi)$ in a straightforward way as follows. Let $D_\psi G$ in (5.14) now represent the Jacobian matrix
$$D_\psi G = \{\partial G_i(\theta, \psi) / \partial \psi_j\}, \quad (i = 1, \cdots, m,\ j = 1, \cdots, n_\psi)$$
so that $H(\theta, \psi)$ denotes a $m \times m$ variance-covariance matrix. Suppose that the vector $G(\theta, \psi)$ is chosen so that $rank H(\theta, \psi) = m$, then the Wald statistic
$$W^{(m)} \equiv T\{G(\hat{\theta}, \hat{\psi}) - G(\theta, \psi)\}^* H(\hat{\theta}, \hat{\psi})^{-1} \{G(\hat{\theta}, \hat{\psi}) - G(\theta, \psi)\} \qquad (5.23)$$

5.2. Wald Tests of the One-way Effect

is asymptotically χ^2-distributed with m degrees of freedom if (θ, ψ) is the true value. Denote G_{0m} the given m vector, the null hypothesis $G(\theta, \psi) = G_{0m}$ is tested by means of $W^{(m)}$. The extension of causality test in Granger's sense can be conducted by setting $G_{0m} = 0$. The test statistic is given by

$$W^{(m)} \equiv T\{G(\hat{\theta}, \hat{\psi})\}^* H(\hat{\theta}, \hat{\psi})^{-1}\{G(\hat{\theta}, \hat{\psi})\}. \tag{5.24}$$

If $W^{(m)} \geq \chi^2_\alpha(m)$ for the α upper quantile of χ^2 distribution with m degrees of freedom, $G_{0m} = 0$ is rejected at α significance level; the asymptotically $(1 - \alpha)$ confidence set of G can be given by the interior and the surface of an ellipsoid; namely

$$[G : T\{G(\hat{\theta}, \hat{\psi}) - G\}^* H(\hat{\theta}, \hat{\psi})^{-1}\{G(\hat{\theta}, \hat{\psi}) - G\} \leq \chi^2_\alpha(m)]. \tag{5.25}$$

It consists of those G which are not rejected at the α significance level by the Wald test. In the case of $m = 2$, for example, set $G(\hat{\theta}, \hat{\psi}) = (\hat{G}_1, \hat{G}_2)$, $G = (G_1, G_2)$ and $H(\hat{\theta}, \hat{\psi})^{-1} = \{\hat{h}_{(ij)}\}$ ($\hat{h}_{(ij)} = \hat{h}_{(ji)}$); then the confidence sets with asymptotic confidence coefficient $(1 - \alpha)$ for various α are given by the set of nested ellipses determined by

$$\{G : F_2(G) \leq \chi^2_\alpha(2)/T\}, \qquad 0 < \alpha < 1, \tag{5.26}$$

where

$$F_2(G) = (G_1 - \hat{G}_1)^2 \hat{h}_{(11)} + (G_2 - \hat{G}_2)^2 \hat{h}_{(22)} + 2(G_1 - \hat{G}_1)(G_2 - \hat{G}_2)\hat{h}_{(12)}.$$

Remark 5.1 Note that our algorithm for evaluating the Wald statistic and the confidence set does not depend upon the kind of measures of one-way effect so that it applies also to the long-run or local one-way effects, $\bar{D}_{Y \to X}(\varepsilon)$ or $\bar{D}_{Y \to X}(t_1, t_2)$ given in Section 3.2.

Chapter 6

Cointegrated Model Identification

Most economic time series exhibit trends, which suggests that they are nonstationary. The time-series notion of cointegration was used to remove the trend component. When Granger (1981) showed that a time-series model with cointegration has a representation as an error-correction model and vice versa, the importance of nonstationary processes for econometric modeling became evident. The empirical analysis of a large number of nonstationary time series can be conducted in view of the cointegrated VAR model. Before conducting the empirical causality analysis of the possibly nonstationary time series in the next chapter, we first need to identify the cointegration model which best fit the data. That is to say, we must first estimate the cointegration rank and cointegration vectors as well as the other parameters, and then evaluate the identified models by the tests of autocorrelation and Gaussainity of the residuals.

6.1 Preliminary Analysis

In the following empirical analysis, the discussions are mainly forced on quarterly observations of GDP (abridged as Y), M2+CD (M), Call Rates (R), Exports (Ex), and Imports (Im) in Japan during the period 1975/I through 1994/IV. The data of GDP and M2+CD as well as Call Rates are based in Japanese yen and are from the 'Economic Statistics Monthly' by Research and Statistics Department of the Bank of Japan. The data of Exports and Imports are in U.S.

Chapter 6. Cointegrated Model Identification

Dollars and are from the summary table of the 'Balance of Payments Monthly' edited by International Department of the Bank of Japan. The original data of GDP, M2+CD, Exports and Imports are nominal and given as logarithms. Figure 6.1 gives the plots of all these original data in levels and in differences.

We begin by analyzing a system with nominal variables which are assumed to be integrated of order 1. Cointegration analysis has provided useful information for specifying and evaluating econometric models. Based on the ML method by Johansen (1988, 1991), we first determined the cointegration rank and the cointegrated vectors themselves in levels of the VAR model and then the other parameters by ML method. For this purpose, we constructed an easy human interface FORTRAN program, CRT95 [Yao (1996a)], which provides the calculation of the $\tau(r)$ statistics [and also $\tau_{\lambda-\max}(r)$ as defined in Chapter 4, but we did not apply it to the cointegrartion test] used in the estimation of cointegration rank in levels of the VAR model.

In the following study, we use model (5.10) with common lag-length $a = 5$. The lag-length of an autoregressive process delimits the range of possible configuration of the *FMO*. In order to avoid the difference of lag-length playing a part in figurative difference of *FMO*, we did not use information criteria which are rather suited for identification of individual models, but used a common lag-length. As will be seen below, the hypotheses tests of the residual auto-correlation and the Gaussianity seem mostly supported for the residuals derived by fitting the lag-length $a = 5$. The model we used is p-dimensional AR(5) in ECM form represented by

$$\Delta Z(t) = \alpha \beta^* Z(t-1) + \sum_{i=1}^{4} \Gamma_i \Delta Z(t-i) + \mu + \sum_{j=1}^{3} \Phi_j P_j(t) + \varepsilon(t), \qquad (6.1)$$

where $\varepsilon(t)$'s $(t = 1, \cdots, T)$ are Gaussian white noise with mean 0 and variance-covariance matrix Σ, α and β are $p \times r$ matrices $(r \leq p)$ such that rank$(\alpha \beta^*) = r$, $P(t)$ the 3×1 vector of centered seasonal dummies so as not to produce seasonal trend effects in the level of $Z(t)$. The first 5 observations of $Z(t)$ are kept for initial values. The effective sample size is 75, which means that we must be careful when making inferences based on the asymptotic distributions for the cointegration rank test statistics.

6.1. Preliminary Analysis

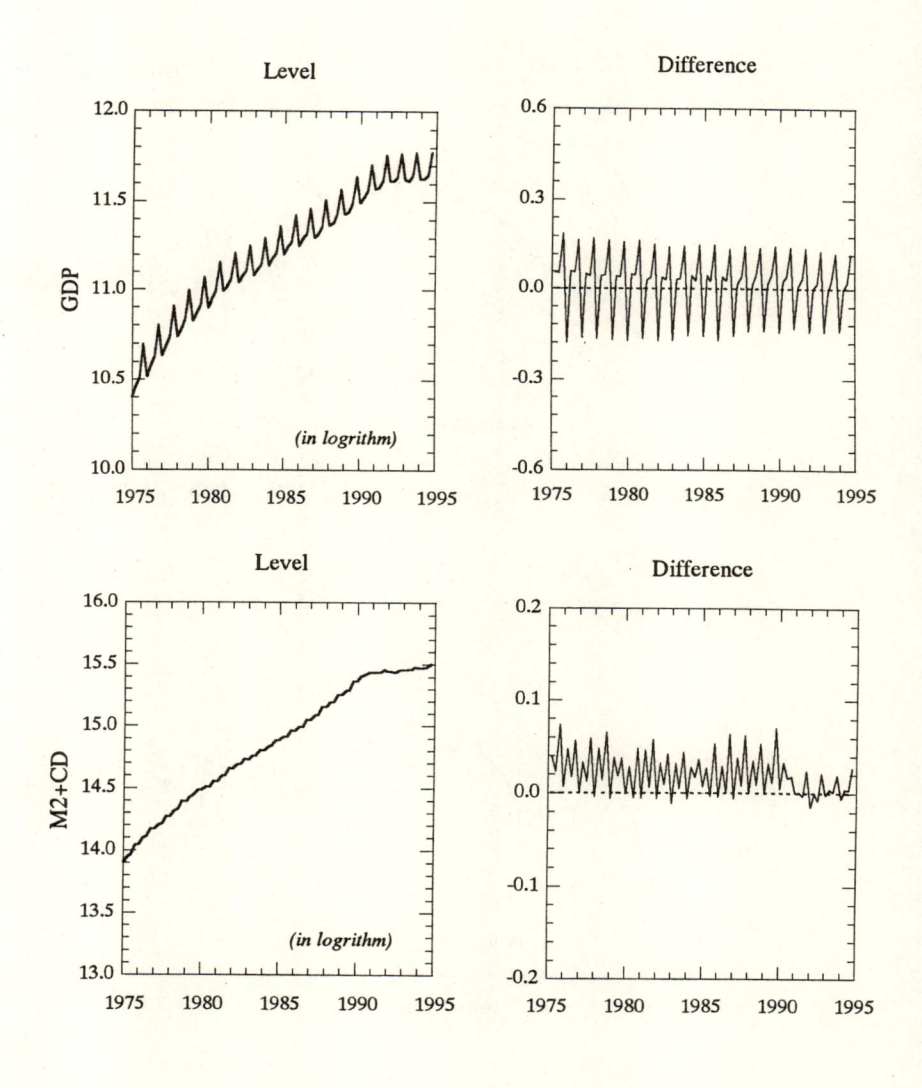

Figure 6.1 Japanese Macroeconomic Data in Levels and Differences

Chapter 6. Cointegrated Model Identification

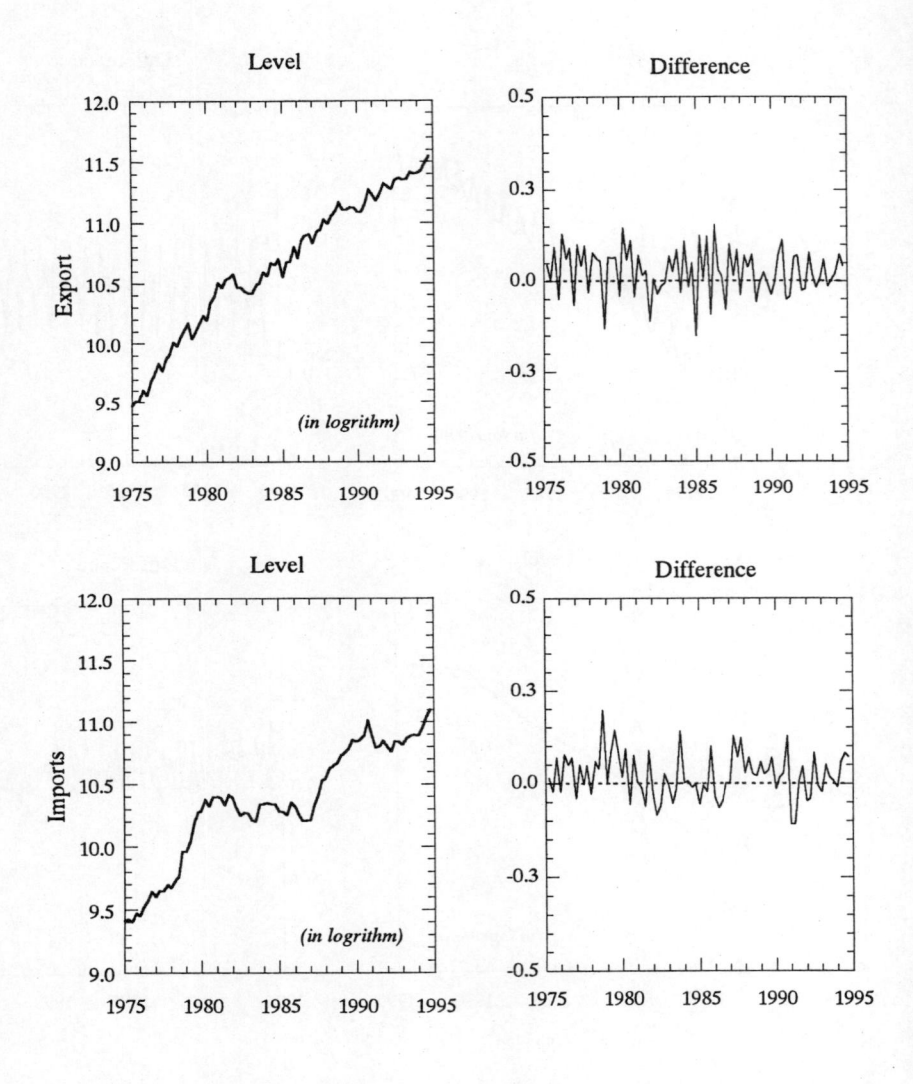

Figure 6.1 Continued

6.1. Preliminary Analysis

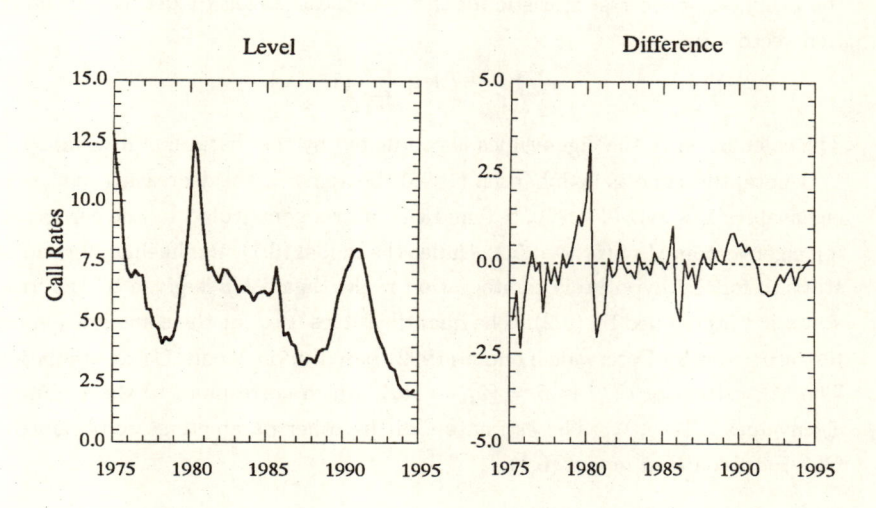

Figure 6.1 Continued

The r cointegrated vectors determine the number of linearly independent stationary relations in levels of the variables, i.e. the number of cointegration vectors in the data. This is very useful for a full understanding of the generating mechanisms of the economic system. This property also makes it possible to use one-way effect causal measures in the analysis of nonstationary integrated processes which can be expressed in a VAR model.

It also seems important to base the final choice on a sensitivity analysis of different values of r. If for instance there exist prior knowledge concerning the number of cointegrated vectors or concerning the number of common trends driving the system, this knowledge should not be neglected. See for details, Johansen and Juselius (1990), Yao and Hosoya (1995), Yao (1996a).

The estimation of r is performed by the $\tau(r)$ statistic defined by (4.17), there

Chapter 6. Cointegrated Model Identification

the likelihood-ratio test statistic for the hypothesis at least existing r cointegration vectors is:
$$\tau(r) = -T\log \sum_{i=r+1}^{p} (1-\hat{\lambda}_i). \tag{6.2}$$
The calculation of the eigenvalues is conducted by the discussion in Chapter 4.

Denote, the same as in Johansen (1995) theorem 6.1, the decreasing sequence of eigenvalues $1 > \hat{\lambda}_1 > \cdots > \hat{\lambda}_p > 0$ and the matrix constituted by the corresponding eigenvectors $\hat{V} = (\hat{v}_1, \cdots, \hat{v}_p)$. Under the model (6.1), the likelihood ratio test statistic for the hypothesis cointegration rank r against p is given by the 'trace' statistic $\tau(r)$ defined by (6.2). The quantile tables used for the cointegration rank test are given by Osterwald-Lenum (1992) based upon Monte Carlo simulations. The ML estimator of β is $\hat{\beta} = (\hat{v}_1, \cdots, \hat{v}_r)$, which correspond to the r non-zero eigenvalues $\hat{\lambda}_1, \cdots, \hat{\lambda}_r$. The estimators of the other parameters are obtained by OLS for given $\hat{\beta}$ in model (6.1).

Remark 6.1 The numerical computations of this book were conducted by FORTRAN program CRT95 written by the author [see Yao and Hosoya (1995) and Yao (1996a)]. By applying this program to the five macroeconomic series, we investigated bivariate, trivariate as well as four-variate models. The necessary cointegration test statistics and all the parameters are calculated by CRT95. Since the size of twenty-year quarterly data cannot be regarded as large, to be conservative, we use $T - n_\psi$ instead of the sample size T in (5.18), (5.19) and (5.21).

6.2 Empirical Cointegrated Relations

The estimated eigenvalues and the corresponding eigenvectors of the bivariate and trivariate as well as four-variate VAR models in error correction form are given in Tables 6.1, 6.2, 6.3, respectively. The variables of the models are indicated in the tables. The observed trace statistics are also listed there. The parameters α and $\Gamma(k)$, which will be used in the following causality analysis, are then estimated by the OLS method and denoted by $\hat{\alpha}, \hat{\Gamma}(k), (k = 1, 2, 3, 4)$, respectively. The 80%, 90%, 95% confidence statistics in Tables 6.1, 6.3 are from Osterwald-Lenum

6.2. Empirical Cointegrated Relations

(1992).

We estimate the cointegration rank r of the ECM based not only on the $\tau(r)$ statistic but also on the consideration of other aspects of the data and the corresponding model. Consider, for example, the determination of the cointegration rank r for bivariate model $Z = (Y, R)^*$, where the necessary quantiles are listed in Table 6.1. Even though the observed test statistics indicate two cointegrated relations, considering the obvious nonstationary nature of the nominal GDP, we chose $\hat{r} = 1$. The investigation of the Gaussianity test of the residuals also supports this conclusion. If we chose $\hat{r} = 2$, then the E_p-statistic would be 4.2744 with a p-value 0.37 (which is less than the p-value 0.89 when choosing $\hat{r} = 1$. For details see Section 6.3).

6.2.1 Bivariate Models

For the empirical analyses of bivariate models, the estimated results of the eigenvalues and the corresponding eigenvectors for 9 pairs of macroeconomic data of Japanese GDP, M2+CD, Call Rates, Exports, and Imports are listed in Table 6.1. The eigenvalues and the eigenvectors show the relationships of the processes as indicated. In view of the formula of (6.2), by using the eigenvalues listed in Table 6.1, the estimation of $\tau(r)$ statistics are also conducted.

In Table 6.1, the likelihood-ratio test statistics are compared to the 90 percent quantiles of appropriate limiting distribution. Based on the estimate of the trace statistic, the procedure of the estimation for the bivariate model of $(Y, M)^*$ is as follows. First, we consider the number of cointegration vectors, beginning with the hypothesis $r = 0$. Using the trace test procedure gives $\hat{\tau}(0) = 14.46$. As the 0.1 critical value of the asymptotic distribution is 13.33, i.e., $\hat{\tau}(0) > 13.33$, the hypothesis $r = 0$ is rejected. This means that there is at least one cointegration relation in the processes of GDP and M2+CD. Furthermore, as $\hat{\tau}(1) = 2.66$, which is less then the 0.1 critical value 2.69, hence we can conclude that there is one cointegration vector for the $(Y, M)^*$ model. From Table 6.1 we see the cointegration vector is $(0.834, -0.551)^*$. In view of this we can get the equilibrium relation

$$0.834Y - 0.551M = 0.$$

Chapter 6. Cointegrated Model Identification

For the bivariate model $(Y, Im)^*$, the number of cointegration vectors is zero. Table 6.1 shows that all the estimated test statistics are less than the corresponding 90 percent quantiles. All of the other estimations are similar to the above discussions. Figure 7.1, plots (a1) to (a8), lists the estimated number of cointegration vectors, or the estimate of the cointegration rank, $\hat{r}$.

Table 6.1 The Eigenvalues and the Eigenvectors and the Trace Statistics for Bivariate Models

	Eigenvalues					Eigenvalues			
	(0.146	0.035)				(0.112	0.055)		
	Eigenvectors		$p-r$	$\hat{\tau}$		Eigenvectors		$p-r$	$\hat{\tau}$
Y	0.834	-0.713	1	2.66	Y	0.986	0.997	1	4.28
M	-0.551	0.702	2	14.46	R	0.166	-0.075	2	13.16
	Eigenvalues					Eigenvalues			
	(0.152	0.049)				(0.119	0.034)		
	Eigenvectors		$p-r$	$\hat{\tau}$		Eigenvectors		$p-r$	$\hat{\tau}$
Y	0.840	0.968	1	3.80	Y	-0.620	0.902	1	2.60
Ex	-0.543	-0.251	2	16.12	Im	0.784	-0.432	2	12.12
	Eigenvalues					Eigenvalues			
	(0.152	0.051)				(0.204	0.036)		
	Eigenvectors		$p-r$	$\hat{\tau}$		Eigenvectors		$p-r$	$\hat{\tau}$
M	0.911	0.999	1	3.95	M	-0.735	0.909	1	2.77
R	0.413	0.018	2	16.33	Ex	0.678	-0.417	2	19.90
	Eigenvalues					Eigenvalues			
	(0.145	0.032)				(0.126	0.015)		
	Eigenvectors		$p-r$	$\hat{\tau}$		Eigenvectors		$p-r$	$\hat{\tau}$
R	0.262	0.259	1	2.45	R	0.316	-0.077	1	1.13
Ex	0.965	-0.966	2	14.19	Im	0.949	0.997	2	11.27
	Eigenvalues								
	(0.146	0.036)					τ-statistic		
	Eigenvectors		$p-r$	$\hat{\tau}$		$p-r$	80%	90%	95%
Ex	-0.574	0.866	1	2.71		1	1.66	2.69	3.76
Im	0.819	-0.499	2	14.53		2	11.07	13.33	15.41

The τ-statistic quantiles are from Table 1 in Osterwald-Lenum (1992).

6.2. Empirical Cointegrated Relations

6.2.2 Trivariate Models

We investigate 4 trivariate models which we are interested in by the combination of the 5 macroeconomic Japanese data. The estimates of the eigenvalues and corresponding eigenvectors as well as the trace statistics are listed in Table 6.2. In view of the estimated eigenvalues and eigenvectors listed there, we can see the cointegrated relationships of the 4 models as indicated.

From Table 6.2 we can see that except the trivariate model of $(M, R, Ex)^*$, all of the other trivariate models have only one cointegration vectors. For example, see the model of $(Y, M, R)^*$. We first consider the hypothesis $r = 0$, by Table 6.2 we have $\hat{\tau}(0) = 38.83 \geq 26.79 = \tau(0|0.9)$. This shows that the hypothesis is not significant. Considering the hypothesis $r \leq 1$, the fact that $\hat{\tau}(1) = 11.75 < 13.33 = \tau(1|0.9)$ shows that there is no evidence in the data for more than one cointegration relation. We then can conclude that there is only one cointegration vector for the model of $(Y, M, R)^*$. From Table 6.2 we see the cointegration vector is $(0.829, -0.560, -0.007)^*$. Then the equilibrium relation is given by

$$0.829Y - 0.560M - 0.07R = 0$$

or

$$Y = 0.676M + 0.0840R.$$

For the model of $(M, R, Ex)^*$, the number of estimated cointegration vectors is two, i.e. $\hat{r} = 2$. We begin with the hypothesis $r = 0$ versus the general hypothesis H_1. Using the trace test procedure gives $\hat{\tau}(0) = 34.70$, which is great than the 90 percent quantile, 26.79. This means that there is at least one cointegrated relation in the processes of M2+CD & Call Rates & Exports. If we test the hypothesis $r \leq 1$ in H_1, we get a test value $\hat{\tau}(1) = 13.93 > 13.33 = \tau(1|0.9)$. This means that there are at least two cointegration relations in this trivariate data process. Because $\hat{\tau}(2) = 2.52 < 2.69 = \tau(2|0.9)$, we can conclude that there are two cointegration vectors for the model of $(M, R, Ex)^*$. From Table 6.2 we see the cointegration vectors are $(-0.747, -0.012, 0.665)^*$ and $(-0.601, -0.066, 0.796)^*$ respectively corresponding to the two eigenvalues of 0.242 and 0.141, i.e.,

$$\hat{\beta}^* = \begin{pmatrix} -0.747 & -0.012 & 0.665 \\ -0.601 & -0.066 & 0.796 \end{pmatrix}.$$

Chapter 6. Cointegrated Model Identification

The cointegration ranks of the trivariate model $(Y, R, Im)^*$ and model $(Y, Ex, Im)^*$ are determined by this way and the results are showed in the following plots (b1) to (b4) in Figure 7.1.

6.2.3 Four-variate Models

Concerning four-variate VAR models, we only show the investigation results of the models of $(Y, M, R, Ex)^*$, $(Y, M, R, Im)^*$ and $(M, R, Ex, Im)^*$. The estimated eigenvalues and the corresponding eigenvectors are listed in Table 6.3. Furthermore, by using the estimated eigenvalues, we also calculate the trace statistics which will be used in the test of cointegration rank. In view of the estimated eigenvalues and eigenvectors listed in Table 6.3, we can see the cointegrated relationships of the five macroeconomic time serieses.

The estimation of the cointegration vectors for the four-variate model is similar to that of the the bivariate or trivariate models. Table 6.3 shows that the trace statistics support the result that all of the three models with four-variate hold only one cointegration vector at a 10% significance level. As an example, see model $(M, R, Ex, Im)^*$. We consider the number of cointegration vectors, beginning with the hypothesis $r = 0$ versus the general hypothesis H_1. By using the trace test procedure, we can see that $\hat{\tau}(0) = 48.73$, which is greater than the 10% significance level 43.95 of the asymptotic distribution. Hence there is an evidence in the data that there exists at least one cointegration relation. When we tested the hypothesis $r \leq 1$ in H_1, we got a test value $\hat{\tau}(1) = 25.38$, which is less than the 90 percent quantile 26.79. This suggests us to receive $\hat{r} = 1$ as the number of estimated cointegration vectors. Table 6.3 shows that the cointegration vector is $(0.737, 0.015, -0.677, 0.041)^*$. The equilibrium relation of the four economic time serieses is

$$0.737M + 0.015R - 0.677Ex + 0.041Im = 0$$

or

$$0.737M + 0.015R = 0.677Ex - 0.041Im.$$

As far as model $(Y, M, R, Ex)^*$, for a given 0.1 critical value, since

$$\hat{\tau}(0) = 53.67 > \tau(0|0.9) = 43.95$$

and
$$\hat{\tau}(1) = 22.76 < \tau(1|0.9) = 26.79,$$

hence, we can conclude that just one cointegration vector exists, which is corresponding to the eigenvalue 0.338. In view of Table 6.3, similar to this procedure, we see the four-variate model $(Y, M, R, Im)^*$ has only one cointegrated relation as well. Based on the two four-variate models, the following two equilibrium relations can finally be obtained

$$0.717Y - 0.673M - 0.006R + 0.185Ex = 0$$

and

$$0.8Y - 0.596M - 0.012R + 0.066Im = 0.$$

Remark 6.2 It should be noted that for the eigenvalue $\hat{\gamma}_i$, the corresponding eigenvector in this book are normalized such that $\sum_{j=1}^{p} \hat{v}_{ij}^2 = 1$. This is different to the choice of Johansen (1988), Johansen and Juselius (1990), but the eigenvalues are not changed.

6.3 Evaluation of the Identified Models

A criterion for the lag-length selection is that the resulting residuals are uncorrelated and keeping Gaussainity to a reasonable degree. In this section, in view of the tests of auto-correlation and Gaussainity, we confirm weather the identified cointegrated models in the above section (for the selected Japanese macoreconomic data) suit for the following causal analysis. For the sake of brevity, we only plotted the estimated residuals and the histograms for the cases of one bivariate model, one trivariate model, and one four-variate model (see Figures 6.2, 6.3, and 6.4).

The uncorrelation of the residual is checked by Portmanteau test. In this paper, different to the Ljung and Box (1978) test which Johansen (1995) used, we use the following modified form given by Hosking (1980), which seems to have better performance for small sample size:

Chapter 6. Cointegrated Model Identification

Table 6.2 The Eigenvalues and the Eigenvectors and the Trace Statistics for Trivariate Models

	Eigenvalues				
	(0.303	0.128	0.020)		
	Eigenvectors			$p-r$	$\hat{\tau}$
Y	0.829	0.886	0.788	1	1.51
M	-0.560	-0.462	-0.615	2	11.75
R	-0.007	0.021	0.010	3	38.83
	Eigenvalues				
	(0.233	0.062	0.029)		
	Eigenvectors			$p-r$	$\hat{\tau}$
Y	0.314	0.911	-0.862	1	2.17
M	-0.779	-0.350	0.486	2	6.94
Ex	0.545	-0.219	0.147	3	26.81
	Eigenvalues				
	(0.211	0.100	0.028)		
	Eigenvectors			$p-r$	$\hat{\tau}$
Y	0.842	-0.867	-0.179	1	2.13
M	-0.539	0.377	0.889	2	10.04
Im	-0.025	0.326	-0.423	3	27.83
	Eigenvalues				
	(0.242	0.141	0.033)		
	Eigenvectors			$p-r$	$\hat{\tau}$
M	-0.746	-0.591	0.845	1	2.52
R	-0.012	0.069	-0.017	2	13.93
Ex	0.665	0.804	-0.535	3	34.70
	Eigenvalues				
	(0.201	0.131	0.031)		
	Eigenvectors			$p-r$	$\hat{\tau}$
M	0.749	-0.508	0.820	1	2.37
R	0.111	0.004	0.016	2	12.93
Im	-0.653	0.861	-0.572	3	29.77
	Eigenvalues				
	(0.258	0.134	0.031)		
	Eigenvectors			$p-r$	$\hat{\tau}$
Y	-0.794	-0.844	0.932	1	2.39
Ex	0.596	0.346	-0.147	2	13.15
Im	-0.120	0.409	-0.331	3	35.53

See the τ-statistic quantiles in the following Table 6.3.

6.3. Evaluation of the Identified Models

Table 6.3 The Eigenvalues and the Eigenvectors and the Trace Statistics for Four-variate Models

	Eigenvalues					
	(0.338	0.173	0.090	0.019)		
	Eigenvectors				$p-r$	$\hat{\tau}$
Y	−0.717	−0.814	0.913	0.847	1	1.42
M	0.673	0.199	−0.296	−0.523	2	8.50
R	0.006	0.054	−0.002	0.005	3	22.76
Ex	−0.185	0.543	−0.279	−0.098	4	53.67
	Eigenvalues					
	(0.338	0.176	0.075	0.041)		
	Eigenvectors				$p-r$	$\hat{\tau}$
Y	−0.800	0.846	−0.880	−0.501	1	3.12
M	0.596	−0.523	0.436	0.829	2	8.97
R	0.012	0.029	−0.010	−0.006	3	23.52
Im	−0.066	0.098	0.186	−0.248	4	54.40
	Eigenvalues					
	(0.268	0.163	0.124	0.028)		
	Eigenvectors				$p-r$	$\hat{\tau}$
M	0.735	0.083	−0.382	0.864	1	2.13
R	0.015	−0.021	0.047	0.006	2	12.07
Ex	−0.677	−0.584	0.781	−0.096	3	25.38
Im	0.041	0.808	−0.492	−0.495	4	48.73

	Trace Statistics : τ		
$p-r$	80%	90%	95%
1	1.66	2.69	3.76
2	11.07	13.33	15.41
3	23.64	26.79	29.68
4	40.15	43.95	47.21

The τ-statistic quantiles are from Osterwald-Lenum (1992).

Chapter 6. Cointegrated Model Identification

$$Hg(s) = T^2 \sum_{j=1}^{s} \frac{1}{T-j} tr\{\hat{C}_{0j}\hat{C}_{00}^{-1}\hat{C}_{0j}^{*}\hat{C}_{00}^{-1}\}, \tag{6.3}$$

where

$$\hat{C}_{0j} = T^{-1} \sum_{t=j+1}^{T} \hat{\varepsilon}_t \hat{\varepsilon}_{t-j}^{*}.$$

Under the null hypothesis of uncorrelation, the distribution of this test statistic is approximated for large T and for $s > a$ by χ^2 distribution with degrees of freedom $f = p^2(s-a)$ where a is the lag length of the model.

For the cases of bivariate, trivariate and four-variate models, we chose the same $s = 18$. The observed statistics are listed in Table 6.4. For a given 0.05 critical value, the estimates of the Hg-statistics for all the models [except (Y, M, R, Ex)] are not significant. Even for a 0.01 critical value, as the Hg-statistic of model (Y, M, R, Ex) is 0.0163 (> 0.01), we know the estimated residuals are uncorrelated. In the whole, the results support that all the residuals in the models we discussed are reasonably uncorrelated.

The Gaussian assumption of the disturbance term is checked by applying the omnibus test for multivariate normality given by Doornik and Hansen (1994) to the residuals of the estimated models. Let R_r^* be the $p \times T$ matrix of the residuals with sample covariance matrix $F = (f_{ij})$. Create a matrix D with the reciprocals of the standard deviations on the diagonal, $D = diag(f_{11}^{-1/2}, \cdots, f_{pp}^{-1/2})$, and then form the correlation matrix $C = DFD$. Define the transformed matrix of R_r by

$$R_c = HL^{-1/2}H^*DR_r^*, \tag{6.4}$$

where L is the diagonal matrix with the eigenvalues of C on the diagonal. The columns of H are the corresponding eigenvectors. Then we compute univariate skewness $\sqrt{b_{1i}}$ and kurtosis b_{2i} of each vector of the transformed $R_c^*, i = 1, \cdots, p$. Under the null hypothesis of multivariate normal distribution of the residuals, the test statistic is asymptotically distributed as:

$$E_p = Z_1^* Z_1 + Z_2^* Z_2 \sim \chi^2(2p), \tag{6.5}$$

where $Z_1 = (z_{11}, \cdots, z_{1p})^*$ and $Z_2 = (z_{21}, \cdots, z_{2p})^*$. For $i = 1, \cdots, p$, the transformation for the skewness $\sqrt{b_{1i}}$ into z_{1i} is due to D'Agostino (1970). For $i = 1, \cdots, p$,

6.3. Evaluation of the Identified Models

the kurtosis b_{2i} is transformed from a gamma distribution to χ^2, and then transformed into standard normal z_{2i} using the Wilson-Hilferty cubed root transformation. The observed test statistics E_p for all the models used in this paper are listed in Table 6.5. Those test statistics seem to indicate that there is no significant departure from Gaussianity. The results in Tables 6.4 and 6.5 ensure us that we may proceed to the analysis of the one-way effect measurement on the basis of the proposed ECM's.

Remarks 6.3 The elements of the Z_1 and Z_2 in model (6.5), i.e. z_{ij} ($i = 1, 2$, $j = 1, 2, \cdots, p$), are calculated as follows:

(i) For $i = 1, \cdots, p$, the transformation for the skewness $\sqrt{b_{1i}}$ into z_{1i} is conducted by the following precess:

$$\begin{aligned}
\beta &= 3(T^2 + 27T - 70)(T+1)(T+3)/(T-2)(T+5)(T+7)(T+9), \\
\omega^2 &= -1 + \{2(\beta - 1)\}^{1/2}, \\
\delta &= 1/\{\log\sqrt{\omega^2}\}^{1/2}, \\
y &= b_{1i}[(\omega^2 - 1)(T+1)(T+3)/\{12(T-2)\}]^{1/2}, \\
z_{1i} &= \delta \log\{y + (y^2 + 1)^{1/2}\}.
\end{aligned} \quad (6.6)$$

(ii) For $i = 1, \cdots, p$, the kurtosis b_{2i} is transformed from a gamma distribution to χ^2, and then transformed into standard normal z_{2i} using the Wilson-Hilferty cubed root transformation:

$$\begin{aligned}
\delta &= (T-3)(T+1)(T^2 + 15T - 4), \\
a &= (T-2)(T+5)(T+7)(T^2 + 27T - 70)/6\delta, \\
c &= (T-7)(T+5)(T+7)(T^2 + 2T - 5)/6\delta, \\
k &= (T+5)(T+7)(T^3 + 37T^2 + 11T - 313)/12\delta, \\
\alpha &= a + b_{1i}c, \\
\chi &= (b_{2i} - 1 - b_{1i})2k, \\
z_{2i} &= \{(\chi/2\alpha)^{1/3} - 1 + (1/9\alpha)\}(9\alpha)^{1/2}.
\end{aligned} \quad (6.7)$$

Chapter 6. Cointegrated Model Identification

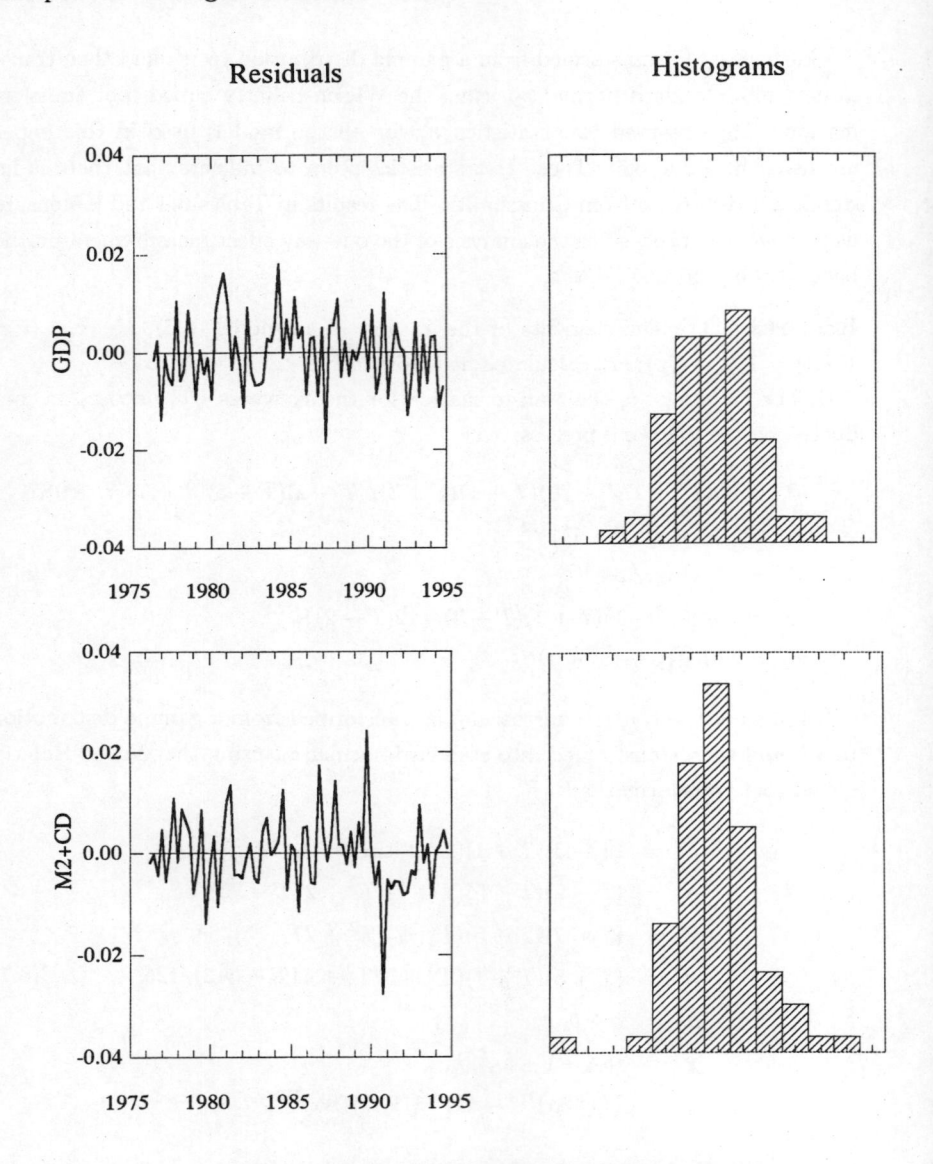

Figure 6.2 Residuals and the Histograms for the Japanese Data (Based on Bivariate Model)

6.3. Evaluation of the Identified Models

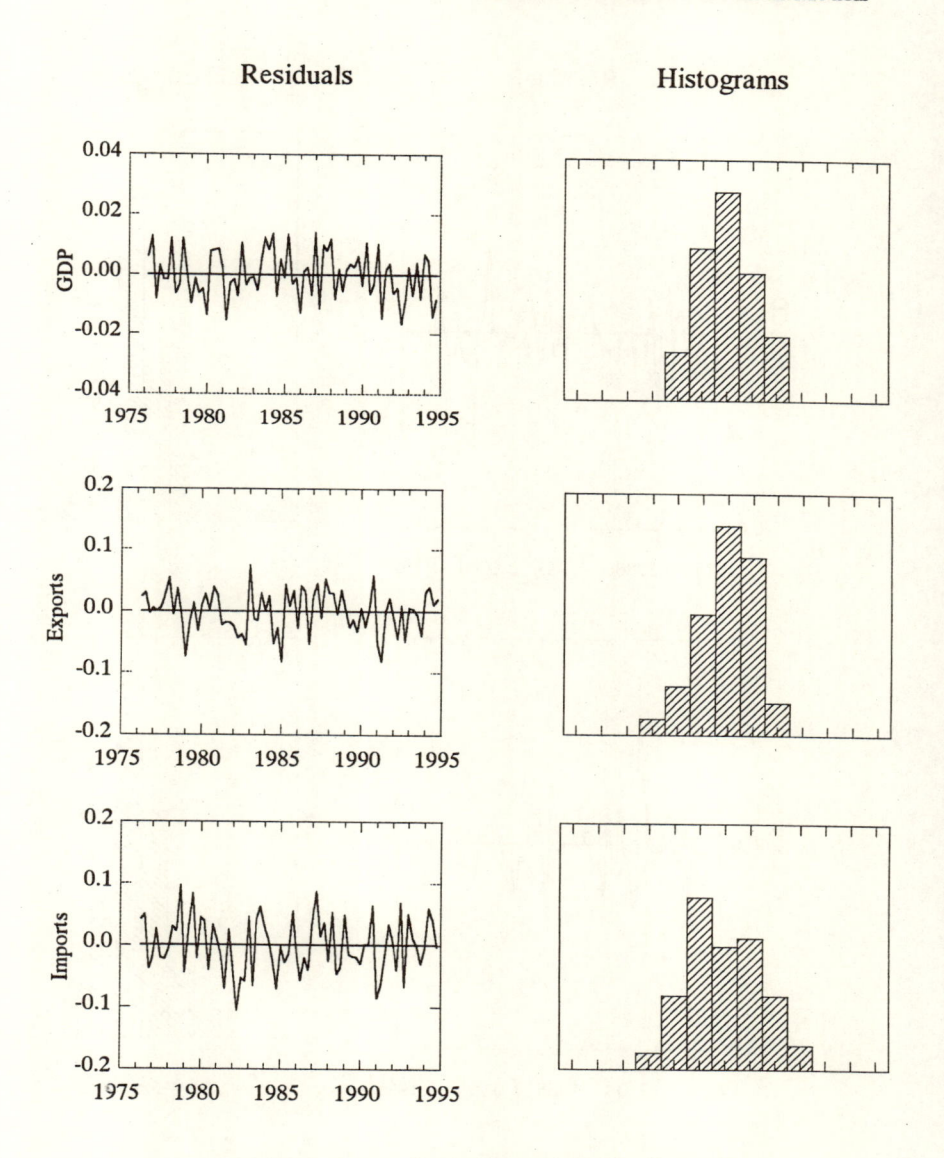

Figure 6.3 Residuals and the Histograms for the Japanese Data (Based on Trivariates Model)

Chapter 6. Cointegrated Model Identification

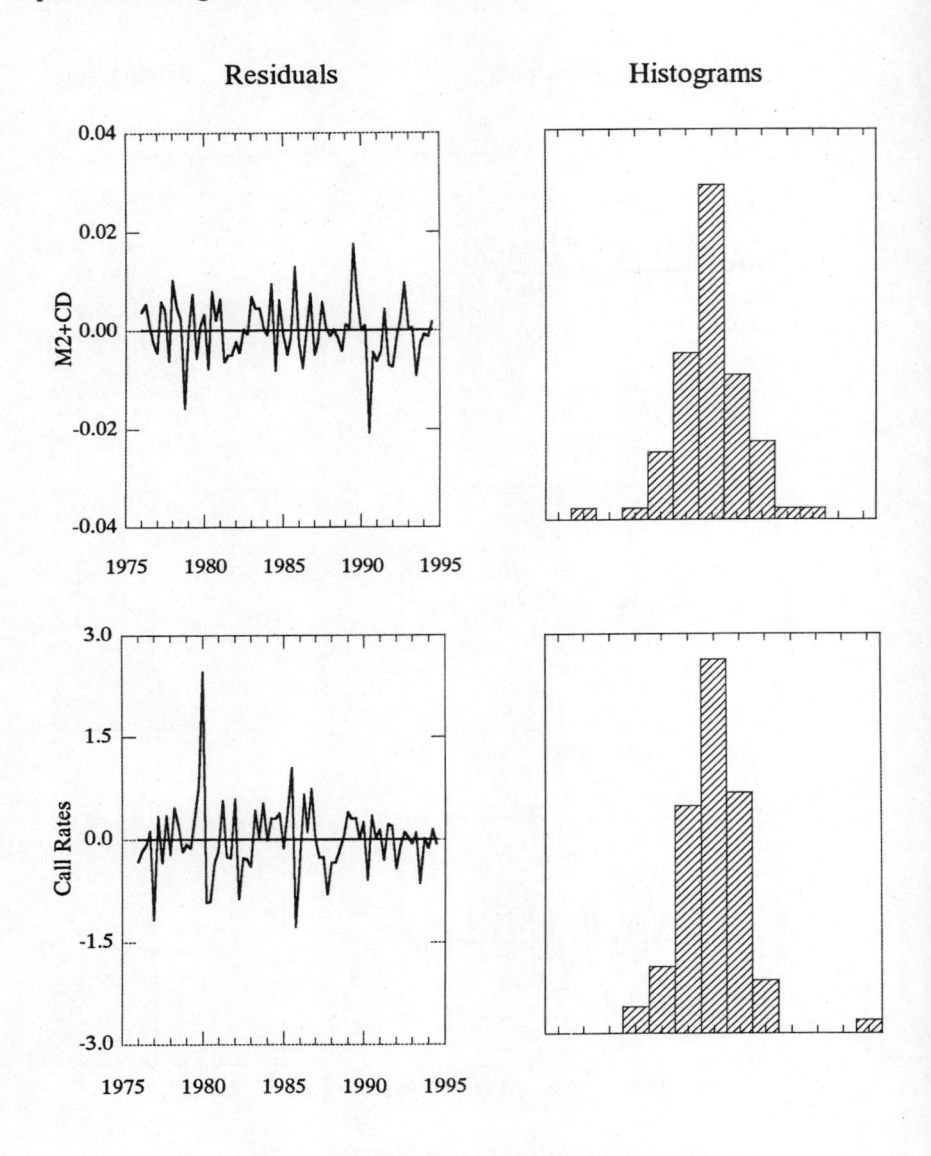

Figure 6.4 Residuals and the Histograms for the Japanese Data (Based on Four-variates Model)

6.3. Evaluation of the Identified Models

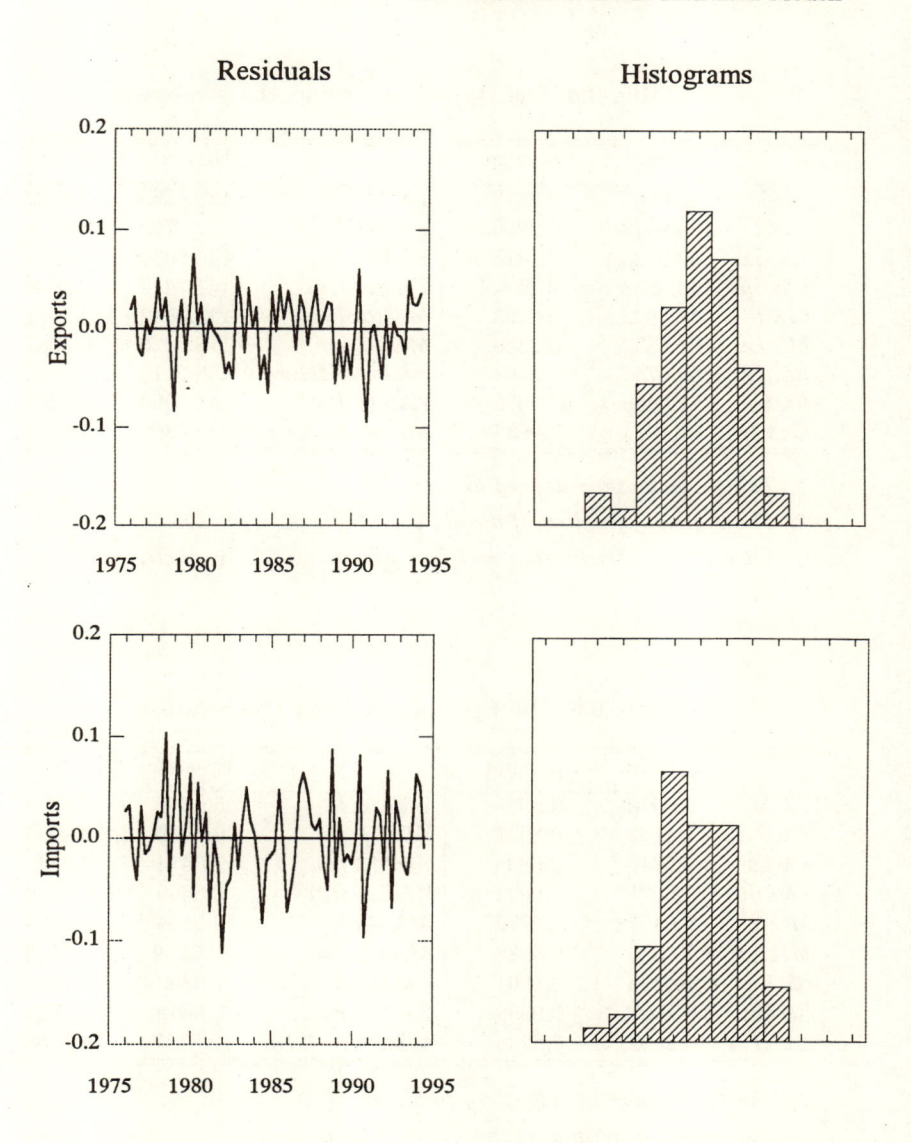

Figure 6.4 Continued

Chapter 6. Cointegrated Model Identification

Table 6.4 The Hg-statistics and the p-values

	Hg-stat.	p-value		Hg-stat.	p-value
$Y\&M$	55.8605	0.3319	$Y\&M\&R$	129.4265	0.2037
$Y\&R$	56.9648	0.2956	$Y\&M\&Ex$	137.0790	0.0990
$Y\&Ex$	62.9925	0.1413	$Y\&M\&Im$	144.9039	0.0410
$Y\&Im$	58.3853	0.2524	$Y\&Ex\&Im$	141.7412	0.0596
$M\&R$	42.1847	0.8325	$M\&R\&Ex$	133.3932	0.1427
$M\&Ex$	61.1332	0.1808	$M\&R\&Im$	116.0028	0.5087
$R\&Ex$	59.6746	0.2168	$Y\&M\&R\&Ex$	253.9510	0.0163
$R\&Im$	51.3956	0.4976	$Y\&M\&R\&Im$	241.2960	0.0565
$Ex\&Im$	68.1974	0.0653	$M\&R\&Ex\&Im$	229.2855	0.1492

1. The Hg-statistic is defined by (6.3).
2. The degree of freedom of the Hg-statistic is 52, 117, 208
    for bivariate, trivariate, and four-variate models, respectively.

Table 6.5 The Ep-statistics and the p-values

	Ep-stat.	p-value		Ep-stat.	p-value
$Y\&M$	0.0940	0.9989	$Y\&M\&R$	5.0317	0.5398
$Y\&R$	1.1102	0.8927	$Y\&M\&Ex$	0.3049	0.9995
$Y\&Ex$	2.2849	0.6835	$Y\&M\&Im$	1.0414	0.9840
$Y\&Im$	0.6071	0.9623	$Y\&Ex\&Im$	0.5600	0.9970
$M\&R$	5.6457	0.2272	$M\&R\&Ex$	8.9454	0.1767
$M\&Ex$	2.7026	0.6088	$M\&R\&Im$	10.3059	0.1123
$R\&Ex$	7.6296	0.1061	$Y\&M\&R\&Ex$	7.9830	0.4351
$R\&Im$	0.1067	0.9986	$Y\&M\&R\&Im$	5.8645	0.6624
$Ex\&Im$	0.8692	0.9289	$M\&R\&Ex\&Im$	12.5157	0.1296

1. The Ep-statistic is defined by (6.5).
2. The degree of freedom of the Ep-statistic is 4, 6, 8
    for bivariate, trivariate, and four-variate models, respectively.

Chapter 7

Empirical Causal Relationships

Following the pre-analysis in the above chapter, we will discuss the empirical results of the measures of one-way effect among GDP, M2+CD, Call Rates, Exports and Imports during the period 1975/I through 1994/IV[see Figure 6.1]. The purpose of the empirical analysis is to show the macroeconomic relationships of Japanese economy in the period we are interested. We especially want to know how money supply and interest rates affect the economy of Japan. The empirical results show that the dramatic development of Japanese economy in the last two decades is mostly due to the international trade and the monetary system. We also want to know the causal relationships of these macroeconomic time series. In section 7.2, using our new approach, the empirical results show the non-competitional economic relationship between Japan and China.

7.1 Estimation and Explanation of the Causal Measures

We investigate the empirical causal relationships of macroeconomic data based the p-dimensional cointegrating process $Z(t) = (X(t)^*, Y(t)^*)^*$ expressed by

$$\Delta Z(t) = \alpha \beta^* Z(t-1) + \sum_{i=1}^{4} \Gamma(i) \Delta Z(t-i) + \mu + \sum_{j=1}^{3} \Phi_j P_j(t) + \varepsilon(t). \quad (7.1)$$

The estimators of the cointegration rank and cointegration vector as well as the other parameters in model (7.1), *i.e.*, $\hat{r}$ (the rank of $\alpha\beta^*$), $\hat{\beta}, \hat{\alpha}, \hat{\Gamma}(i)$ ($i = 1, 2, 3, 4$),

Chapter 7. Empirical Causal Relationships

and $\hat{\Sigma}$ are determined by the discussions in Chapter 4 and the above Section 6.1. As the causal relationships are not affected by the dummy variables and the intercept (time trend) in model (7.1), let $C(e^{-i\lambda})$ be the cofactor matrix of

$$I_p - (I_p + \hat{\alpha}\hat{\beta}^*)e^{-i\lambda} - \sum_{k=1}^{4} \hat{\Gamma}(k)(e^{-ik\lambda} - e^{-i(k+1)\lambda}), \tag{7.2}$$

then the measure of one-way effect from $\{Y(t)\}$ to $\{X(t)\}$ can be estimated based on the frequency response estimate

$$\hat{\Lambda}(e^{-i\lambda}) = \hat{C}(e^{-i\lambda})\hat{\Sigma}^{1/2}$$

and the spectral density estimate

$$\hat{f}(e^{-i\lambda}) = \frac{1}{2\pi}\hat{\Lambda}(e^{-i\lambda})\hat{\Lambda}(e^{-i\lambda})^*.$$

Since the causal measure of one-way effect in the frequency domain is symmetric with zero point in the period of $(-\pi, \pi]$, we only plotted the estimated results in $(0, \pi]$. We chose the left of the period being open due to the properties of trigonometry and periodic function. The causal measure in the frequency domain at zero point represents the causal relation at an infinite time period. In the long-run relationship analysis, what we are interested in is the properties of the estimated $FMO(\lambda)$ while λ is near original point but not zero.

Economic phenomena are generally observed in a periodic manner. While stock prices and commodity exchanges are recorded continuously, most data collection methods restrict observations to daily, weekly, monthly, or yearly intervals. An economic time series is therefore usually the result of sampling a phenomenon at equally spaced points in time. In economics, one phenomenon can be considered as a sum of oscillations at different frequencies. An oscillation described by $1/T$ is measured in cycles per unit time, where T is the length of time required for one complete oscillation. The quantity λ in the period $(-\pi, \pi]$ is simply angular frequency,

$$\lambda = 2\pi/T,$$

which is the number of revolusions around the unit circle per unit time. For details see Fishman (1969).

7.1. Estimation and Explanation of the Causal Measures

A notable peak of the estimated $FMO_{Y \to X}(\lambda)$ at $\lambda = \pi/2$, for example for quarterly data, would indicate that there may be a significant one-way effect from $\{Y(t)\}$ to $\{X(t)\}$ in a one-year period cycle. It should be noted that this does not imply that $\{Y(t)\}$ causes $\{X(t)\}$ with a one-year lag. The time-lag relationship in $\{Y(t)\}$ causing $\{X(t)\}$ should be observed in Sims' distributed-lag representation [see (3.5), there we discussed the relations of sationary processes], which connects $\{Y_{0,-1}(t)\}$ and $\{X_{-1,0}(t)\}$ in the time domain. The causal measure of one-way effect at the frequency $\lambda = \pi/20$ corresponding to a 40-cycle movement shows the effect of a ten-year cycle. The FMO at frequency $\lambda = \pi/40$ shows the relation of twenty-year cycle components. For different definitions of the "long-run" relation, for example, over ten-year period cycle, over twenty-year period cycle, or over fifty-year period cycle, the overall one-way effects are expressed by the local measures of the OMO in the frequency bands of $(0, \pi/20]$, $(0, \pi/40]$, or $(0, \pi/100]$, respectively.

For the purpose of causal analysis in view of the measures of one-way effect presented by Hosoya (1991, 1997) based on the ECM model, we have constructed a good interface FORTRAN program, HOCM98 [see also HOCM95 in Yao (1996a)]. HOCM98 provides the calculation of the causal measures of one-way effect based on a cointegrated model in the time domain and the frequency domain. The input of the program are p-dimensional observations and the sample size. For modeling a cointegrated ECM, the constant term, deterministic time trend, seasonal dummies, the order of the ECM can be freely determined. Furthermore, the dimensions p_1 and p_2 as well as the combinations of the variables can also be freely selected. The main output of program HOCM98 is the estimated FMO in $(0, \pi]$, the estimated OMO and its Wald test statistic, and the 95% confidence interval of the estimated OMO in case the non-causality null hypothesis is rejected at a 0.05 critical value. In the case of the null hypothesis is accepted at the given confidence level, in stead of the confidence interval, the p-value of the Wald test is given. For the details of the computational algorithm of the Wald statistic, see Section 5.2.

For the calculation of the causal measures of one-way effect in the frequency domain, we take 200 equal-division of the period $(0, \pi]$, and get a frequency set of $\{i = 1, 2, \cdots, 200\}$. For each model we calculated 200 causal measures of the

Chapter 7. Empirical Causal Relationships

one-way effect in the frequency domain, $M(\lambda_i), i = 1, 2, \cdots, 200$. Each of the plots in the following Figure 7.1 are plotted by 200 estimated causal measures of the one-way effect in the frequency domain in $(0, \pi]$. Before we chose 200 as the number of interval division of $(0, \pi]$, we have tested many cases of interval division until 1200 equal-divisions of period $(0, \pi]$. We find that 200 equal-divisions of the period is good enough to plot a smoothly figure that can express the causal measure of one-way effect in the frequency domain. For small number of divisions of the period $(0, \pi]$, the estimated causal measures of the one-way effect may not express the true measures especially at smaller frequencies. So we think 200 is a proper equal-division of the period $(0, \pi]$, at least it is suited for the selected Japanese macro economic data dealt with in this article.

Remark 7.1 The existence of the Nyquist frequency [see for example Yao (1985)] should not be ignored. The discernible highest frequency at $\lambda = \pi$, which corresponds to two time periods ($T = 2\pi/\lambda = 2$); namely, half a year for quarterly data. The economic implication is that, we cannot discern the one-way effect shorter than half a year for quarterly data.

7.2 Causal Relations of Japanese Macroeconomic Data

In this section, in view of the cointegrated ECM and calculation algorithm discussed in the above section and Chapter 6, we summarize the main results of the causal relationships of Japanese macroeconomic data. Based on bivariate, trivariate and four-variate cointegrated models, we will analyze causal relations from one (may be multiple) economic time series to another of the nominal GDP, M2+CD, Call Rates, Exports and Imports. We will also investigate how the economic indices affect each other in Japanese economic activity. The empirical results of the causal measures of one-way effect in the frequency domain are plotted in Figure 7.1.

For bivariate models, we investigated 18 groups of one-way effect causal relations from one time series to another. Figure 7.1 (a1) through (a8) shows the estimated $\hat{M}_{Y \to X}(\lambda)$ of the bivariate models for the respective cases where X and Y are as indicated. For the trivariate models, we investigated a large number

7.2. Causal Relations of Japanese Macroeconomic Data

of the 2-to-1 causal relations which are of interest to our study. Figure 7.1 (b1) through (b10) show the estimated results of $\hat{M}_{Y \to X}(\lambda)$ of the trivariate model for respective cases where X and Y are as indicated. As far as four-variate models, even there have many possible combinations of 2-to-2 and 3-to-1 causal relations, we only show the main estimated results of $\hat{M}_{Y \to X}(\lambda)$ of four-variate model for respective cases where X and Y are as indicated [see Figure 7.1 (c1) to (c4)]. The cointegration rank, OMO, confidence intervals of OMO, and the p-value (in the case that the null hypothesis of noncausality is not rejected) are also listed there.

Although many computations were conducted on possible combinations of the five macroeconomic time series, only a few that are of interest to our study are shown here. The causal measure in the frequency domain can give a clear explanation of the long-run and short-run economic relationships in the last twenty years of Japanese economy. An observation of the plots in Figure 7.1 will yield the following notable findings.

1. The estimated OMO from M2+CD to nominal GDP is about three times that in the reverse direction, but neither of the two measures is significant at a 0.05 critical level [see plot (a1)]. Since the p-value of the Wald test for testing the one-way effect from money supply to GDP is 0.08, even though the effect is small, but significant at a 10 percent significance level. The plot (a1) also shows that there is no one-way effect in the frequency band $[0.4\pi, \pi]$ or in a period band shorter than one year and a quarter. The estimate of the FMO of money to GDP has a peak in the interval of $[0.25\pi, 0.4\pi]$, which shows the significant local effects between five-quarter time period and two-year time period. The second peak near the origin point indicates the existence of the long-run effect.

2. In general, Call Rate has conspicuous one-way effects to the other variables. In contrast, the effects in the reverse direction are small and not significant [see (a3) to (a6) in Figure 7.1]. The estimated properties of the FMO near zero show that all the effect are long-run. We can also see that except the one-way effect of Call Rates to Exports, the other three one-way effects are very stable. A very interesting finding is that the effect of Call Rates to Exports has one comparatively short peak getting at frequency 0.06π,

Chapter 7. Empirical Causal Relationships

which correspond to 10/3 cycles (nearly ten months) time period. The estimated OMO of interest rates to exports is 8.1 [with a confidence interval (6.11, 10.08)], which is about twice of the others. The presence of the one-way effect from interest rates would seem rather conformable to the conventional understanding of macroeconomic activities. Moreover, the role of interest rates seems to be consistent with Sims (1980)'s findings in the macroeconomic data of the U.S.

3. Plot (a7) shows that the one-way effect from Exports to GDP is significant. The corresponding one-way effect in the frequency domain shows that the effect is not long-run. The estimate of the OMO from Imports to GDP is 2.61 and W=2.79 with a p-value 0.095, the main effect are concentrated in the time period less than one year [see plot (a8)]. It is only significant at 0.1 critical level. The one-way effect from Exports and Imports to GDP is 3.82 and W=3.27 with a p-value 0.07 [see Figure 7.1, plot (b1)]. The effects from GDP to Exports and to Imports are not significant. On the whole, it shows that during the period we analyzed, the Japanese economic growth can be thought derived by the external trades.

4. As far as the bivariate cointegration model between Exports and Imports is concerned, the OMO from Exports to Imports is 0.01, and the test statistic is estimated as W=2.93 with p-value 0.086, whereas the OMO from Imports to Exports is 0.06 and the test statistic is W=1.88 with a p-value 0.17. Namely, at a 0.05 critical level, there is no significant one-way causality between Japanese Exports and Imports. This also shows that at a 0.1 critical value, there exists a comparatively weak one-way effect from Exports to Imports.

5. The one-way effect from M2+CD and Call Rates to GDP is significant and the corresponding one-way effect in the frequency domain get its peak at frequency 0.4π [see plot (b2)], implying that the highest effect comes from about one year and a quarter period. The one-way effect of GDP and Call Rates to M2+CD is large and significant ($\hat{W} = 7.19$), and the mainly one-way effect in the frequency domain are concentrated in the time band where

7.2. Causal Relations of Japanese Macroeconomic Data

the time period less than two year [see plot (b3)]. The estimate of OMO is 7.77, which is the highest value of the overall measures of one-way effect in all the trivariate model cases we have studied. Both of the one-way effects from M2+CD and Call Rates to Exports and to Imports are not significant at a 0.05 significance level [see plot (b4), (b5)]. These findings seem to indicate that money supply is ineffective to the Japanese external trades in this period of the floating exchange-rate of Japanese Yen.

6. The estimated OMO of money supply and exports to nominal GDP is 2.60 with a Wald statistic $\hat{W} = 15.6$ [See plot (b6), Figure 7.1]. The peak of the one-way effect is occurred in the 5th seasonal time period for about just one season. The effect from money supply and imports to nominal GDP is 3.5 and significant at a 95% confidence level. The one-way effect is long-run [see plot (b7)]. Plots (b8) in Figure 7.1 shows that the causal measure from GDP and Imports to M2+CD is 3.22 and significant. The one-way effect is not long-run and the causal measure of one-way effect in the frequency domain down quickly after the point of last peak, $\lambda = 0.2\pi$, correspond to two and a half years time period. The overall measure of GDP and Exports to M2+CD is only 2.6 and the p-value of its Wald test is 0.34.

7. Our Wald test shows that the effect of interest rates and exports to money supply is significant at a 0.05 critical value, and the effect from interest rates and imports to money supply is also significant at the same critical value. The former one-way effect is greater than the latter [see (b9) and (b10)]. Both effects are stable in the entire frequency region $(0, \pi]$ and are long-run. The evidence also indicates that the one-way effect from exports to money is not significant and we have

$$M_{Y \to M} = 0.03, \quad M_{R \to M} = 4.53, \quad M_{Ex \to M} = 1.89,$$

whereas

$$M_{Y+R \to M} = 7.77, \quad M_{R+Ex \to M} = 5.86.$$

These results imply that, for some cases, a policy mix is needed and is perhaps more effective than pursuing a single-policy objective.

Chapter 7. Empirical Causal Relationships

8. The effect from money supply and interests rate as well as exports to nominal gross domestic production is observed. See plot (c1) of Figure 7.1. The overall measure of one-way effect from $(M, R, Ex)^*$ to GDP is about 3.77, which with a 95% confidence interval (3.18, 4.35). Both long-run and short-run effects are observed. The effects of money supply and interests rate as well as imports to nominal GDP is also observed. From plot (c2) we can see the overall measure of one-way effect from $(M, R, Im)^*$ to GDP is 3.78. Even though the effects are not steady, both long-run and short-run effects are observed. Comparatively, the effect from money supply and interests rate as well as imports to GDP keeps a high level effect for the time periods less than two and half years.

9. The effect from exports and imports to money supply and interest rates is strong and significant [see plot (c3)]. The effect in the reverse direction, the effect of money supply and interest rates to exports and imports [see plot (c4)], is comparatively large in value ($OMO = 4.82$) but not significant ($W = 1.15$ with a p-value=0.23). We have also find that even the estimated OMO of $(M, R, Im)^*$ to Ex is comparatively large ($OMO = 3.45$) but not significant (p-value=0.21). This means that the magnitude of the estimated OMO itself does not tell us whether a one-way effect is statistically significant or not, and a test is therefore needed to judge the significance. As a whole, the findings imply that in the Japanese economy recent years, the external trades have had a significant one-way effect on the monetary side of the Japanese economy.

To summarize, the above empirical analyses show that there is no significant one-way effect from income to money but that the reverse effect is significant at a critical value of 0.1 but not of 0.05. In general, interest rates affect the other variables, but not vice versa. The international trade affects the monetary economy, but the opposite is not the case. Concerning the effects of external trades on Japanese economic growth in the period of concern, the cause is mainly from exports, but it is not long-run. The empirical results also indicate the cases for which policy mixing might be more effective.

7.2. Causal Relations of Japanese Macroeconomic Data

In the remainder of this section, we will illustrate the confidence-set construction given in (3.15). Based on the trivariate model (4.1) for the variable $Z = (Y, M, R)^*$, and for the case of vector-valued OMO, $G = (G_1, G_2)^*$, we have the estimated matrix

$$H(\hat{\theta}, \hat{\psi})^{-1} = \begin{pmatrix} 0.0026 & -0.0012 \\ -0.0012 & 0.3705 \end{pmatrix}, \quad (7.3)$$

where G_1 is the OMO from Y and R to M, and G_2 is the OMO from M and R to Y, respectively. We have the Wald statistic $W^{(2)} = 307.89$, which means that the two one-way effects are simultaneously significant. Following to the argument of Section 3, we can determine the confidence set of the two OMO, G_1 and G_2; the 0.9 confidence set of the two one-way effect causal measures is given by

$$0.14(G_1 - 7.77)^2 - 0.13(G_1 - 7.77)(G_2 - 3.93) + 19.64(G_2 - 3.93)^2 \leq 4.61. \quad (7.4)$$

To visualize the nested ellipses graphically, we give three plots in Figures 7.2 and 7.3 [the scale of γ axis in Figure 7.3 (a) is set to be four times as much as that in Figure 7.2]. Figure 7.2 depicts the confidence surface for confidence coefficients γ ranging from 0 to 0.975. For $\gamma = 0$, the ellipse is degenerated to one point on the plane of $\gamma = 0$. The degenerated point is nothing but the ML estimate $(\hat{G}_1, \hat{G}_2) = (7.77, 3.93)$. For a specific confidence coefficient $\gamma = \gamma_1$, the confidence ellipse is determined as the section cut by the plane in the right angle to the γ axis at the height of $\gamma = \gamma_1$. Figure 7.3 (a) shows the nested ellipses which correspond to the confidence sets for γ in the interval $[0.90, 0.95]$. It is just the portion cut out from the body in Figure 7.2 by the parallel planes $\gamma = 0.90$ and $\gamma = 0.95$. One cut end of the portion (the smaller ellipse) shows the 90 percent confidence set of the one-way effect measures determined by (4.8). Figure 7.3 (b) is the confidence sets for γ in the interval $[0.90, 0.95]$ projected onto the $(G1, G2)$ plane.

Chapter 7. Empirical Causal Relationships

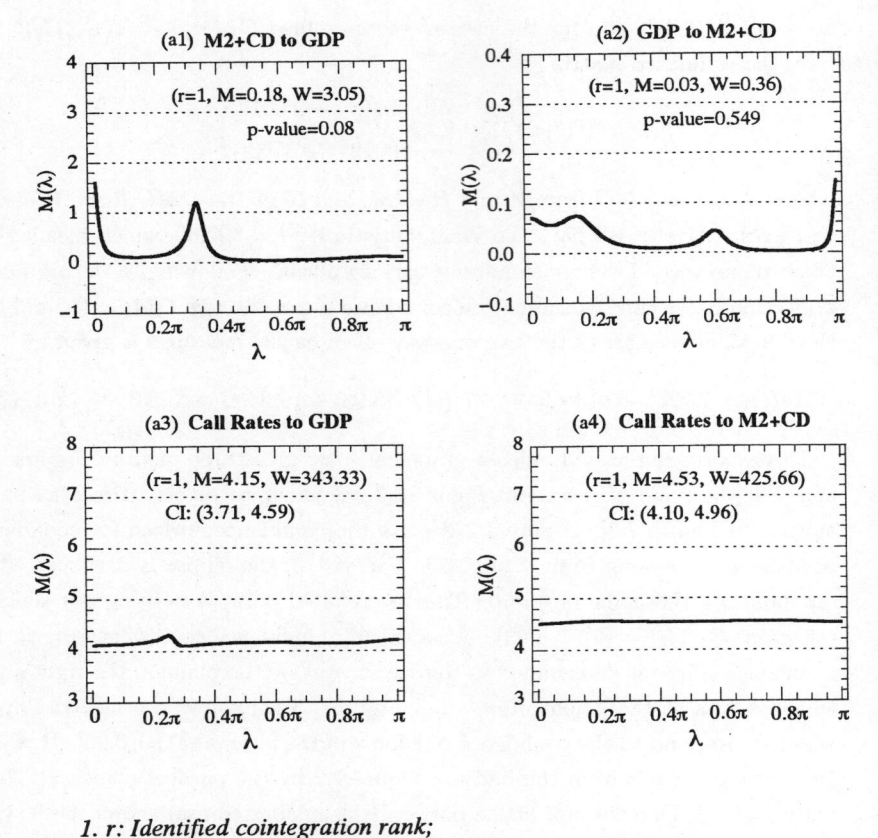

(a1) M2+CD to GDP
(r=1, M=0.18, W=3.05)
p-value=0.08

(a2) GDP to M2+CD
(r=1, M=0.03, W=0.36)
p-value=0.549

(a3) Call Rates to GDP
(r=1, M=4.15, W=343.33)
CI: (3.71, 4.59)

(a4) Call Rates to M2+CD
(r=1, M=4.53, W=425.66)
CI: (4.10, 4.96)

1. *r: Identified cointegration rank;*
2. *W: Wald statistic given by (5.21)*
3. *CI: The 95% confidence interval of OMO*
   (in case the non-causality null hypothesis is rejected).

Figure 7.1 Estimated Measures of One-way Effect, Identified Cointegration Ranks, Wald Statistics and Confidence Intervals

7.2. Causal Relations of Japanese Macroeconomic Data

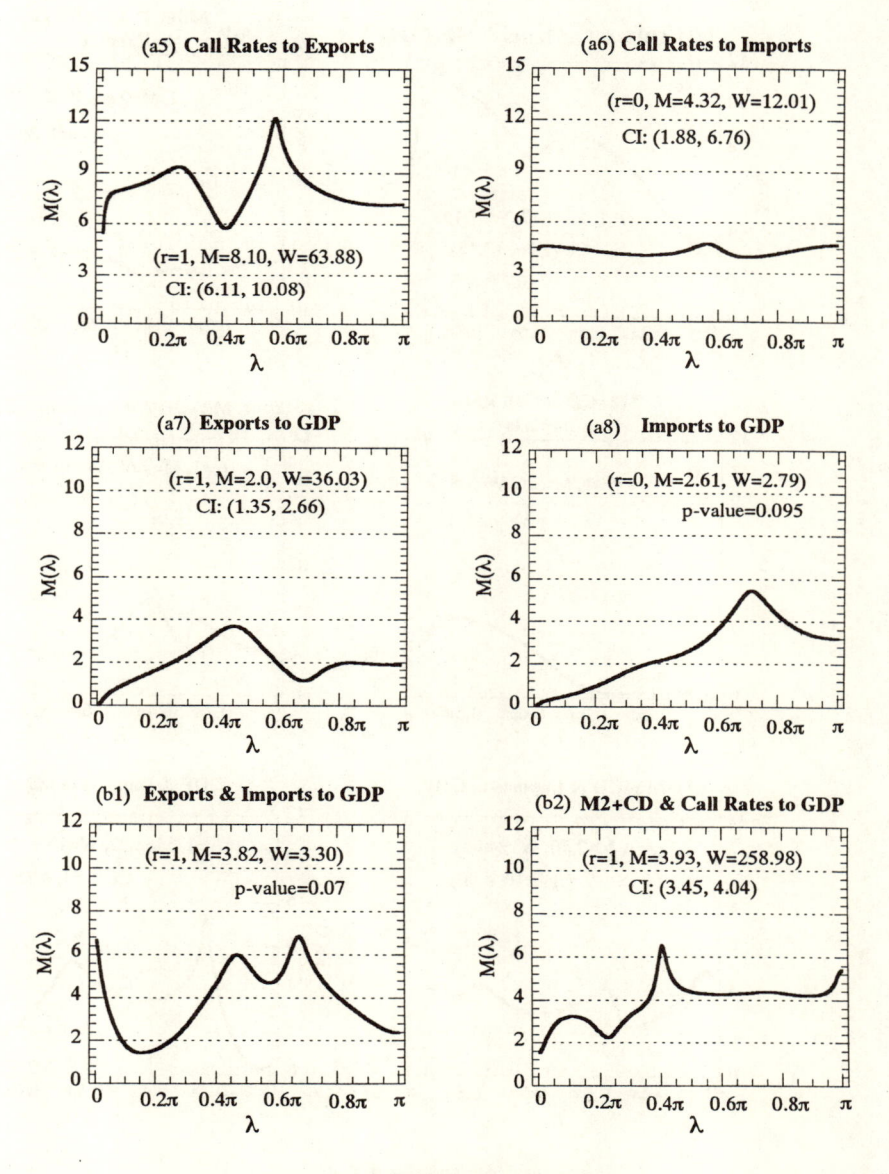

(a5) Call Rates to Exports
(r=1, M=8.10, W=63.88)
CI: (6.11, 10.08)

(a6) Call Rates to Imports
(r=0, M=4.32, W=12.01)
CI: (1.88, 6.76)

(a7) Exports to GDP
(r=1, M=2.0, W=36.03)
CI: (1.35, 2.66)

(a8) Imports to GDP
(r=0, M=2.61, W=2.79)
p-value=0.095

(b1) Exports & Imports to GDP
(r=1, M=3.82, W=3.30)
p-value=0.07

(b2) M2+CD & Call Rates to GDP
(r=1, M=3.93, W=258.98)
CI: (3.45, 4.04)

Figure 7.1 Continued

Chapter 7. Empirical Causal Relationships

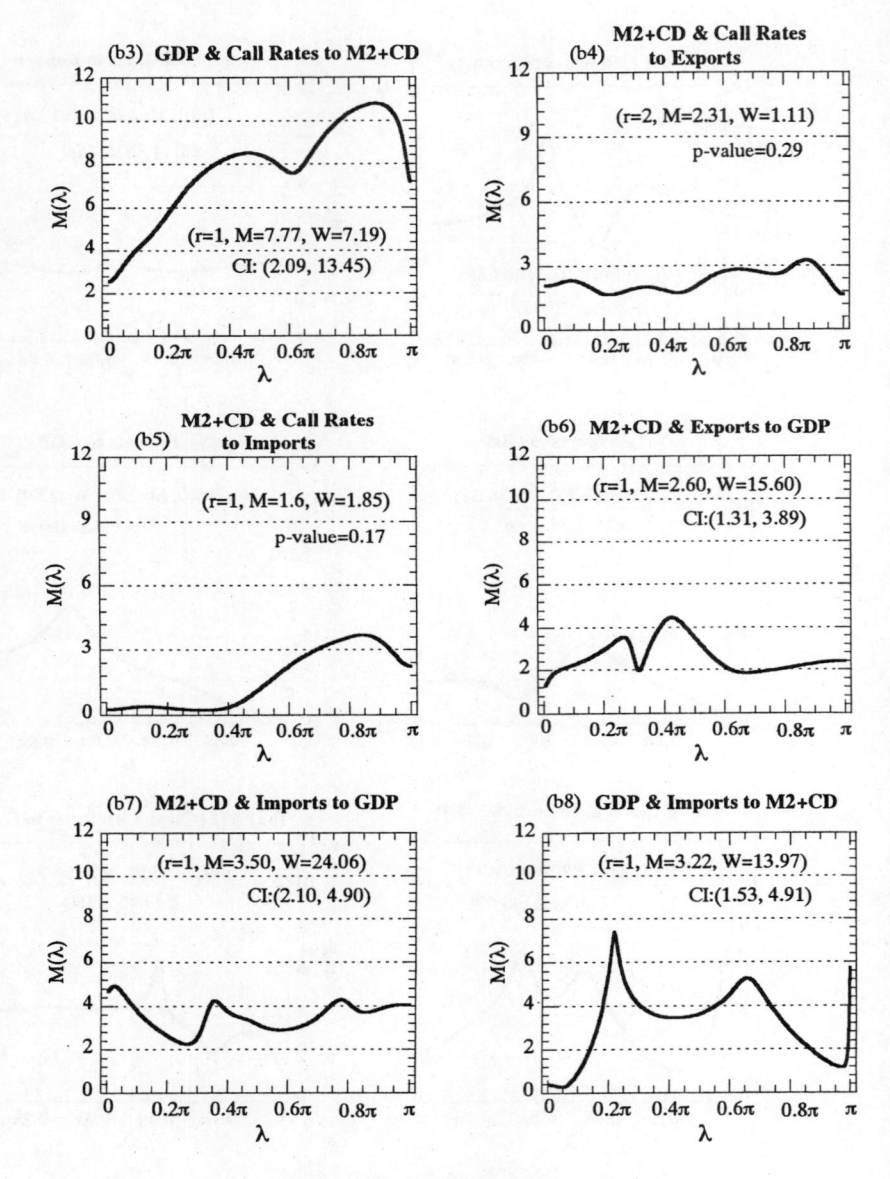

(b3) **GDP & Call Rates to M2+CD**
(r=1, M=7.77, W=7.19)
CI: (2.09, 13.45)

(b4) **M2+CD & Call Rates to Exports**
(r=2, M=2.31, W=1.11)
p-value=0.29

(b5) **M2+CD & Call Rates to Imports**
(r=1, M=1.6, W=1.85)
p-value=0.17

(b6) **M2+CD & Exports to GDP**
(r=1, M=2.60, W=15.60)
CI:(1.31, 3.89)

(b7) **M2+CD & Imports to GDP**
(r=1, M=3.50, W=24.06)
CI:(2.10, 4.90)

(b8) **GDP & Imports to M2+CD**
(r=1, M=3.22, W=13.97)
CI:(1.53, 4.91)

Figure 7.1 Continued

7.2. Causal Relations of Japanese Macroeconomic Data

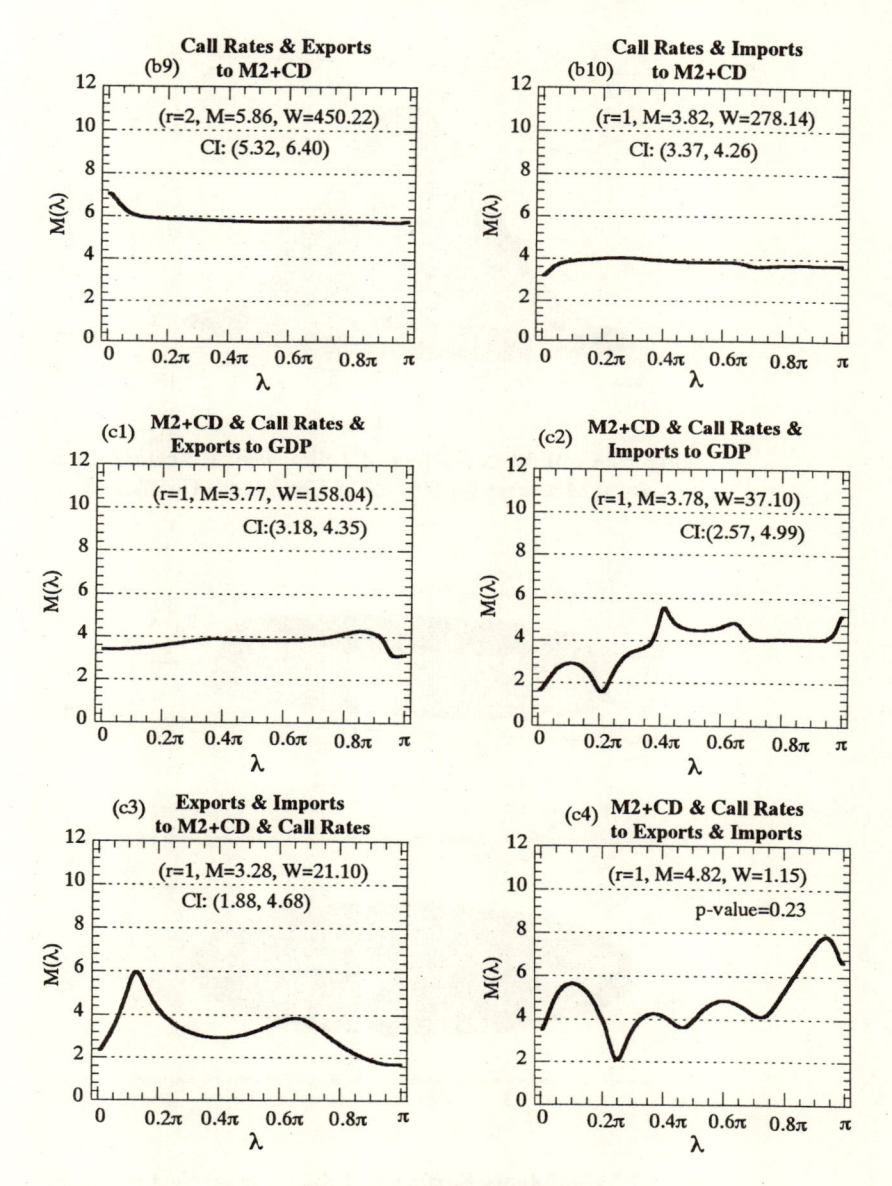

(b9) Call Rates & Exports to M2+CD
(r=2, M=5.86, W=450.22)
CI: (5.32, 6.40)

(b10) Call Rates & Imports to M2+CD
(r=1, M=3.82, W=278.14)
CI: (3.37, 4.26)

(c1) M2+CD & Call Rates & Exports to GDP
(r=1, M=3.77, W=158.04)
CI: (3.18, 4.35)

(c2) M2+CD & Call Rates & Imports to GDP
(r=1, M=3.78, W=37.10)
CI: (2.57, 4.99)

(c3) Exports & Imports to M2+CD & Call Rates
(r=1, M=3.28, W=21.10)
CI: (1.88, 4.68)

(c4) M2+CD & Call Rates to Exports & Imports
(r=1, M=4.82, W=1.15)
p-value=0.23

Figure 7.1 Continued

Chapter 7. Empirical Causal Relationships

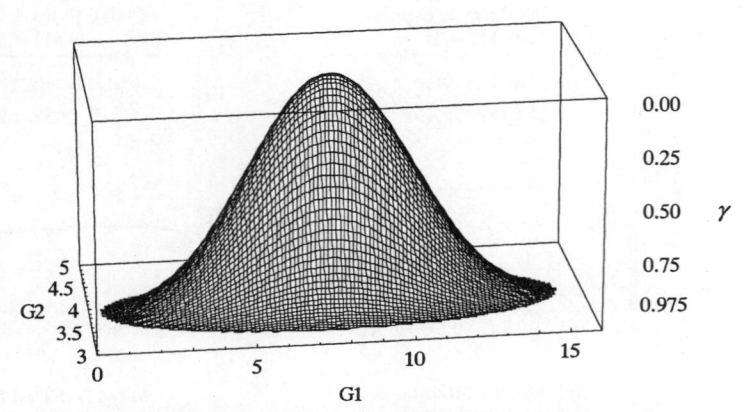

Figure 7.2 Confidence Surface of 2-dimensional Vector-valued Causal Measures for 0 to 0.975 Confidence Coefficient

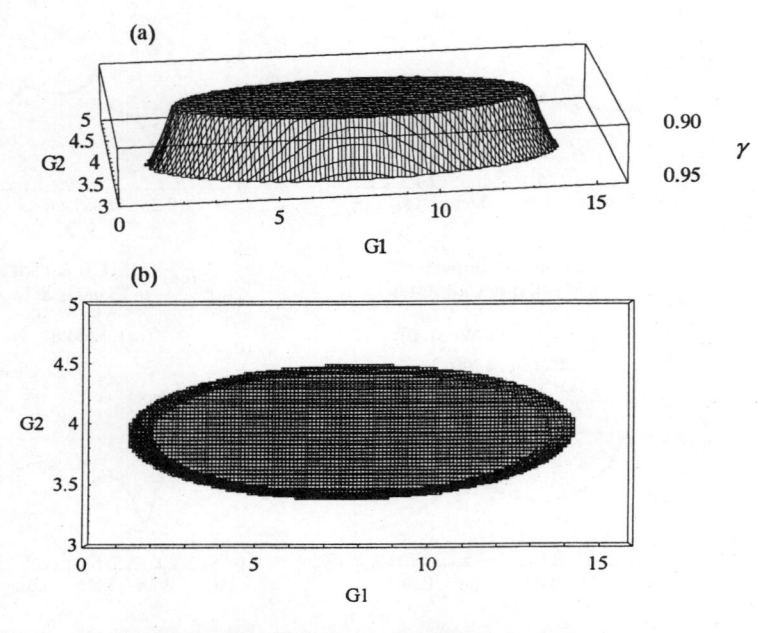

Figure 7.3 Confidence Surface of 2-dimensional Vector-valued Causal Measures for 0.90 to 0.95 Confidence Coefficient

7.3 Causality Between Japanese and Chinese Data

In this section, we apply the approach of the one-way-effect causal measures developed in the foregoing chapters to the analysis macroeconomic relations between two countries. This is the first attempt to apply our new approach to the analysis of economic relations between two large regional sectors. This section aims to show the characterization of the causal structures in the recent Japanese and Chinese macroeconomy. In view of the estimated causal measures (in the frequency domain and the time domain) based on a cointegrated VAR model, the long-run and short-run economic relationships between Japan and China are showed. The empirical result supports the general understanding that the economic relationship between Japan and China, at least in the meaning of international trade, is not competitional in the last two decades.

7.3.1 Cointegrated Model Identification

We used the Japanese data discussed above and the exports to China (Ec or Exports-JC) as well as the imports from China (Ic or Imports-JC) during the same period of the first quarter of 1975 through the fourth quarter of 1994. The Ec and Ic are the sum of monthly data (originally based on The Summary Report on Trade of Japan) from Nikkei NEEDS Macro Database. Both the Ec and the Ic are in U.S. Dollars. Figure 7.4 depicts the original data in levels and in differences of the Ec and Ic. The two time series appear to be, to a reasonable extent, non-stationary with stationary differences.

In the following study, we apply the common lag-length $a = 5$. The lag-length of autoregressive process delimits the range of possible configuration of the FMO. In order to avoid the lag-length playing a part in differentiation of the configuration, we do not use information criteria which are rather suited for identification of individual models. As is seen below, the uncorrelation and the Gaussianity hypotheses seem mostly supported for the residuals derived by fitting the lag-length $a = 5$. The fitted model we used is the cointegrated p-dimensional AR(5) in ECM form represented by model (6.1).

Chapter 7. Empirical Causal Relationships

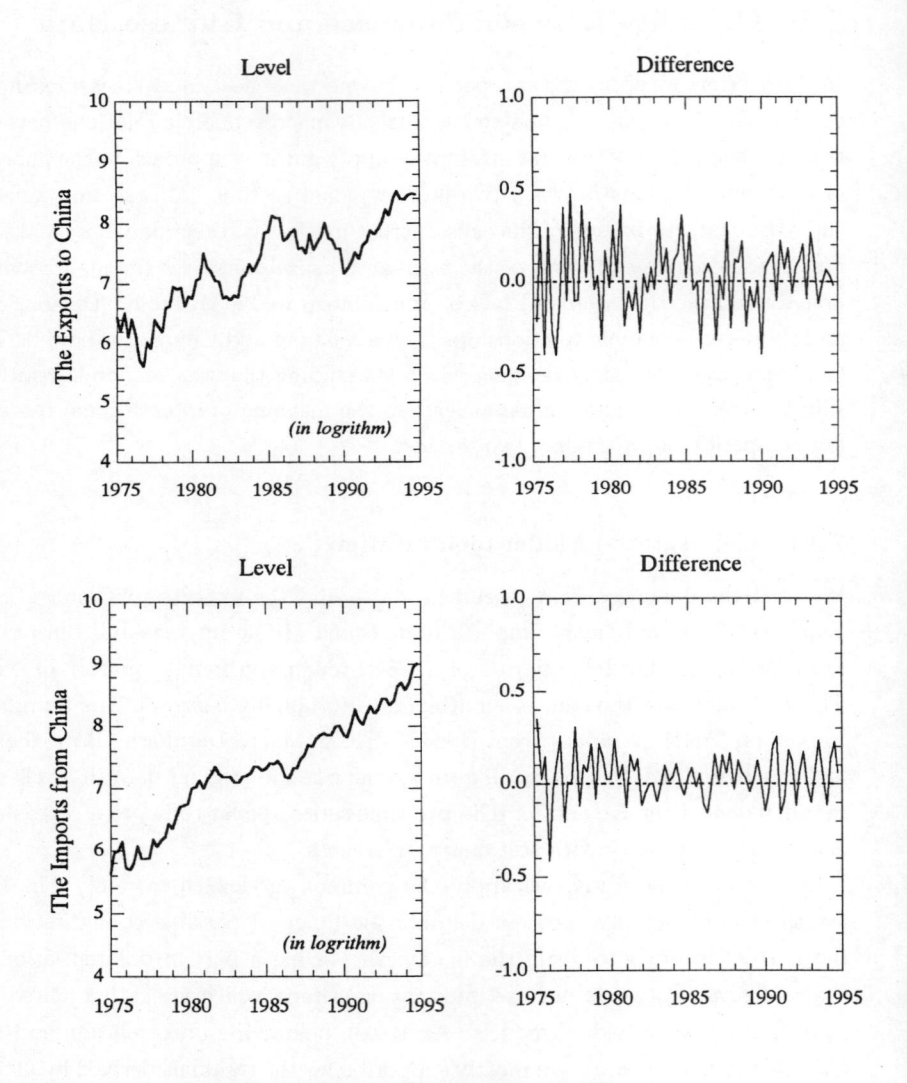

Figure 7.4 The International Trade between Japan and China

7.3. Causality Between Japanese and Chinese Data

The estimated eigenvalues and the corresponding eigenvectors of the bivariate and trivariate as well as four-variate in ECM are given in Tables 7.1, 7.2, 7.3. The variables of the models are indicated in the tables respectively. The observed trace statistics for different cointegration rank are also listed in the tables. As far as the bivariate models (see Table 7.1), Johansen's cointegration test suggests that there existing only one cointegration rank in model $(Y, Ec)^*$ and $(R, Ec)^*$. For these two models with one cointegration rank, we also get two equilibrium relations of

$$0.766Y - 0.643Ec = 0$$

and

$$0.902R + 0.432Ec = 0.$$

The estimated $\hat{\tau}$ statistics in Figure 7.2 show that there is no cointegrations in the trivariate models, i.e., for the cases of the trivariate models we discussed, the identified models which will be used in the following causal analysis are the traditional difference VAR model. As for the four-variate model $(M, R, Ec, Ic)^*$, Figure 7.3 tells us even $\hat{\tau}(0) = 43.65 < 43.95 = \tau(0|0.9)$, as the p-value of $\hat{\tau}(0) = 43.65$ is very near to 0.1 and that $\hat{\tau}(1) = 22.97 < 26.79 = \tau(1|0.9)$, then we can choose $\hat{r} = 1$. In the case of choosing the cointegration rank 1, we can get the equilibrium relation as follows

$$0.369M + 0.566R - 0.731Ec + 0.097Ic = 0$$

or

$$0.369M + 0.566R = 0.731Ec - 0.097Ic.$$

The tests of residual autocorrelation and Gaussainity of the identified cointegration models, which include the exports and imports between China and Japan, are listed in Table 7.4 and Table 7.5. For both of the tests of the Hg and the E_p, we hoped to get a comparatively large p-value. Table 7.4 shows that the smallest p-value of the Hg test is 0.0242, which is obtained for the four-variate model $(M, R, Ec, Ic)^*$. Concerning the E_p test, the smallest p-value is 0.109, which is obtained for the bivariate model $(R, Ec)^*$. For a given 0.01 critical value, the test statistics in Table 7.4 and Table 7.5 show that all the identified models are suitable for the following empirical causal analysis.

Chapter 7. Empirical Causal Relationships

Table 7.1 The Eigenvalues and the Eigenvectors and the Trace Statistics for Bivariate Models

	Eigenvalues (0.183 0.047)					Eigenvalues (0.094 0.004)			
	Eigenvectors		$p-r$	$\hat{\tau}$		Eigenvectors		$p-r$	$\hat{\tau}$
Y	-0.766	0.993	1	3.64	Ec	7.405	7.691	1	0.29
Ec	0.643	-0.115	2	18.78	Ic	0.286	0.286	2	7.69
	Eigenvalues (0.152 0.049)					Eigenvalues (0.077 0.028)			
	Eigenvectors		$p-r$	$\hat{\tau}$		Eigenvectors		$p-r$	$\hat{\tau}$
M	0.840	0.968	1	3.80	M	0.583	-0.319	1	2.13
Ec	-0.543	-0.251	2	16.12	Ic	-0.812	0.948	2	8.14
	Eigenvalues (0.145 0.013)					Eigenvalues (0.113 0.000)			
	Eigenvectors		$p-r$	$\hat{\tau}$		Eigenvectors		$p-r$	$\hat{\tau}$
R	0.902	0.991	1	1.01	R	0.601	-0.105	1	0.01
Ec	0.432	-0.137	2	12.78	Ic	0.799	0.994	2	8.97

See Table 6.1 for the τ-statistic quantiles.

Table 7.2 The Eigenvalues and the Eigenvectors and the Trace Statistics for Trivariate Models

	Eigenvalues				
	(0.164	0.106	0.034)		
		Eigenvectors		$p-r$	$\hat{\tau}$
M	0.934	-0.797	0.919	1	2.59
R	0.358	-0.018	0.012	2	10.99
Ic	0.021	0.603	-0.394	3	24.42
	Eigenvalues				
	(0.169	0.115	0.032)		
		Eigenvectors		$p-r$	$\hat{\tau}$
M	0.749	-0.508	0.820	1	2.44
Ec	0.388	-0.365	0.069	2	11.58
Ic	0.331	0.773	-0.443	3	25.48

See Table 6.3 for the τ-statistic quantiles.

7.3. Causality Between Japanese and Chinese Data

Table 7.3 The Eigenvalues and the Eigenvectors and the Trace Statistics for Four-variate Models

	Eigenvalues					
	(0.241	0.162	0.093	0.032)		
	Eigenvectors				$p-r$	$\hat{\tau}$
M	0.369	-0.477	-0.518	0.110	1	2.42
R	0.566	-0.069	0.781	-0.508	2	9.73
Ec	-0.731	0.871	-0.342	0.854	3	22.97
Ic	0.097	0.097	-0.074	0.021	4	43.65

See Tables 6.3 for the τ-tatistic quantiles.

Table 7.4 The Hg-statistics and the p-values

	Hg-stat.	p-value		Hg-stat.	p-value
$Y\&Ec$	60.6232	0.1928	$Ec\&Ic$	62.4273	0.1525
$M\&Ec$	50.4564	0.5348	$M\&Ec\&Ic$	125.2771	0.2836
$M\&Ic$	58.1883	0.2581	$M\&R\&Ic$	122.7860	0.3388
$R\&Ec$	63.3306	0.1349	$M\&R\&Ec\&Ic$	250.1354	0.0242
$R\&Ic$	58.1436	0.2595			

1. The Hg-statistic is defined by (6.3).
2. The degree of freedom of the Hg-statistic is 52, 117, 208 for bivariate, trivariate, and four-variate models, respectively.

Table 7.5 The Ep-statistics and the p-values

	Ep-stat.	p-value		Ep-stat.	p-value
$Y\&Ec$	2.6474	0.6184	$Ec\&Ic$	0.5454	0.9689
$M\&Ec$	2.5871	0.6291	$M\&Ec\&Ic$	3.5588	0.7361
$M\&Ic$	1.1489	0.8864	$M\&R\&Ic$	1.4793	0.9609
$R\&Ec$	7.5628	0.1090	$M\&R\&Ec\&Ic$	0.5714	0.9998
$R\&Ic$	0.1205	0.9983			

1. The Ep-statistic is defined by (6.5).
2. The degree of freedom of the Ep-statistic is 4, 6, 8 for bivariate, trivariate, and four-variate models, respectively.

Chapter 7. Empirical Causal Relationships

7.3.2 Empirical Measures of the One-way Effect

Figure 7.5 lists 12 plots of the estimated FMO for the cases of bivariate, trivariate and four-variate models, as indicated. Plots (d1) through (d7) show the bivariate cases, (e1) through (e3) show the trivariate cases, and plots (f1) to (f2) are for the four-variate models. The estimates of the cointegrating rank (r) and the OMO (M) as well as the Wald test statistic W are also presented in the plots in Figure 7.5. The 95 percent confidence intervals of the OMO, in case the null hypothesis of non-causality is rejected, are also listed in the corresponding plots. The estimated OMO are obtained by numerical integration of the estimated FMO's by dividing $(0, \pi]$ into 200 equal intervals. For each of the models we calculate the FMO for frequency points $\lambda_i = i\pi/200$, $i = 1, 2, \cdots, 200$. As for the number of division of $(0, \pi]$, we also checked many cases of interval division up to 1200, and we found that the 200 equal-division of the interval $(0, \pi]$ is fine enough.

Although similar computations were conducted on possible combinations and pairing of the seven macroeconomic time series of Japan and China, this book only focuses on a few that are of interest to us, especially those cases in which the null hypothesis of non-causality in Granger's sense is rejected. Figure 7.5 shows the following notable findings of the causal relations between Japanese and Chinese macroeconomic data.

1. The significant one-way effects from Japanese GDP to the exports to China and to the imports from China are not observed. The Exports to China has one-way effect to GDP [see plot (d1), $OMO = 7.09$ and $W = 127.34$] but the Imports from China does not. Plot (b1) shows us that the comparatively short-run effect of the Exports to China to Japanese GDP. The estimated one-way effect from Exports-JC to M2+CD is significant [see plot (d2), $OMO = 6.85$, with a 95 percent confidence region $(5.73, 7.96)$]. The FMO is very low around the frequency 0.32π. The one-way effect of Imports-JC to M2+CD is significant [$OMO = 4.06$, the Wald-statistic $W = 105.04$, see plot (d3)]. The effect is comparatively steady in the lower frequency band and is not long-run. Plot (e1) shows that the one-way effect from Exports-JC and Imports-JC to M2+CD is significant and long-run

7.3. Causality Between Japanese and Chinese Data

($OMO = 5.61$, $W = 55.81$). The three plots, (d2), (d3) and (e1), show that Japanese money supply is partially effected by the external trade between Japan and China.

2. The one-way effect of Imports-JC to Exports-JC is significant but very small in value [the estimated $OMO = 0.05$, $W = 17.17$]. Plot (d4) shows that the one-way effect is only long-run. The reverse of the OMO, the one-way effect from Imports-JC to Exports-JC, is comparatively large but not significant in the whole region of $(0, \pi])$. Plot (d5) implies that, in a short frequency band including the frequency 0.45π, the OMO may be significant (the work of statistical test will be left for the next study). The empirical results show that at 95% confidence level there is no significant one-way effects between Exports and Imports. A further investigation can tell us that at a comparatively large critical value, there exists a comparatively weak one-way effect from Exports to Imports, and the one-way effect is only long-run.

3. It is observed that interest rates have a one-way effect on the international trade between Japan and China. Plot (d6) shows the one-way effect from Call Rates to Exports-JC. The third-quarter time period is comparatively weak. Based on a traditional difference model, the empirical results show that the one-way effect from Call Rates to Imports-JC is comparatively large (over twice of the measure from Call Rates to Exports-JC) and significant. The effect appears at half a year time period and down quickly in the third quarter time period band. Then, it goes up very quickly and takes a sharp peak just at the one year time period [see plot (d7)]. Even when neither of the one-way effects from interest rates to Imports-JC or to Exports-JC is long-run, the results support the conclusion that interest rates in general affect other economic indices, as pointed out in the discussions of Japanese macroeconomic data in the above section.

4. The one-way effect of M2+CD and Call Rates to Imports-JC is significant and the short-runt effect seems comparatively more larger [see plot (e2)]. The one-way effect of M2+CD and Imports-JC to Exports-JC is 0.3 with a 95% confidence region $(0.04, 0.55)$. Plot (e3) shows that the one-way effect

Chapter 7. Empirical Causal Relationships

are only concentrated to two narrow frequency bands including 0.25π and 0.65π. This may mean that the instant effect that the money and imports policy has on the exports to China occurs only two times. The one is very weak and coming at the third-quarter time period, the other one coming at about two-year time period.

5. In view of plot (f1), we see that the one-way effect causal measure of Exports-JC and Imports-JC to M2+CD and Call Rates (the estimated $OMO = 5.6$) is significant at 95% confidence level (the Wald test statistic $W = 25.26$). The one-way effect is not only short-run but also long-run. The effect of M2+CD and Call Rates to Exports-JC and Imports-JC [see plot (f2)] is comparatively large in value ($OMO = 5.77$) but not significant ($W = 1.26$ with a p-value=0.26) in the whole frequency region $(0, \pi]$). As a whole, the findings support that in the recent Japanese economy, the external trades have a significant one-way effect on the monetary side of the Japanese economy.

In general, the external trade between Japan and China influences the monetary economy, but the opposite is not the case. Even so, the monetary economy affects the imports from China. The empirical results of the imports from China do not affect Japanese economic growth. This may support the common understanding that the economy of Japan and that of China are cooperative, especially in the field of external trade. The empirical results also suggest the conclusion that interest rates commonly affect other economic time series but receive no effect from others. A very important contribution of this section to the econometric analysis is that our causal measure approach based on a cointegration system can present a new way in the analysis of the causal relationships of the nonstationary macroeconomic time series between two or more countries.

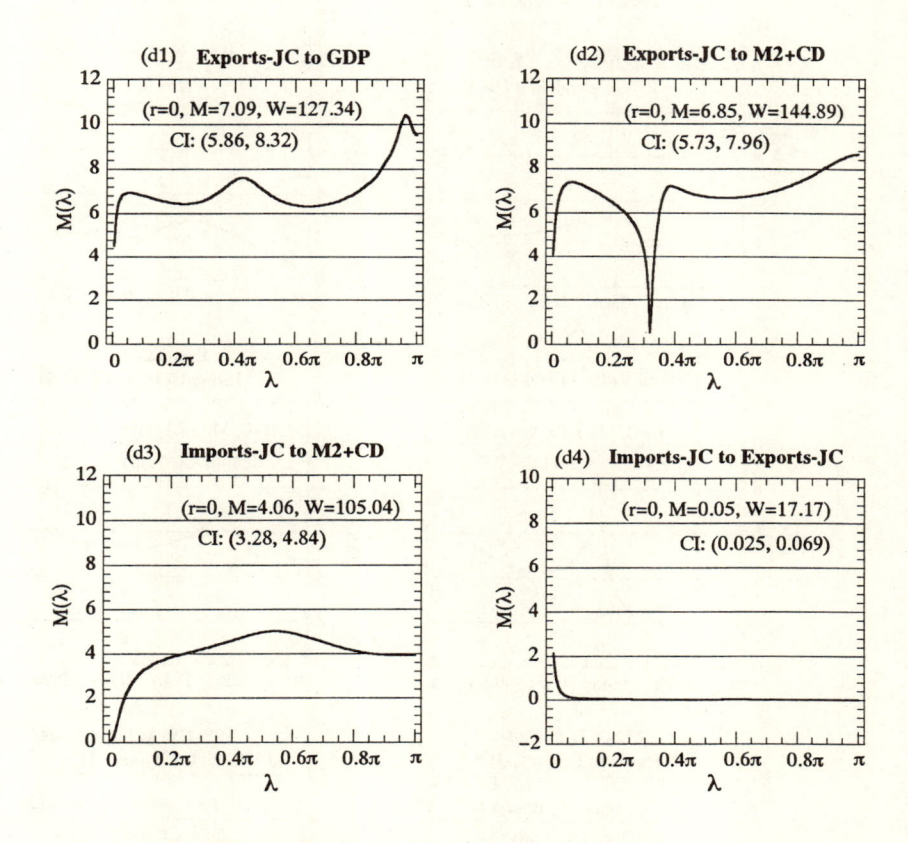

7.3. Causality Between Japanese and Chinese Data

(d1) Exports-JC to GDP
(r=0, M=7.09, W=127.34)
CI: (5.86, 8.32)

(d2) Exports-JC to M2+CD
(r=0, M=6.85, W=144.89)
CI: (5.73, 7.96)

(d3) Imports-JC to M2+CD
(r=0, M=4.06, W=105.04)
CI: (3.28, 4.84)

(d4) Imports-JC to Exports-JC
(r=0, M=0.05, W=17.17)
CI: (0.025, 0.069)

1. *r: Identified cointegration rank;*
2. *W: Wald statistic given by (5.21)*
3. *CI: The 95% confidence interval of OMO*
   (in the case the non-causality null hypothesis is rejected).

Figure 7.5 Estimated Measures of One-way Effect, Identified Cointegration Ranks, Wald Statistics and Confidence Intervals

Chapter 7. Empirical Causal Relationships

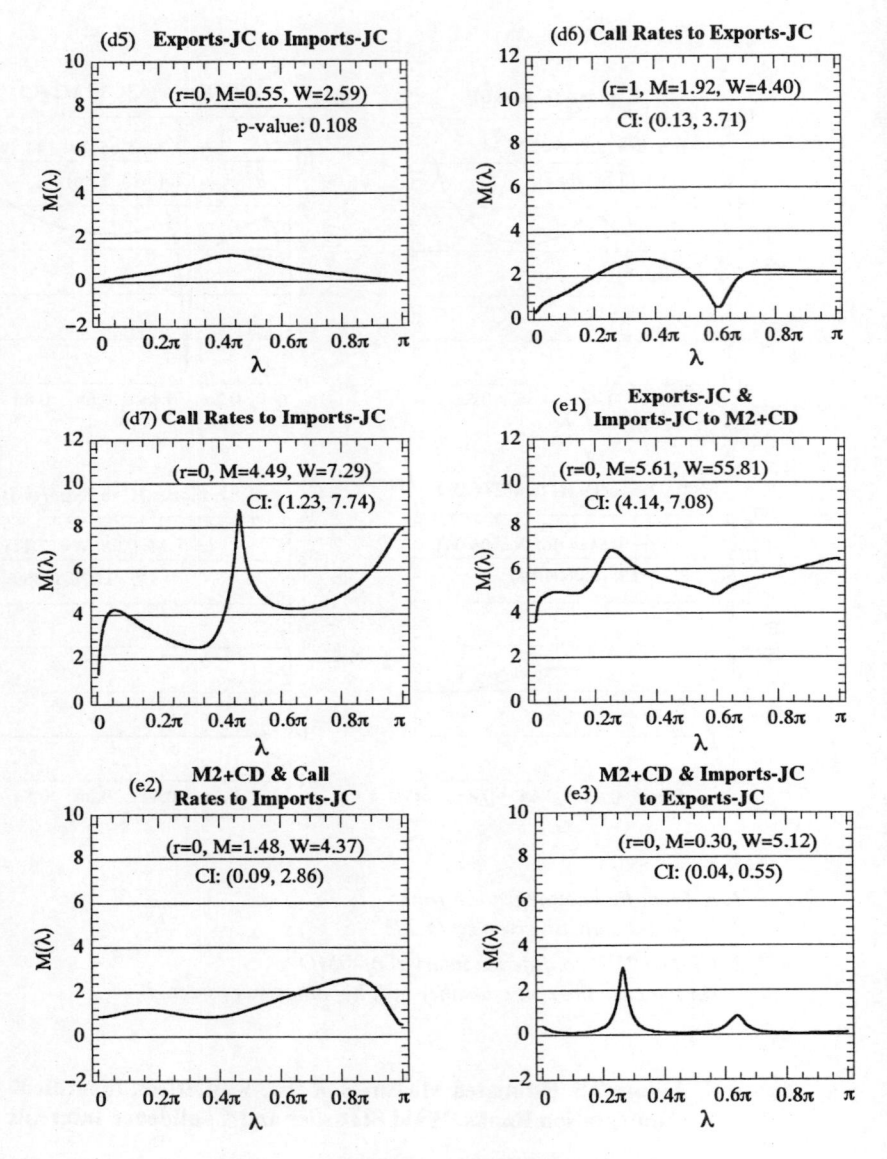

(d5) Exports-JC to Imports-JC
(r=0, M=0.55, W=2.59)
p-value: 0.108

(d6) Call Rates to Exports-JC
(r=1, M=1.92, W=4.40)
CI: (0.13, 3.71)

(d7) Call Rates to Imports-JC
(r=0, M=4.49, W=7.29)
CI: (1.23, 7.74)

(e1) Exports-JC & Imports-JC to M2+CD
(r=0, M=5.61, W=55.81)
CI: (4.14, 7.08)

(e2) M2+CD & Call Rates to Imports-JC
(r=0, M=1.48, W=4.37)
CI: (0.09, 2.86)

(e3) M2+CD & Imports-JC to Exports-JC
(r=0, M=0.30, W=5.12)
CI: (0.04, 0.55)

Figure 7.5 Continued

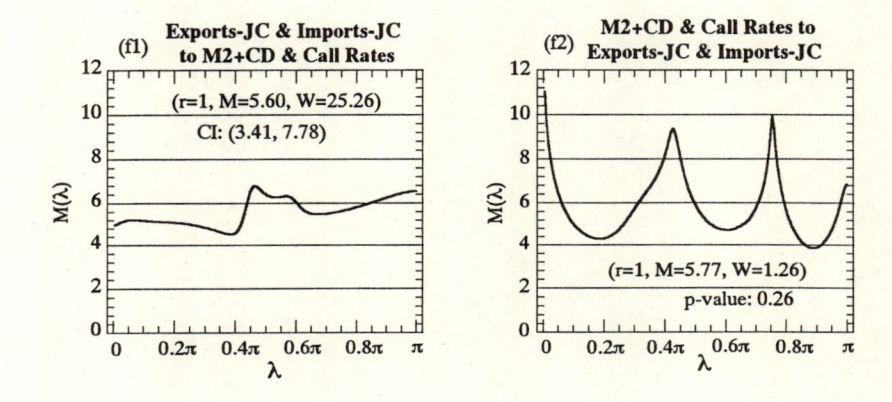

7.3. Causality Between Japanese and Chinese Data

(f1) Exports-JC & Imports-JC to M2+CD & Call Rates
(r=1, M=5.60, W=25.26)
CI: (3.41, 7.78)

(f2) M2+CD & Call Rates to Exports-JC & Imports-JC
(r=1, M=5.77, W=1.26)
p-value: 0.26

Figure 7.5 Continued

Part II

Econometric Analysis of Nonlinear Processes

Chapter 8

The BCT Model and Cross-entropy Risk

The discussions so far are for the nonstationary time series based on a cointegrated model with Gaussian disturbance term processes. In the practical analysis of economics or business, we often meet some macroeconomic data which do not follow a Gaussian process. This is one of the main reasons stimulating the development of identification methods for the nonlinear processes. In this chapter, we will investigate the Box-Cox transformation (BCT), which has been proved very useful in the analysis of nonlinear processes. The BCT model identification will be conducted by using the methods of the nested χ^2 test [Hosoya (1986, 1989)] and the general information criterion (GIC) as well as the extention of Akaike's information criterion (AIC) [Akaike (1973), Hosoya (1984), Yao (1992, 1994), Yao and Hosoya (1994)]. The main results in the following five chapters are the summations of the studies by Hosoya (1984, 1989), Yao (1992, 1994, 1995, 1996c, 1998), and Yao and Hosoya (1994).

In this chapter, we will first give an overview of the results concerning the theory and application of the BCT. In Section 8.2, the inference of the estimation of the cross-entropy risk is shown. Then the definition of the GIC (which is different to Takeuchi (1976)'s definition, and would be used in the identification of the BCT model) is given. In the line of arguments given in Hosoya (1989), Yao (1992, 1995), and Yao and Hosoya (1994).

Chapter 8. The BCT Model and Cross-entropy Risk

8.1 The Box-Cox Transformation

The analytic techniques of linear models as exemplified by the variance analysis and multiple regression analysis usually assume that the expectation of the random variables hold a simple structure. In multiple regression problems, it is assumed that the expectation of the dependent variable is adequately represented by a rather simple function of the independent variables, and constancy of error variance and the independence of the observations are also assumed. In some cases, the transformation of dependent as well as independent variables may be desirable to produce the simplest possible regression model in the transformed variables. The general idea is to restrict attention to transformations indexed by the unknown parameter λ and then to estimate λ and the other parameters of the model by standard methods of inference.

For the analysis of nonlinear process, there is a method of Box-Cox transformation [see Box-Cox (1964)]. As a special power transformation, for any positive variable Y, the Box-Cox transformation (BCT) is defined as

$$Y^{[\lambda]} = \begin{cases} \dfrac{Y^\lambda - 1}{\lambda} & \lambda \neq 0 \\ 0 & \lambda = 0 \end{cases} \tag{8.1}$$

or for the case Y is negative but for some positive a, $Y > -a$ (then $Y + a > 0$),

$$Y^{[\lambda]} = \begin{cases} \dfrac{(Y+a)^\lambda - 1}{\lambda} & \lambda \neq 0 \\ 0 & \lambda = 0, \end{cases} \tag{8.1}'$$

where λ is an unknown parameter called the BCT parameter. In general, it is assumed that for each λ, $Y^{[\lambda]}$ is a monotonic function of Y over the admissible range. Because of (8.1) is continuous at $\lambda = 0$ [see Yao (1992), Yao and Hosoya (1994), or the following Remark 8.2], so it is more preferable for theoretical analysis.

Remark 8.1 The following investigations are only based on the nonlinear transformation defined by (8.1). It is very clearly that all the results will be hold for the case $Y < 0$ if only we make a parallel change of Y by (8.1)' in the following discussions.

8.1. The Box-Cox Transformation

As for the BCT regression model, since the explanatory variables can be also transformed, so that the general BCT model has the form

$$Y^{[\lambda_0]} = \beta_1 X_1^{[\lambda_1]} + \beta_2 X_2^{[\lambda_2]} + \cdots + \beta_p X_p^{[\lambda_p]} + \varepsilon. \tag{8.2}$$

The BCT regression model expressed in (8.2) can be specified and the parameters can be estimated by the methods that will be discussed below. For $\lambda_0 = 1, 0$ and -1, Y enters into model (8.2) linearly, as log and as the reciprocal of Y. This property is also true for the BCT to the independent variables. Thus, the estimation procedure itself determines which transformation best fits the data. The main purpose of the nonlinear inference used in this book is to present the methods of the information criteria and the nested χ^2 test which can simultaneously estimate the BCT parameter and the other parameters.

For different λ, (8.2) can be simplified into the following three models [see spitzer (1982)]:

$$Y^{[\lambda]} = \beta_1 X_1 + \beta_2 X_2 + \cdots + \beta_p X_p + \varepsilon, \tag{8.3}$$

$$Y^{[\lambda]} = \beta_1 X_1^{[\lambda]} + \beta_2 X_2^{[\lambda]} + \cdots + \beta_p X_p^{[\lambda]} + \varepsilon, \tag{8.4}$$

$$Y^{[\lambda_0]} = \beta_1 X_1^{[\lambda_1]} + \beta_2 X_2^{[\lambda_1]} + \cdots + \beta_p X_p^{[\lambda_1]} + \varepsilon. \tag{8.5}$$

There are further three types of BCT regression models that can be written as the following forms [see Yao and Hosoya (1994)]:

$$\begin{aligned} Y^{[\lambda]} &= \beta_{11} X_{11} + \beta_{12} X_{12} + \cdots + \beta_{1p} X_{1p} \\ &\quad + \beta_{21} X_{21}^{[\lambda]} + \beta_{22} X_{22}^{[\lambda]} + \cdots + \beta_{2q} X_{2q}^{[\lambda]} + \varepsilon, \end{aligned} \tag{8.6}$$

$$\begin{aligned} Y^{[\lambda_0]} &= \beta_{11} X_{11} + \beta_{12} X_{12} + \cdots + \beta_{1p} X_{1p} \\ &\quad + \beta_{21} X_{21}^{[\lambda]} + \beta_{22} X_{22}^{[\lambda]} + \cdots + \beta_{2p} X_{2p}^{[\lambda]} + \varepsilon, \end{aligned} \tag{8.7}$$

$$\begin{aligned} Y^{[\lambda_0]} &= \beta_{11} X_{11} + \beta_{12} X_{12} + \cdots + \beta_{1p} X_{1p} \\ &\quad + \beta_{21} X_{21}^{[\lambda_{21}]} + \beta_{22} X_{22}^{[\lambda_{22}]} + \cdots + \beta_{2q} X_{2q}^{[\lambda_{2q}]} + \varepsilon. \end{aligned} \tag{8.8}$$

The above seven models cover all the main possible versions of the BCT regression models. There is essentially no real difference between these models, and the statistical analysis procedure is almost the same as well. In the following chapters we mainly deal with model (8.3) and model (8.4). For a discussion of the interpretation of estimated coefficients in the BCT models, see Poirier and Melino (1978) or Huang and Kelingos (1979). The related topics of the BCT model are briefly discussed in Zarembka (1990).

Poirier (1978) discussed the use of the BCT in limited dependent variable models. He concluded that the BCT parameter can be estimated fairly accurately even in models which involve substantial nonlinearities. Spitzer (1978) investigated the BCT in small samples using a Monte Carlo experiment. The small sample properties of models which transform both the dependent and independent variables using the same BCT are investigated. Spitzer (1982) gave a fast and efficient algorithm for the estimation of parameters in models with the BCT. A modification of a full Newton-type algorithm for the solution of the least squares problem for models containing a BCT was presented.

Gemmill (1980) correctly indicated that, by applying different transformation parameters to different variables in a demand equation, a more desirable behavior of income and the price elasticities of demand may be obtained. James and David (1982) investigated income and food expenditure distribution by the use of the BCT. Chang (1977, 1980) gave a successful example of use of the BCT in the analysis of the demand for meat in the United States. There he pointed out that the linear or logarithm function is not suited for the analysis of demand for meat in the United States.

The other details of the theoretical works and applications can be mainly seen in: Bickel and Doksum (1981), Box and Cox (1964, 1982), Huang and Grawe (1980), Hosoya (1983, 1984), Mallela (1980), Seaks and Layson (1983), Tse (1984), White (1972), Zarembka (1968, 1974) etc. But all of the works what have been done for the estimation of the parameter in the BCT models are based on the traditional maximum likelihood method for fixed order of the regression model. For the purpose of simultaneous identification of the model order and the BCT parameter, Hosoya (1983) has first introduced the idea of the general information criterion (GIC). A new numerical evaluation of the GIC for the BCT model is given by Yao (1992), Yao and Hosoya (1994).

Remark 8.2 The BCT that be defined by (8.1) being a function of λ, is differentiable. Here we give out the first two derivatives.

$$\frac{\partial Y^{[\lambda]}}{\partial \lambda} = \begin{cases} [-(Y^\lambda - 1) + \lambda Y^\lambda \log Y]/\lambda^2 & \lambda \neq 0 \\ \frac{1}{2}(\log Y)^2 & \lambda = 0 \end{cases} \quad (8.9)$$

and

$$\frac{\partial^2 Y^{[\lambda]}}{\partial \lambda^2} = \begin{cases} [2(Y^\lambda - 1) - 2\lambda Y^\lambda \log(Y) + \lambda^2 Y^\lambda (\log Y)^2]/\lambda^3 & \lambda \neq 0 \\ \frac{1}{3}(\log Y)^3 & \lambda = 0. \end{cases} \quad (8.10)$$

For $\lambda \neq 0$, the results can be easily obtained by a direct calculation. For $\lambda = 0$, it can be proved by the use of Taylor expansion.

8.2 Estimation of Cross-entropy Risk and the GIC

In this section, we will show the inference of the estimate of cross-entropy risk. The definition of the general information criterion (GIC) is based on the result of an estimate of cross-entropy risk. Here we only show the basic result of the GIC defined by an asymptotic estimation of the cross-entropy risk. The application details of the GIC to the BCT model will be discussed in Chapters 9 and 10. There, we can see that the GIC used in the investigation of the BCT model is different from Takeuchi's [see Takeuchi (1976)].

Let $Y_1, Y_2, \cdots, Y_n$ be a set of random variables which has the joint distribution function $G_n(y_1, y_2, \cdots, y_n|\theta)$ in R, and θ be a parameter such that $\theta = (\theta_1, \theta_2, \cdots, \theta_p) \in \Theta$ where Θ be a non-empty open-subset of R^p. Let $f_n(y_1, y_2, \cdots, y_n|\theta)$ be a probability density function on R^n. The cross-entropy loss accompanied by the use of $f(Y_1, Y_2, \cdots, Y_n|\theta)$ for modeling $(Y_1, Y_2, \cdots, Y_n)$ is the expectation of $[-(1/2)f_n(y_1, y_2, \cdots, y_n)]$ and is given by

$$LCE_n(\theta, f_n) = \int_{R^n} -f_n(y_1, y_2, \cdots, y_n|\theta) dG_n(y_1, y_2, \cdots, y_n). \quad (8.11)$$

The cross-entropy risk of $f_n(Y|\tilde{\theta}_n(Y))$ for an estimate $\tilde{\theta}_n$ is the expectation of the corresponding cross-entropy loss and is given by

Chapter 8. The BCT Model and Cross-entropy Risk

$$\begin{aligned}R_n(\tilde{\theta}, f_n) &\equiv E_{\tilde{\theta}}[LCE_n(\theta, f_n)] \\ &= \int_{R^n}\int_{R^n}\Big\{\frac{1}{n}\log f_n(y_1, y_2, \cdots, y_n|\tilde{\theta}(z_1, z_2, \cdots, z_n)) \\ &\quad dG_n(y_1, y_2, \cdots, y_n)\Big\}dG_n(z_1, z_2, \cdots, z_n).\end{aligned} \quad (8.12)$$

Assume that there is a unique θ, say θ^0, such that

$$LCE_n(\theta^0, f_n) = \min(LCE_n(\theta, f_n)|\theta \in \Theta),$$

and assume that $f_n(y_1, y_2, \cdots, y_n|\theta)$ is a sufficiently smooth function of θ for all values of $y_1, y_2, \cdots, y_n$. Then for $j = 1, 2, \cdots, p$

$$\int_{R^n} \frac{\partial f_n(y_1, y_2, \cdots, y_n|\theta^0)}{\partial \theta_j} dG_n(y_1, y_2, \cdots, y_n) = 0. \quad (8.13)$$

Let $\hat{\theta}_n$ be the maximum-likelihood estimate based on the model $f(Y|\theta)$. An approximately unbiased estimate of the cross-entropy risk of $\hat{\theta}_n$ is constructed by comparison of the formal asymptotic expansion of the risk and the expansion of the log-likelihood evaluated at $\hat{\theta}_n$; in view of (8.10) we can get the following results

$$\begin{aligned}R_n(\hat{\theta}, f_n) &= -E_{\hat{\theta}}\bigg[\int_{R^n}\frac{1}{n}\log f_n(y_1, y_2, \cdots, y_n|\hat{\theta})dG_n(y_1, y_2, \cdots, y_n)\bigg] \\ &= -E_{\hat{\theta}}\bigg[\int_{R^n}\frac{1}{n}\Big\{\log f_n(y_1, y_2, \cdots, y_n|\theta^0) \\ &\quad +\sum_{j=1}^p \frac{\partial f_n(y_1, y_2, \cdots, y_n|\theta^0)}{\partial \theta_j}(\hat{\theta}_{n,j} - \theta_j^0) \\ &\quad +\frac{1}{2}\sum_{j,k=1}^p \frac{\partial^2 f_n(y_1, y_2, \cdots, y_n|\theta^0)}{\partial \theta_j \partial \theta_k}(\hat{\theta}_{n,j} - \theta_j^0)(\hat{\theta}_{n,k} - \theta_k^0) \\ &\quad +o(1)\Big\}dG_n(y_1, y_2, \cdots, y_n)\bigg].\end{aligned} \quad (8.14)$$

In view of (8.13), it is easy to prove that the second item on the right hand side of (8.14) is equal to zero, and the last item on the right hand side of (8.14) is $o(1/n)$. So we can get

$$R_n(\hat{\theta}, f_n) = LCE_n(\theta^0, f_n) + \frac{1}{2}K_n(\hat{\theta}_n, f_n|\theta^0) + o(\frac{1}{n})$$

8.2. Estimation of Cross-entropy Risk and the GIC

$$= -\int_{R^n} \frac{1}{n} \log f_n(y_1, y_2, \cdots, y_n|\hat{\theta}_n) dG_n(y_1, y_2, \cdots, y_n)$$
$$+ \frac{1}{2} K_n(\hat{\theta}_n, f_n|\theta^0) + o(\frac{1}{n}), \tag{8.15}$$

where

$$\frac{1}{2} K_n(\hat{\theta}_n, f_n|\theta^0) = \frac{1}{n} \sum_{j,k=1}^p E[(\hat{\theta}_{n,j} - \theta_j^0)(\hat{\theta}_{n,k} - \theta_k^0)]$$
$$\times \int_{R^2} \frac{\partial^2 f_n(y_1, y_2, \cdots, y_n|\theta^0)}{\partial \theta_j \partial \theta_k} dG_n(y_1, y_2, \cdots, y_n). \tag{8.16}$$

On the other hand, if we expand $(1/n) \log f_n(y_1, y_2, \cdots, y_n|\theta^0)$ around $\hat{\theta}_n$ by Taylor asymptotic expansion theory and take the expectation on both side, then by a straight-forward calculation

$$E_Y[(1/n) \log f_n(y_1, y_2, \cdots, y_n|\theta^0)]$$
$$= \int_{R^n} \frac{1}{n} \log f_n(y_1, y_2, \cdots, y_n|\theta_0) dG_n(y_1, y_2, \cdots, y_n)$$
$$+ \frac{1}{2} K_n(\hat{\theta}_n, f_n|\theta^0) + o(\frac{1}{n}). \tag{8.17}$$

It follows from (8.15) and (8.17) that the quantity

$$-(1/n) \log f_n(y_1, y_2, \cdots, y_n|\theta^0) + K_n(\hat{\theta}_n, f_n|\theta^0) \tag{8.18}$$

has the expectation whose formal expansion coincides with that of $R_n(\hat{\theta}, f_n)$ up to the order $o(1/n)$. If $G_n(y_1, y_2, \cdots, y_n)$ has the density function $f_n(y_1, y_2, \cdots, y_n|\theta^0)$, then

$$K_n(\hat{\theta}_n, f_n|\theta^0) = p/n + o(1/n) \tag{8.19}$$

and the quantity

$$l_n(\hat{\theta}_n) = -(1/n) \log f_n(y_1, y_2, \cdots, y_n|\theta^0) + p/n \tag{8.20}$$

is an unbiased [up to order $o(1/n)$] estimate of $R_n(\hat{\theta}, f_n)$. If we multiply both side of (8.20) by $2n$, then the right hand side of (8.20) is just Akaike's AIC [Aakaike (1973)].

$$\text{AIC}(p) = -2 \log f_n(y_1, y_2, \cdots, y_n|\theta^0) + 2p.$$

Chapter 8. The BCT Model and Cross-entropy Risk

Let $y_1, y_2, \cdots, y_n$ are i.i.d. with the probability density function $f(Y|\theta)$ and so that
$$f_n(y_1, y_2, \cdots, y_n|\theta) = \Pi_{t=1}^n f(y_t|\theta),$$
then the AIC can be defined by
$$\text{AIC}(p) = -2 \sum_{t=1}^n \log f(y_t|\theta) + 2p. \tag{8.21}$$

However, in practice, $G_n(y_1, y_2, \cdots, y_n)$ in (8.11) may not be a member of $\{f_n(Y|\theta; \theta \in \Theta)\}$. In order to have an asymptotically unbiased estimator of $R_n(\hat{\theta}, f_n)$, we need an unbiased estimator of K_n which is defined in (8.16). This is the key point to construct the GIC which will be used in the identification of the BCT regression model.

Set the information matrices $I(\theta^0)$ and $J(\theta^0)$ as follows:
$$I(\theta^0) = -\frac{1}{n}\Big[\int_{R^n} \frac{\partial^2 f_n(y_1, y_2, \cdots, y_n|\theta^0)}{\partial \theta_i \partial \theta_j} dG_n(y_1, y_2, \cdots, y_n)\Big] \tag{8.22}$$
and
$$J(\theta^0) = -\frac{1}{n}\Big[\int_{R^n} \frac{\partial f_n(y_1, y_2, \cdots, y_n|\theta^0)}{\partial \theta_i}$$
$$\frac{\partial f_n(y_1, y_2, \cdots, y_n|\theta^0)}{\partial \theta_j} dG_n(y_1, y_2, \cdots, y_n)\Big]. \tag{8.23}$$

Suppose that $\hat{\theta}_n \to \theta^0$ ($\hat{\theta}_n$ convergence to θ^0 in proberbility), it can be proved that the information matrix $I(\hat{\theta}_n)$ and $J(\hat{\theta}_n)$ are convergence to $I(\theta^0)$ and $J(\theta^0)$ respectively. Then a natural estimate of $K_n(\hat{\theta}_n, f_n|\theta^0)$ can be given by
$$\frac{1}{n} tr I(\theta^0)^{-1} J(\theta^0) = -\frac{1}{n} tr I(\hat{\theta}_n)^{-1} J(\hat{\theta}_n) + o(1/n). \tag{8.24}$$
Finally we see that
$$-(1/n) \log f_n(y_1, y_2, \cdots, y_n|\hat{\theta}_n) + \frac{1}{n} tr I(\hat{\theta}_n)^{-1} J(\hat{\theta}_n) \tag{8.25}$$
is an asymptotically unbiased estimator of the cross-entropy risk of $f(Y|\theta)$ for the given estimator $\hat{\theta}_n$.

For the cases $y_1, y_2, \cdots, y_n$ are i.i.d., then
$$K_n(\hat{\theta}_n, f_n|\theta^0) = tr T^{-1} U, \tag{8.26}$$

8.2. Estimation of Cross-entropy Risk and the GIC

where T and U are $p \times p$ matrices whose (i,j)-th element is given by

$$T(i,j) = \frac{1}{n}\sum_{t=1}^{n} \frac{\partial^2 f(y_t|\theta^0)}{\partial \theta_i \partial \theta_j} \tag{8.27}$$

and

$$U(i,j) = \frac{1}{n}\sum_{t=1}^{n} \frac{\partial f(y_t|\theta^0)}{\partial \theta_i} \frac{\partial f(y_t|\theta^0)}{\partial \theta_j}. \tag{8.28}$$

So at this situation, in view of (8.25)

$$-\frac{1}{n}\sum_{t=1}^{n} \log f(y_t|\hat{\theta}_n) + \frac{1}{n} tr T^{-1} U \tag{8.29}$$

is an asymptotically unbiased estimator of the cross-entropy risk of $f(Y|\theta)$ for the given estimator $\hat{\theta}_n(y_1, y_2, \cdots, y_n)$ [which is the ML estimate based on $f(Y|\theta)$, See also Takeuchi (1976)]. By multiply $2n$ to (8.29), we define GIC by

$$\text{GIC}(p) = -2\sum_{t=1}^{n} \log f(y_t|\theta) + 2tr T^{-1} U. \tag{8.30}$$

From (8.21) and (8.30), we can see that the difference between the AIC and the GIC is only the last item at the right-hand side. In (8.30), $tr T^{-1} U$ may not be a function of the number of free parameters in the model.

Chapter 9

Identification Methods for Nonlinear Processes

In this chapter, we summarize the theoretical results of the GIC applied to the identification of the BCT model. The simultaneous identification of the BCT parameter and the order of the regression part of the BCT model constitute our main purpose. Therefore, it is not suitable to treat the BCT parameter as a nuisance parameter. In the case of Takeuchi's GIC [Takeuchi (1976)], the parameters, except for the model order, are treated as nuisance parameters and are deleted, and the information criterion is only a function of the model order. The GIC we developed is the function of both the model order and the BCT parameter [see Hosoya (1984), Yao (1994)].

AIC, another method that can be used in the identification of the BCT model, will be discussed in the following section. The AIC was first introduced as a basis of comparison and selection among several models [Akaike (1973)]. Being an extension of the ML principle, it can be regarded as a method of asymptotic realization of an optimum estimate with respect to a very general information theoretic criterion. The introduction of an objective criterion enables the objective comparison of models that are usually selected subjectively by analysts and also stimulates the development of more appropriate models. Details of the AIC theory can be found in Sakamoto and Ishiguro and Kitagawa (1986).

Chapter 9. Identification Methods for Nonlinear Processes

9.1 Inference of the GIC for BCT Model

Here we deal with the BCT defined by (8.1) in the last chapter. That is to say we deal with a parametric family of transformation from Y to $Y^{[\lambda]}$, the parameter λ defining a particular transformation, while Y is a dependent variable in the multiple BCT regression model.

$$Y^{[\lambda]} = \beta_1 X_1 + \beta_2 X_2 + \cdots + \beta_p X_p + \varepsilon,$$

where ε is supported to be *i.i.d.* with mean 0 and constant variance σ^2.

Suppose $y_1, y_2, \cdots, y_n$ be independent, positive random variables and consider the set of probability density function indexed by λ

$$f_n(y_1, y_2, \cdots, y_n | \beta, \sigma^2, \lambda) \qquad (9.1)$$
$$= \frac{1}{(2\pi)^{n/2} \sigma^n} \exp\left\{ -\frac{\sum_{t=1}^{n}(y_t^{[\lambda]} - \sum_{k=1}^{p} \beta_k x_{tk})}{2\sigma^2} \right\} \Pi_{t=1}^{n} y_t^{\lambda - 1}.$$

where $y_t^{[\lambda]}$ ($t = 1, 2, \cdots, n$) is defined by (8.1); the design matrix $\mathcal{X} = \{x_{tk} : t = 1, 2, \cdots, n; k = 1, 2, \cdots, p\}$ has rank p [see Box and Cox (1964)], β is the $p \times 1$ coefficient column vector.

Let $\hat{\beta}(\lambda)$ and $\hat{\sigma}(\lambda)^2$ (abbreviated $\hat{\beta}$ and $\hat{\sigma}^2$ in the following discussions) be the ML estimator of β and σ^2 based on the BCT model (9.1) for a given λ. Then

$$\hat{\sigma}^2 = \frac{1}{n} \sum_{t=1}^{n} (y_t^{[\lambda]} - X\hat{\beta})^2 = \frac{1}{n} \sum_{t=1}^{n} (y_t^{[\lambda]} - \sum_{k=1}^{p} \hat{\beta}_k x_{tk})^2. \qquad (9.2)$$

From (9.1), by taking the logarithm of the likelihood function, if we denote the $\hat{\sigma}^2$ hereafter by $\sigma^2(p, \lambda)$, the maximum likelihood estimate of σ^2 for given (p, λ), we obtain the log-likelihood function

$$\log f_n(y_1, y_2, \cdots, y_n | \hat{\beta}, \hat{\sigma}^2, \lambda)$$
$$= \frac{n}{2}(1 + \log 2\pi) - \frac{n}{2} \log \hat{\sigma}^2(p, \lambda) + (\lambda - 1) \sum_{t=1}^{n} \log y_t. \qquad (9.3)$$

We ow consider the calculation of the corresponding matrix T and U that be defined by (8.27) and (8.28). As $y_1, y_2, \cdots, y_n$ are independent, so the logarithmic density distribution function for each y_t ($t = 1, 2, \cdots, n$) is

$$\log f(y_t | \beta, \hat{\sigma}^2, \lambda) = \frac{1}{2}(1 + \log 2\pi) - \frac{s_t^2}{2\sigma^2} + (\lambda - 1) \sum_{t=1}^{n} \log y_t, \qquad (9.4)$$

9.1. Inference of the GIC for BCT Model

where $s_t = (y_t^{[\lambda]} - \sum_{k=1}^{p} \beta_k x_{tk})^2$. Then for $i, j = 1, 2, \cdots, p$, it follows that

$$\frac{\partial}{\partial \beta_i} \log f(y_t|\beta, \hat{\sigma}^2, \lambda) = \frac{s_t x_{ti}}{\sigma^2},$$

$$\frac{\partial}{\partial \sigma} \log f(y_t|\beta, \hat{\sigma}^2, \lambda) = \frac{s_t^2 - \sigma^2}{\sigma^3},$$

$$\frac{\partial^2}{\partial \beta_i \partial \sigma} \log f(y_t|\beta, \hat{\sigma}^2, \lambda) = -\frac{2 s_t x_{ti}}{\sigma^3}, \quad (9.5)$$

$$\frac{\partial}{\partial \beta_i \partial \beta_j} \log f(y_t|\beta, \hat{\sigma}^2, \lambda) = -\frac{x_{ti} x_{tj}}{\sigma^2},$$

$$\frac{\partial^2}{\partial \sigma^2} \log f(y_t|\beta, \hat{\sigma}^2, \lambda) = \frac{\sigma^2 - 3 s_t^2}{\sigma^4}.$$

Let $\hat{s}_t = (y_t^{[\lambda]} - \sum_{k=1}^{p} \hat{\beta}_k x_{tk})^2$, then $n\hat{\sigma}^2 = y_t^{[\lambda]} - \sum_{t=1}^{n} \hat{s}_t$. For $i, j = 1, 2, \cdots, p$; and $\hat{\theta}_n = (\hat{\beta}, \hat{\sigma}^2)$, the elements of matrix $T = T(\hat{\theta}_n, \lambda)$ for given λ are:

$$T(i,j) = \sum_{t=1}^{n} x_{ti} x_{tj} \Big/ \sum_{t=1}^{n} \hat{s}_t^2,$$

$$T(i, p+1) = 2n^{1/2} \sum_{t=1}^{n} x_{ti} \hat{s}_t \Big/ (\sum_{t=1}^{n} \hat{s}_t^2)^{3/2}, \quad (9.6)$$

$$T(p+1, i) = T(i, p+1)$$

$$T(p+1, p+1) = 2n \Big/ \sum_{t=1}^{n} \hat{s}_t^2.$$

The elements of matrix $U = U(\hat{\theta}_n, \lambda)$ for given λ are:

$$U(i,j) = \sum_{t=1}^{n} \hat{s}_t^2 x_{ti} x_{tj} \Big/ (\sum_{t=1}^{n} s_t^2)^2,$$

$$T(i, p+1) = -\frac{1}{2} T(i, p+1) + n^{3/2} \sum_{t=1}^{n} x_{ti} \hat{s}_t^3 \Big/ (\sum_{t=1}^{n} \hat{s}_t^2)^{5/2}, \quad (9.7)$$

$$U(p+1, i) = U(i, p+1),$$

$$U(p+1, p+1) = n^2 \sum_{t=1}^{n} \hat{s}_t^4 \Big/ (\sum_{t=1}^{n} \hat{s}_t^2)^3 - n \Big/ \sum_{t=1}^{n} \hat{s}_t^2.$$

Denote $S = (\hat{s}_1, \hat{s}_2, \cdots, \hat{s}_n)^*$, $S^2 = (\hat{s}_1^2, \hat{s}_2^2, \cdots, \hat{s}_n^2)^*$, S_d^3 be n by n diagonal matrix whose (i,i)-th element is $\hat{s}_i^3, i = 1, 2, \cdots, n$. Then we can write matrix $T = T(\hat{\theta}_n, \lambda)$ for given λ as the partitioned form

$$\begin{pmatrix} (X^*X)(S^*S)^{-1} & 2\sqrt{n}(X^*S)(S^*S)^{3/2} \\ 2\sqrt{n}(S^*X)(S^*S)^{3/2} & 2n(S^*S)^{-1} \end{pmatrix} \quad (9.8)$$

Chapter 9. Identification Methods for Nonlinear Processes

and the matrix $U = U(\hat{\theta}_n, \lambda)$ for given λ as partitioned form

$$\begin{pmatrix} \dfrac{n(X^*S)(X^*S)^*}{(S^*S)^2} & \dfrac{\sqrt{n}(X^*S - nX^*S_d^3/S^*S)}{(S^*S)^{3/2}} \\ \dfrac{\sqrt{n}(S^*X - nS_d^{3*}X/S^*S)}{(S^*S)^{3/2}} & \dfrac{(n^2S^*S^2S - n(S^*S)^4)}{(S^*S)^3} \end{pmatrix}. \quad (9.9)$$

By (9.6) and (9.7), or (9.8) and (9.9), we can calculate the trace of the information matrix of the BCT model (9.1) for given (p, λ), the trace can be expressed by:

$$tr(p, \lambda) = tr(T(\hat{\theta}_n, \lambda)^{-1} U(\hat{\theta}_n, \lambda)). \quad (9.10)$$

From (8.27) and (9.10), the general information criterion of the BCT model (9.1) for given (p, λ) is:

$$\text{GIC}(p, \lambda) = \mathcal{C} + n \log \hat{\sigma}^2(p, \lambda) - 2(\lambda - 1) \sum_{t=1}^{n} \log y_t + tr(p, \lambda), \quad (9.11)$$

where, here and after, $\mathcal{C} = n(1 + \log 2\pi)$. Because the number of free parameters in the BCT model (9.1) for given (p, λ) is $p + 1$, therefor the AIC for the BCT model is

$$\text{AIC}(p, \lambda) = \mathcal{C} + n \log \hat{\sigma}^2(p, \lambda) - 2(\lambda - 1) \sum_{t=1}^{n} \log y_t + 2(p + 1). \quad (9.12)$$

The identification problem between two given probability density functions can be conducted by the information criteria, the AIC, or the GIC. Model selection is based on the minimum principle of the GIC or the AIC. For a given $p_i, i = 1, 2$, the probability density functions $f(p_1, \lambda)$ and $f(p_2, \lambda)$, which are indexed by the pairs of the parameters (p_1, λ) and (p_2, λ) for a different BCT parameter λ, determine two classes of the BCT models. Note that

$$\text{GIC}(p_1, \hat{\lambda}_1) = \min\{\text{GIC}(p_1, \lambda | \lambda)\},$$

$$\text{AIC}(p_1, \hat{\lambda}_1) = \min\{\text{AIC}(p_1, \lambda | \lambda)\}$$

and

$$\text{GIC}(p_2, \hat{\lambda}_2) = \min\{\text{GIC}(p_2, \lambda | \lambda)\},$$

9.1. Inference of the GIC for BCT Model

$$\text{AIC}(p_2, \hat{\lambda}_2) = \min\{\text{AIC}(p_2, \lambda|\lambda)\}$$

In view of the AIC method, choose the model $f(p_1, \hat{\lambda}_1)$ if

$$\text{AIC}(p_1, \hat{\lambda}_1) < \text{AIC}(p_2, \hat{\lambda}_2) \qquad (9.13)$$

and the model $f(p_2, \hat{\lambda}_2)$ otherwise.

If we use the GIC method, choose the model $f(p_1, \hat{\lambda}_1)$ if

$$\text{GIC}(p_1, \hat{\lambda}_1) < \text{GIC}(p_2, \hat{\lambda}_2) \qquad (9.14)$$

otherwise choose the model $f(p_2, \hat{\lambda}_2)$.

In the case of (9.13) and/or (9.14) take equality, *i.e.*, $\text{AIC}(p_1, \hat{\lambda}_1) = \text{AIC}(p_2, \hat{\lambda}_2)$ and/or $\text{GIC}(p_1, \hat{\lambda}_1) = \text{GIC}(p_2, \hat{\lambda}_2)$, we prefer to choose the model which with a lower order. The lower order model with fewer parameters has many advantages especially in the small sample empirical analysis. In some cases where the estimated $\text{GIC}(p_1, \hat{\lambda}_1)$ and $\text{GIC}(p_2, \hat{\lambda}_2)$ are very near, we may also prefer to choose the lower order BCT model.

In the following discussions, we consider some of the BCT regression models generally used. The GIC and the AIC for the corresponding BCT regression model are given. The details of the calculation of the

$$tr(p, \lambda) = tr(T(\hat{\theta}_n, \lambda)^{-1} U(\hat{\theta}_n, \lambda))$$

for different models are also pointed out.

1. Multiple Regression Model: For a multiple regression model with the BCT: $(Y, X_1, X_2, \cdots, X_p | \lambda)$, here we only consider the case which is defined as

$$Y^{[\lambda]} = \beta_0 + \beta_1 X_1 + \beta_1 X_2 + \cdots + \beta_p X_p + \varepsilon, \qquad (9.15)$$

with an expression of density function

$$f_n(y_1, y_2, \cdots, y_n | \beta_0, \beta_1, \cdots, \beta_p, \sigma^2, \lambda)$$

$$= \frac{1}{(2\pi)^{n/2} \sigma^n} \exp\Big\{-\frac{1}{2\sigma^2} \sum_{t=1}^n (y_t^{[\lambda]} - \beta_0 - \sum_{k=1}^p \beta_k x_{tk})\Big\} \Pi_{t=1}^n y_t^{\lambda-1}.$$

Chapter 9. Identification Methods for Nonlinear Processes

For a set of n independent observations $\{y_i, x_{i1}, x_{i1}, \cdots, x_{ip}\}_{i=1}^n$, the AIC and the GIC of model $(Y, X_1, X_2, \cdots, X_p|\lambda)$ for fixed BCT parameter λ are respectively given by

$$\text{AIC}(Y, X_1, X_2, \cdots, X_p|\lambda) = \mathcal{C} + \mathcal{C}_1 + 2(p+2), \qquad (9.16)$$

$$\text{GIC}(Y, X_1, X_2, \cdots, X_p|\lambda) = \mathcal{C} + \mathcal{C}_1 + 2tr(p, \lambda), \qquad (9.17)$$

where

$$\mathcal{C}_1 = n \log \hat{\sigma}^2(Y, X_1, X_2, \cdots, X_p|\lambda) - 2(\lambda - 1) \sum_{t=1}^n \log y_t.$$

The $tr(p, \lambda)$ can be calculated by the same way as (9.10) if only we set $X_0 = (1, 1, \cdots, 1)^*$ and rewrite the index i to $i+1$, p to $p+1$.

2. Polynomial Regression Model: Now consider a p-th order BCT polynomial regression model, say model

$$Y^{[\lambda]} = \beta_0 + \beta_1 X^1 + \beta_1 X^2 + \cdots + \beta_p X^p + \varepsilon, \qquad (9.18)$$

with an expression of density function

$$f_n(y_1, y_2, \cdots, y_n | \beta_0, \beta_1, \cdots, \beta_p, \sigma^2, \lambda)$$
$$= \frac{1}{(2\pi)^{n/2}\sigma^n} \exp\Big\{-\frac{1}{2\sigma^2} \sum_{t=1}^n (y_t^{[\lambda]} - \beta_0 - \sum_{k=1}^p \beta_k x_t^k)\Big\} \Pi_{t=1}^n y_t^{\lambda-1}.$$

For a set of n independent observations $\{y_i, x_i\}_{i=1}^n$, the AIC and the GIC are respectively given by

$$\text{AIC}(Y, X|p, \lambda) = \mathcal{C} + \mathcal{C}_2 + 2(p+2), \qquad (9.19)$$

$$\text{GIC}(Y, X|p, \lambda) = \mathcal{C} + \mathcal{C}_2 + 2tr(p, \lambda), \qquad (9.20)$$

where

$$\mathcal{C}_2 = n \log \hat{\sigma}^2(Y, X|p, \lambda) - 2(\lambda - 1) \sum_{t=1}^n \log y_t.$$

The $tr(p, \lambda)$ can be calculated by the same way as (9.10) if only we set $X_0 = (1, 1, \cdots, 1)^*$ and rewrite the index i to be the i-th exponent.

3. Autoregressive Model: Now consider a q-th order BCT autoregressive model, say model

$$X_t^{[\lambda]} = \beta_1 X_{t-1}^{[\lambda]} + \beta_2 X_{t-2}^{[\lambda]} + \cdots + \beta_q X_{t-q}^{[\lambda]} + \varepsilon. \qquad (9.21)$$

For the independent observations $\{x_i\}_{i=1}^n$, we can have the expression of density function

$$f_n(x_1, x_2, \cdots, x_n | \beta_1, \cdots, \beta_q, \sigma^2, \lambda)$$
$$= \frac{1}{(2\pi)^{n/2}\sigma^n} \exp\left\{-\frac{1}{2\sigma^2} \sum_{t=1}^n (x_t^{[\lambda]} - \beta_0 - \sum_{k=1}^q \beta_k x_{t-k}^{[\lambda]})\right\} \Pi_{t=1}^n x_t^{\lambda-1}.$$

The AIC and GIC are respectively given by

$$\text{AIC}(X|\ q, \lambda) = \mathcal{C} + \mathcal{C}_3 + 2(q+2), \tag{9.22}$$

$$\text{GIC}(X|\ q, \lambda) = \mathcal{C} + \mathcal{C}_3 + 2tr(q, \lambda), \tag{9.23}$$

where

$$\mathcal{C}_3 = n \log \hat{\sigma}^2(X|q,\lambda) - 2(\lambda - 1) \sum_{t=1}^n \log x_t.$$

The $tr(q, \lambda)$ can be calculated by the same way as (9.10) if only we treat $X_t^{[\lambda]}$ as $Y^{[\lambda]}$, $X_{t-k}^{[\lambda]}$ as X_k, $k = 1, 2, \cdots, q$.

Remark 9.1 For the observation $\{y_t\}_{i=1}^n$ of the random variable Y and it's geometric mean $\dot{Y}$, if we apply the normalized transformation $Z^{[\lambda]} = Y^{[\lambda]}/\dot{Y}^{(\lambda-1)}$, then the GIC and the AIC defined by (9.11) and (9.12) as the results of new variable Z, can be simplified by removing the third term on the right hand of the equations, respectively.

9.2 Nested χ^2 Test for the BCT Model

Besides the information criterion methods used in the identification of the BCT regression model, we have also another method called the nested χ^2 test. In this section we summarize the method of the nested χ^2 test, which was first introduced by Hosoya (1986). It applies the generalized likelihood ratio (GLR) test of equal marginal error rate to the model selection problems. The application to hierarchical statistical models was studied by Hosoya (1986, 1989). Yao (1992), Yao and Hosoya (1994) showed the process and computational algorithm of applied this method to the investigation of the BCT model.

Chapter 9. Identification Methods for Nonlinear Processes

Suppose that the parameter $\theta = (\theta_1, \theta_2, \cdots, \theta_p)$ specifying a density function of observations, where the parameter θ_j is r_j dimensional vector. The hypothesis H_j implies that

$$H_j: \quad \theta_{j+1} = \theta_{j+2} = \cdots = \theta_p = 0, \qquad (9.24)$$

and H_p implies that no such specification is imposed.

For $i < j$ ($1 \leq i, j \leq p$), denote by L_{ij} the log-likelihood ratio for testing H_i against H_j. The test for H_i in the presence of such nested alternative hypotheses would use L_{ij}, by using a test with critical region $R = \{L_{ij} \leq c_j$, for some $j \in (i+1, \cdots, p)\}$ where the c_j's are determined so that $Pr\{R|H_i\}$ is equal to the required size. The p-value which corresponds to this test is evaluated as $P(q^*) = Pr\{Q \leq q^*|H_i\}$ where $Q = \min(P_j| \; i+1 \leq j \leq p)$ is the p-value based on L_{ij} and q^* is the observed value of Q. The test for the critical region will here be termed a GLR test [see Hosoya (1989)]. For the case all degrees of freedom are 1 and $p \leq 13$, the algorithm for the p-value is available in Hosoya and Katayama (1987). See also Terui (1990) for the small-sample GLR test for the nested regression models.

Now we consider the p-th order BCT polynomial regression model, say model

$$Y^{[\lambda]} = \beta_0 + \beta_1 X + \beta_1 X^2 + \cdots + \beta_p X^p + \varepsilon, \qquad (9.25)$$

with an expression of density function

$$f(Y, X|\beta_0, \beta_1, \cdots, \beta_p, \sigma^2, \lambda)$$
$$= \frac{1}{(2\pi)^{n/2}\sigma^n} \exp\left\{-\frac{1}{2\sigma^2}\sum_{t=1}^{n}(y_t^{[\lambda]} - \beta_0 - \sum_{k=1}^{p}\beta_k x_t^k)\right\}\Pi_{t=1}^{n} y_t^{\lambda-1}.$$

For a set of n independent observations $\{y_i, x_i\}_{i=1}^{n}$, the simultaneous estimation of the BCT parameter λ and the order p of the regression model by the nested χ^2 test proceeds by the following steps:

1. For a given p, we consider a family of polynomial regression models in which each of the orders is less than or equals to p. We first calculate the $n_1 \times p$ matrix of the maximum log-likelihood (MLL) for a given n_1 and a different fixed $\lambda_i = 1, 2, \cdots, n_1$. Then, by the MLL estimation, the BCT parameter $\hat{\lambda}_j$ for the j-th order polynomial regression model can be determined. We denote the MLL by $L(j, \hat{\lambda}_j), j = 1, 2, \cdots, p$.

9.2. Nested χ^2 Test for the BCT Model

2. For $k = 1, 2, \cdots, p-1$, we calculate the difference of the two MLL ratios $LR(k, j)$ defined as follows:

$$LR(k, j) = 2[L(j, \hat{\lambda}_j) - L(k, \hat{\lambda}_k)], \quad j = k+1, \cdots, p, \qquad (9.26)$$

where k is the order of the polynomial regression model. We treat this to be the input to the subroutine program given by Hosoya and Katayama (1987). By this way, the p-values $\{p_k\}_{k=1}^{p-1}$ can be obtained.

3. For the given significance level α_0, if there existed some index k that satisfied $p_k > \alpha_0$, we chose the first k to be the estimator of the order of the BCT polynomial regression model. That is to say, $\hat{p} = k$. If $p_k \leq \alpha_0$ for all $k = 1, 2, \cdots$, then we have $\hat{p} = p$. The corresponding $\hat{\lambda}_{\hat{p}}$, which we want to estimate, is the estimator of the BCT parameter that best fits the model.

Chapter 10

Numerical Evaluation of the GIC and the AIC

In this chapter, in view of the Monte Carlo experiment, we show the performance of the maximum-likelihood estimate (MLE) and the GIC applied to the identification of the BCT regression model. We intend to confirm that the GIC is an extension of the classical ML method and should have an approximately equal performance in estimating the BCT parameter for fixed-order BCT model. The comparison of the performance of the GIC and the AIC in the identification of the BCT regression model is also shown. The results in this chapter are mainly based on Yao (1992, 1994), Yao and Hosoya (1994).

Just as we expected, as an extension of the MLE, the GIC plays almost the same role in the identification of the fixed-order BCT model. The Monte Carlo experiment shows that there is no significant difference between the GIC method and the AIC method. A closer observation of the simulation results reveals that in estimating the BCT parameter, the GIC is a little precise than the AIC. The opposite holds for the identification of the BCT polynomial model order.

We only give very briefly empirical examples in this chapter in order to show the procedure of applying the presented methods to the finite sample empirical analysis. The applications to the Tokyo stock price index and a textile experiment are illustrated. The analysis of the Tokyo stock price index gives a new empirical model but not the often-used logarithmic model. The empirical analysis of the textile experiment presented in Box and Cox (1964) is re-examined by the use of

Chapter 10. Numerical Evaluation of the GIC and the AIC

our approach. We see that the optimal value for the transformation parameter by the MLE method is the same as the result of Box-Cox (1964). The empirical results also show that, in view of the GIC and the AIC, the applications of the BCT model to the investigation of economic activities become more interesting.

The numerical calculations are performed by the Fortran programs presented by Yao (1992). They are named as: PMRMM92, PBMGM92, PBMAM192, and PBMAM292.

10.1 Simulation Models

For the purpose of using the Mote Carlo experiment in the following numerical evaluation of the performances of the information criteria method and the nested χ^2 test, we need to construct a random data set for our investigation. Let us first consider a second-order BCT polynomial regression model:

$$Y^{[\lambda]} = Z = \beta_0 + \beta_1 X + \beta_2 X^2 + \varepsilon, \tag{10.1}$$

where $\beta_0 = 2.1, \beta_1 = 0.81, \beta_2 = 0.64$, the values of ε is random number and be obtained from $N(0,1)$. The sample size is chosen to be $N(=100)$. The independent variable are defined as $x_t = t/40$, for $t = 1, 2, \cdots, N$. The data set of the dependent observations is determined by

$$y_t = \begin{cases} (\lambda z_t + 1)^{1/\lambda} & \lambda \neq 0 \\ \exp z_t & \lambda = 0 \end{cases} \tag{10.2}$$

The parameters β_1 and β_2 are chosen so that the contributions of $X^j (j = 1, 2)$ to the variance of Z are approximately equalized by the use of these parameters. That is to say, each of the parameter has approximately equal importance in explaining the variation in Z. The parameter β_0 is chosen so that Y or $(\lambda Z + 1)$ and Z are positive or the mathematical relations in (10.2) hold true.

We also investigated a third order polynomial regression BCT model

$$Y^{[\lambda]} = 2.1 + 0.81X - 0.49X^2 + 0.64X^3 + \varepsilon. \tag{10.3}$$

The constant and the coefficients in model (10.3) are determined in the same way as for model (10.1). As the simulation results in the following discussions

10.2. Monte Carlo Experiments by the GIC and the MLE

expressed very similar properties, we mainly discuss the results based on model (10.1). For some cases, some of the results based on model (10.3) are listed with no further explanation.

For a given BCT parameter λ_0 and sample size N ($t = 1, 2, \cdots, N$), we first create random data set $\{\varepsilon_t\}_{t=1}^N$ which has mean zero and variance σ_0^2. We then create data set $\{z_t\}_{t=1}^N$ from $\{\varepsilon_t\}_{t=1}^N$ and $\{x_t\}_{t=1}^N$ by model (10.1),

$$z_t = 0.21 + 0.81 x_t + 0.64 x_t^2 + \varepsilon_t. \tag{10.4}$$

The dependent variable data set $\{y_t\}_{t=1}^N$ is created by (10.2). Following these steps, we have constructed a data set that satisfied the BCT polynomial regression model, and we know that the true BCT parameter is λ_0 and the true order of the BCT regression model is $k_0 = 2$ (or for the case of using the model (10.3), $k_0 = 3$).

The simulation experiment consists of identifying the order of polynomial regression and the BCT parameter by a large number of replications. At the same time, we can compare the power of different methods used in the identification of the BCT regression model.

10.2 Monte Carlo Experiments by the GIC and the MLE

To compare the performances of the GIC and the MLE in the identification of the fixed order BCT regression model, we investigated three true constructed models defined by (10.1) with the disturbance term variance $\sigma_0^2 = 1$ and the BCT parameters $\lambda_0 = 0, 0.1, 0.2$, respectively. We will identify the BCT parameter λ and other statistical coefficients in model

$$Y^{[\lambda]} = Z = \beta_0 + \beta_1 X + \beta_2 X^2 + \varepsilon. \tag{10.5}$$

Based on the discussions above, for a given $\{\lambda_j\}_{j=1}^{n_1}$ (in this experiment we set $n_1 = 13$) and pre-created data set $\{y_t, x_t\}_{t=1}^N$, where $N = 100$. Let us suppose that the true parameter λ_0 is not known. Now, we identify model (10.4) by the use of the GIC defined in (9.20) and the MLE method so as to search the best BCT parameter $\hat{\lambda}$. That is to say we need to estimate λ_g and λ_l respectively by

$$\text{GIC}(\hat{\beta}, \hat{\sigma}^2 | \hat{\lambda}_g) = \min\{\text{GIC}(\hat{\beta}, \hat{\sigma}^2 | \lambda_j)\} \tag{10.6}$$

Chapter 10. Numerical Evaluation of the GIC and the AIC

and
$$L(\hat{\beta}, \hat{\sigma}^2|\hat{\lambda}_l) = \min\{L(\hat{\beta}, \hat{\sigma}^2|\lambda_j)\} \tag{10.7}$$

where $\hat{\lambda}_g$ and $\hat{\lambda}_l$ are the estimators determined by the GIC and the MLE, respectively, $\hat{\beta}$ and $\hat{\sigma}^2$ are the ML estimator of β and σ^2 based on model (10.1) for a given λ, respectively, and $tr(\hat{\beta}, \hat{\sigma}^2|\lambda)$ used in (10.5) can be calculated in the way discussed in (9.20). We repeated this experiment ten thousand times.

Table 10.1 gives the main results of ten thousand replicated Monte Carlo experiments. The main part of column (1) gives the frequencies in the total 10,000-times experiment for the GIC and the MLE, respectively, when the true BCT parameter is $\lambda_0 = 0$. The 'mean $\hat{\lambda}$' is the weighed mean of $\{\lambda_j\}_{j=1}^{n_1}$

$$\text{Mean}\hat{\lambda} = \sum_{j=1}^{n_1} \hat{\lambda}_j \times \frac{N(\hat{\lambda}_j)}{N}, \tag{10.8}$$

where $N(\hat{\lambda}_j)$ is the frequency against $\hat{\lambda}_j$ and $N = \sum_{j=1}^{n_1} N(\hat{\lambda}_j)$. The 'Var $\hat{\lambda}$' is the weighted mean of the variance of $\{\lambda_j\}_{j=1}^{n_1}$. Columns (2) and (3) are the results for models with $\lambda_0 = 0.1, 0.2$, respectively.

From Table 10.1, we can see that for all the three models indexed by the BCT parameter $\lambda_0 = 0.1, 0.1, 0.2$, both of the GIC and the MLE have very good simulation results. The results also show that there are no significant differences between the two methods when used in the BCT model identification.

Example 10.1 This example re-examine the example which was presented in Box and Cox (1964). It described the experiment on the behavior of worsted yarn under cycles of repeated loading. The number of cycles to failure, y, obtained in a single replicate of a 3^3 experiment in which the factors are:

- X_1: length of test specimen (250, 300, 350 mm.),

- X_2: amplitude of loading cycle (8, 9, 10 mm.),

- X_3: load (40, 45, 50 mm.).

10.2. Monte Carlo Experiments by the GIC and the MLE

Table 10.1 Distribution of the Estimated Frequencies in the 10,000-Times Iterated Monte Carlo Experiment

$\hat{\lambda}$	(1) $\lambda_0 = 0.0$		(2) $\lambda_0 = 0.1$		(3) $\lambda_0 = 0.2$	
	GIC	MLE	GIC	MLE	GIC	MLE
-0.30	0	0	0	0	2	2
-0.25	0	0	0	0	5	5
-0.20	0	0	4	4	59	57
-0.15	2	2	101	98	332	316
-0.10	198	182	762	730	1058	1045
-0.05	2264	2195	2387	2357	2193	2186
λ_0	5025	5053	3599	3619	2864	2864
0.05	2284	2321	2354	2384	2133	2157
0.10	223	242	704	716	1010	1015
0.15	4	5	84	86	299	304
0.20	0	0	5	6	40	44
0.25	0	0	0	0	5	5
0.30	0	0	0	0	0	0
Mean$\hat{\lambda}$	0.0004	0.0013	0.0990	0.0998	0.1983	0.1990
Var$\hat{\lambda}$	0.0396	0.0396	0.0550	0.0555	0.0710	0.0709

The simulation results for model (10.1) with $\sigma_0^2 = 1$.

It is the same with the original paper of Box-Cox (1964), the levels of the x's are denoted conventionally by $-1, 0, 1$. Since the relative range of the x's is not very great, transformation of the x's does not have a big effect on the linearity of the regression, so we only use a transformation of the dependent variable alone. We rewrite the original data set in Table 10.2. In this example we define the BCT as

$$y_i^{[\lambda]} = (y_i/1000)^{[\lambda]}/\dot{Y}^{(\lambda-1)}, \tag{10.9}$$

where $\dot{Y}$ is the geometric mean of $\{y_i/1000\}_{i=1}^{27}$. We do not pay more attention to the physical meaning of the experiment and only list the identification results determined by the methods of GIC and MLE in Table 10.3. In view of Table

Chapter 10. Numerical Evaluation of the GIC and the AIC

10.3, the identified model determined by the GIC and the MLE are

$$Y^{[-0.07]} = -0.3336 + 0.4692X_1 - 0.3559X_2 - 0.2211X_3, \tag{10.10}$$

and

$$Y^{[-0.06]} = -0.3321 + 0.4691X_1 - 0.3555X_2 - 0.2211X_3. \tag{10.11}$$

The natural logarithm transformation model is given by

$$\log Y = -0.3336 + 0.4692X_1 - 0.3559X_2 - 0.2211X_3. \tag{10.12}$$

This shows that, by the MLE method, the optimal value for the transformation parameter is $\lambda_0 = -0.06$, which is the same as that of Box-Cox (1964). Furthermore, it is seen that, by the GIC method, the optimal value for the transformation parameter is $\lambda_0 = -0.07$. Because both of the estimators determined by the two methods are very near zero, the advantages of a log transformation corresponding to the choice $\lambda_0 = 0$ are considerable, and such a choice is strongly supported by the results obtained by both the GIC method and the MLE method.

**Table 10.2 3^3 Factorial Experiment
Cycles to Failure of Worsted Yard**

x_1	x_2	x_3	y	x_1	x_2	x_3	y	x_1	x_2	x_3	y
-1	-1	-1	674	0	-1	-1	1114	1	-1	-1	3636
-1	-1	0	370	0	-1	0	1198	1	-1	0	3184
-1	-1	1	292	0	-1	1	634	1	-1	1	2000
-1	0	-1	338	0	0	-1	1022	1	0	-1	1568
-1	0	0	266	0	0	0	620	1	0	0	1070
-1	0	1	210	0	0	1	438	1	0	1	556
-1	1	-1	170	0	1	-1	442	1	1	-1	1140
-1	1	0	118	0	1	0	332	1	1	0	884
-1	1	1	90	0	1	1	220	1	1	1	360

x_i: *factor levels, $i = 1, 2, 3$; y: cycles to failure.*
Source: Box-Cox (1964), p223, Table 4.

10.2. Monte Carlo Experiments by the GIC and the MLE

Table 10.3 The Estimated GIC and MLL for a Textile Experiment

λ	GIC	MLL	Trace	Var
-0.10	-117.7233	63.3486	4.4870	0.2474
-0.09	-117.8520	63.4433	4.5173	0.2457
-0.08	-117.9241	63.5119	4.5498	0.2444
-0.07	<u>-117.9400</u>	63.5539	4.5839	0.2437
-0.06	-117.9000	<u>63.5692</u>	4.6192	0.2434
-0.05	-117.8049	63.5578	4.6553	0.2436
-0.04	-117.6557	63.5196	4.6918	0.2443
-0.03	-117.4537	63.4550	4.7282	0.2455
-0.02	-117.2002	63.3643	4.7642	0.2471
-0.01	-116.8968	63.2480	4.7996	0.2493
0.00	-116.5452	63.1066	4.8340	0.2519

MLL: the value of maximum log-likelihood

Example 10.2 In this example, we deal with the Tokyo stock price index. The data are monthly averages from the year 1981 to the year 1990, and they are listed in Table 10.4. The original data are listed in Table 66 in *Annual Report on Business Cycle Indicators*, 1991 (in Japanese). We represent the time series by $P_t = P_{yy+mm-1981}$, where $yy = 1981, 1982, \cdots, 1990$; $mm = 1, 2, \cdots, 12$; $t = 1, 2, \cdots, 120$, indicates time periods.

Here we consider the following BCT regression model with the transformation of $P_t^{[\lambda]} = (P_t/100)^{[\lambda]}/\dot{P}^{(\lambda-1)}$,

$$P_t^{[\lambda]} = \beta_0 + \beta_1 P_{t-1}^{[\lambda]} + \varepsilon, \tag{10.13}$$

where $t = 1, 2, \cdots, 120$, and $\dot{P}$ is the geometric mean of $P_t/100)^{[\lambda]}$. The minimum GIC and maximum log-likelihood (MLL) are obtained at the same BCT parameter $\hat{\lambda} = -0.5$. This result can be seen in Table 10.5. The minimum GIC is -180.454 and the maximum MLL is 93.99. The identified models determined by the GIC and the MLE are the same:

$$P_t^{[-0.5]} = 0.0184 + 0.989 P_{t-1}^{[-0.5]}. \tag{10.14}$$

Chapter 10. Numerical Evaluation of the GIC and the AIC

In view of formula (10.13), we can get an intuitional interesting regression relation of Tokyo stock price index:

$$\frac{1}{\sqrt{P_t}} = 0.0016 + \frac{0.989}{\sqrt{P_{t-1}}}. \tag{10.15}$$

The natural logarithmic transformation regression model is given by

$$\log P_t = 0.0337 + 0.991 \log P_{t-1}. \tag{10.16}$$

Table 10.4 Tokyo Stock Price Index

Jan. 4, 1968=100

Month	1981	1982	1983	1984	1985
1	505.68	572.84	588.77	759.63	927.20
2	505.87	570.70	585.86	772.60	941.18
3	515.78	536.85	601.16	813.28	994.51
4	546.03	534.98	618.29	857.00	972.46
5	554.96	555.72	633.30	822.35	983.88
6	568.67	540.55	644.50	785.77	1010.86
7	590.00	530.85	661.54	774.56	1040.04
8	596.74	523.53	669.89	804.81	1011.82
9	564.58	531.75	684.49	815.76	1010.72
10	545.04	541.43	686.21	840.00	1028.35
11	558.10	566.04	686.46	855.83	1006.23
12	566.10	583.09	705.43	888.85	1031.64
Month	1986	1987	1988	1989	1990
1	1034.69	1648.99	1828.36	2437.49	2758.91
2	1066.03	1742.31	1985.47	2470.84	2680.39
3	1162.99	1851.08	2109.32	2417.04	2401.41
4	1233.83	2050.98	2165.74	2463.50	2163.47
5	1264.45	2140.02	2167.79	2522.56	2365.92
6	1329.78	2171.44	2185.63	2475.28	2379.77
7	1394.75	1996.17	2177.78	2526.71	2339.80
8	1496.38	2101.60	2195.02	2631.40	2024.40
9	1503.96	2085.39	2124.77	2626.01	1815.28
10	1414.25	2023.68	2123.30	2668.29	1757.88
11	1432.65	1852.26	2217.24	2725.65	1736.44
12	1553.47	1828.15	2302.54	2859.57	1744.42

Table 10.5 The Estimated GIC and MLL for Tokyo Stock Price Index

λ	GIC	MLL	Trace	Var
-0.60	-180.6430	93.6405	3.3190	0.0092
-0.58	-180.9391	93.7727	3.3031	0.0102
-0.56	-180.1626	93.8706	3.2893	0.0112
-0.54	-180.3259	93.9411	3.2782	0.0123
-0.52	-180.4230	93.9809	3.2694	0.0136
-0.50	-180.4540	93.9900	3.2629	0.0150
-0.48	-180.4222	93.9700	3.2589	0.0166
-0.46	-180.3202	93.9171	3.2570	0.0183
-0.44	-180.1563	93.8356	3.2575	0.0202
-0.42	-180.9306	93.7257	3.2603	0.0224
-0.40	-180.6399	93.5853	3.2653	0.0248

10.3 Comparison of the GIC and the AIC

The model-selection problem of the BCT polynomial regression model has been theoretically and empirically discussed above. In this section, we discuss the Monte Carlo investigation of the simultaneous identification of the BCT parameter and the order of regression model. We want to know the performance of the GIC and the AIC. We can see that the former is a little more precise than the latter in the estimation of the BCT parameter λ; but it is the reverse of estimating the order of the BCT polynomial regression model.

In this study, we conducted a 2,000-times iterated Monte Carlo experiment, where the sample size is the same, $N = 100$. The models discussed here are the second-order model (10.1) ($k_0 = 2$) and the third-order BCT polynomial regression model (10.3) ($k_0 = 3$). The true BCT parameter λ_0 is chosen to be $0, 0.1, 0.2$. The variance of the disturbance term is $\sigma_0^2 = 1$.

Now, for a known generated data set $\{y_t, x_t\}_{t=1}^{100}$, let us consider the following k-th order BCT polynomial regression model

$$y_i^{[\lambda]} = \beta_0 + \beta_1 x_i + \cdots + \beta_i^k. \tag{10.17}$$

Chapter 10. Numerical Evaluation of the GIC and the AIC

According to the procedure mentioned above, we constructed a second order BCT polynomial regression model, and known that whose true BCT parameter for dependent variable Y is $\lambda = \lambda_0$. Supposing that the true BCT parameter λ_0 and the order k_0 are unknown, the identification of the BCT model for the generated data set is conducted by the AIC and the GIC. For $\lambda = \lambda_j$ ($j = 1, 2, \cdots, n_1$), $k = 1, 2, \cdots, K$ (in this investigation we choose $n_1 = 13$ and $K = 5$), we search for the best fitted BCT polynomial regression model, *i.e.* for the given data set $\{y_t, x_t\}_{i=1}^{100}$ to determine a pair of parameter $(\hat{\lambda}, \hat{k})$ that satisfy

$$\text{AIC}(\hat{\lambda}_a, \hat{k}_a) = \min\{\text{AIC}(\lambda, k)\} \tag{10.18}$$

and

$$\text{GIC}(\hat{\lambda}_g, \hat{k}_g) = \min\{\text{GIC}(\lambda, k)\}. \tag{10.19}$$

The AIC and the GIC are described in (9.19) and (9.20), respectively. The identification results are formulated in Table 10.6 and Table 10.7 for the two information criterion methods. Furthermore, the simulation results for model (10.3) are listed in Table 10.8 and Table 10.9 without further explanation.

Table 10.6 is divided into three main parts for the GIC method. The first row lists thirteen BCT parameters around the true parameter λ_0 with a step of ± 0.05. The main parts of the numbers in Table 10.6 describe the distribution of the estimated frequencies against the BCT parameter λ and against the order k of the polynomial regression model. The experiment is repeated two thousand times. The three parts from top to bottom are the results corresponding to the true BCT parameters $\lambda_0 = 0, 0.1, 0.2$, respectively. Table 10.7 lists the results for the AIC method. These two tables demonstrate that both of the two information criterion methods have satisfactorily identified the true models. The Monte Carlo experiment powerfully estimated the order of the BCT polynomial regression model. Closer inspection reveals that the GIC method is slightly better than the AIC method in the estimation of the BCT parameter

This conclusion is not based on the estimated parameters themselves, for both of the estimated parameters are very near the true values and the frequencies that can determine the estimator of λ almost have the same distribution. The slight difference between the two estimators of λ determined by the GIC and the AIC

10.3. Comparison of the GIC and the AIC

is suggested on the meaning of the symmetry of the frequencies against λ for the true (or best-fitted) order. Here, the symmetry is measured by the weights of the frequencies on the two sides of the true order. For example, considering the result by the GIC method for the case of $k_0 = 2$ and the true BCT parameter $\lambda_0 = 0.1$, the left weight and the right weight are 42.2309 and 57.7691, respectively; for the AIC method, the left and the right weight is 41.1224 and 58.8776, respectively. The closer to 50 the weights are, the better the estimator is. Furthermore, for intuitional purposes, we can see the difference by plotting a balance line against 50% level line. The closer to the 50% level line the balance line is, the better the model is. From these viewpoints, we can say that the GIC method is slightly better than the AIC method in the estimation of the BCT parameter. For the detail see Yao (1992).

Table 10.6 and Table 10.7 show that the AIC method is better than the GIC method in the decision of the order of the BCT polynomial regression model because, when using the AIC method, the frequencies around the true order are more concentrated than when using the GIC method

Chapter 10. Numerical Evaluation of the GIC and the AIC

Table 10.6 Simulaton for Polynomial Regression Model by the 2,000-Times Iterated Monte Carlo Experiment — by the GIC Method, $k_0 = 2, N = 100$

λ	k=1	k=2	k=3	k=4	k=5	Tatol
-0.20	0	0	0	0	0	0
-0.15	2	0	0	0	0	2
-0.10	24	15	3	3	8	53
-0.05	93	236	57	26	52	464
$\lambda_0 = 0.0$	36	648	116	93	81	974
0.05	5	293	58	46	58	460
0.10	0	23	8	3	10	44
0.15	0	0	3	0	0	3
0.20	0	0	0	0	0	0
$N(k)$	160	1215	245	171	209	2000
Mean λ	-0.0444	0.0030	0.0041	0.0058	0.0024	-0.0005
-0.20	2	0	0	0	0	2
-0.15	13	5	2	1	2	23
-0.10	59	76	21	5	24	185
-0.05	60	272	55	28	48	463
$\lambda_0 = 0.1$	29	457	92	71	55	704
0.05	3	304	55	38	51	451
0.10	1	85	20	18	27	151
0.15	0	7	4	4	3	18
0.20	0	0	3	0	0	3
$N(k)$	167	1206	252	165	210	2000
Mean λ	0.0341	0.1023	0.1032	0.1136	0.1029	0.0977
-0.25	2	0	0	0	0	2
-0.20	11	2	2	0	0	15
-0.15	31	30	10	4	13	88
-0.10	57	106	23	14	29	229
-0.05	34	264	49	23	46	416
$\lambda_0 = 0.2$	25	358	70	54	38	545
0.05	2	302	47	40	43	434
0.10	3	114	28	22	33	200
0.15	0	33	10	8	9	60
0.20	0	5	0	0	3	8
0.25	0	0	3	0	0	3
$N(k)$	165	1214	242	165	214	2000
Mean λ	0.1127	0.2031	0.2031	0.2136	0.2012	0.1963

10.3. Comparison of the GIC and the AIC

Table 10.7 Simulaton for Polynomial Regression Model by the 2,000-Times Iterated Monte Carlo Experiment — by the AIC Method, $k_0 = 2, N = 100$

λ	k=1	k=2	k=3	k=4	k=5	Tatol
-0.20	0	0	0	0	0	0
-0.15	2	0	0	0	0	2
-0.10	24	14	2	2	3	45
-0.05	103	256	58	25	26	468
$\lambda_0 = 0.0$	42	683	127	88	40	980
0.05	5	324	58	43	25	455
0.10	0	30	6	7	4	47
0.15	0	0	3	0	0	3
0.20	0	0	0	0	0	0
$N(k)$	176	1307	254	165	98	2000
Mean λ	-0.0432	0.0038	0.0033	0.0085	0.0005	-0.0002
-0.20	2	0	0	0	0	2
-0.15	17	5	2	0	2	26
-0.10	58	71	22	8	9	168
-0.05	62	286	53	27	25	453
$\lambda_0 = 0.1$	32	509	95	65	27	728
0.05	3	340	55	42	26	466
0.10	2	93	17	15	9	136
0.15	0	10	2	4	2	18
0.20	0	0	3	0	0	3
$N(k)$	176	1314	249	161	100	2000
Mean λ	0.0347	0.1043	0.1008	0.1127	0.1005	0.0982
-0.25	1	0	0	0	0	1
-0.20	12	2	1	0	2	17
-0.15	32	26	11	3	5	77
-0.10	62	116	28	11	11	228
-0.05	40	280	48	27	21	416
$\lambda_0 = 0.2$	30	382	74	50	23	559
0.05	2	326	51	40	23	442
0.10	3	134	24	19	9	189
0.15	0	39	8	7	4	58
0.20	0	5	0	3	1	9
0.25	0	0	3	0	0	3
$N(k)$	183	1310	248	160	99	2000
Mean λ	0.115	0.2051	0.1994	0.2166	0.1955	0.1966

Chapter 10. Numerical Evaluation of the GIC and the AIC

Table 10.8 Simulaton for Polynomial Regression Model by the 2,000-Times Iterated Monte Carlo Experiment — by the GIC Method, $k_0 = 3, N = 100$

λ	k=1	k=2	k=3	k=4	k=5	Tatol
-0.20	0	0	0	0	0	0
-0.15	0	0	0	0	0	0
-0.10	0	4	0	0	3	7
-0.05	0	233	108	36	51	428
$\lambda_0 = 0.0$	0	338	579	148	134	1199
0.05	0	10	205	74	69	358
0.10	0	0	3	2	3	8
0.15	0	0	0	0	0	0
0.20	0	0	0	0	0	0
$N(k)$	0	585	895	260	260	2000
Mean λ	–	-0.0197	0.0058	0.0081	0.0035	-0.0017
-0.20	0	0	0	0	0	0
-0.15	0	0	0	0	1	1
-0.10	0	59	10	6	16	91
-0.05	0	259	164	49	59	531
$\lambda_0 = 0.1$	0	232	413	104	97	846
0.05	0	30	272	73	67	442
0.10	0	1	39	20	24	84
0.15	0	0	3	1	1	5
0.20	0	0	0	0	0	0
$N(k)$	0	581	901	253	265	2000
Mean λ	–	0.0703	0.1097	0.1109	0.1045	0.0977
-0.25	0	0	0	0	0	0
-0.20	0	0	0	0	1	1
-0.15	0	23	3	3	6	35
-0.10	0	109	40	15	28	192
-0.05	0	216	184	41	59	500
$\lambda_0 = 0.2$	0	178	318	84	81	661
0.05	0	39	256	63	60	418
0.10	0	2	91	29	45	167
0.15	0	1	10	7	5	23
0.20	0	0	2	1	0	3
0.25	0	0	0	0	0	0
$N(k)$	0	568	904	243	285	2000
Mean λ	–	0.1598	0.2112	0.2136	0.2049	0.196

10.3. Comparison of the GIC and the AIC

Table 10.9 Simulaton for Polynomial Regression Model by the 2,000-Times Iterated Monte Carlo Experiment — by the AIC Method, $k_0 = 3, N = 100$

λ	k=1	k=2	k=3	k=4	k=5	Tatol
-0.20	0	0	0	0	0	0
-0.15	0	0	0	0	0	0
-0.10	0	5	0	0	0	5
-0.05	0	246	99	28	22	395
$\lambda_0 = 0.0$	0	364	617	150	77	1208
0.05	0	16	242	82	43	383
0.10	0	0	3	3	3	9
0.15	0	0	0	0	0	0
0.20	0	0	0	0	0	0
$N(k)$	0	631	961	263	145	2000
Mean λ	–	-0.019	0.0078	0.0114	0.0093	-0.0001
-0.20	0	0	0	0	0	0
-0.15	0	0	1	0	0	1
-0.10	0	62	9	5	3	79
-0.05	0	267	177	43	27	514
$\lambda_0 = 0.1$	0	258	432	108	54	852
0.05	0	32	307	82	40	461
0.10	0	1	50	23	12	86
0.15	0	0	4	2	1	7
0.20	0	0	0	0	0	0
$N(k)$	0	620	980	263	137	2000
Mean λ	–	0.0712	0.1113	0.1154	0.1124	0.0995
-0.25	0	1	0	0	0	1
-0.20	0	0	0	0	0	0
-0.15	0	26	4	3	0	33
-0.10	0	117	42	11	10	180
-0.05	0	238	178	44	29	489
$\lambda_0 = 0.2$	0	203	333	87	41	664
0.05	0	44	287	76	39	446
0.10	0	2	104	33	17	156
0.15	0	1	18	7	2	28
0.20	0	0	2	1	0	3
0.25	0	0	0	0	0	0
$N(k)$	0	632	968	262	138	2000
Mean λ	–	0.1601	0.2146	0.2176	0.2109	0.1975

Chapter 11

Information Criteria and the Nested χ^2 Test

This chapter deals with the identification problem of the BCT model in view of the information criteria and the nested χ^2 test. The emphases here are on the simultaneous identification of the transformation parameter and on the order of the regression part of the BCT model. Monte Carlo experiments are performed for polynomial regression models in order to compare the performance of these methods. Applications to earthquakes, consumer expenditure, and Tokyo stock price index data are also discussed. The results are based on Yao (1995, 1996a).

We consider the second-order BCT polynomial regression model as discussed in Chapter 10,

$$Y_i^{[\lambda]} = Z_i = 2.1 + 0.81 X_i + 0.64 X_i^2 + \varepsilon_i, \qquad (11.1)$$

where $\varepsilon_i's$ are random disturbance term and obtained from $i.i.d. N(0, \sigma_0^2)$. The sample size is set to be $N = 100$. For $i = 1, 2, \cdots, N$, the independent variable is chosen as $x_i = i/40$.

The Monte Carlo simulation results capture the basic characteristics of the three identification methods quite well. The properties of the AIC and the GIC are very similar in identification performance. This result further confirms the results obtained by the information criterion method in the levels of the variance of the disturbance term $\sigma_0^2 = 0.5$ (in Chapter 10, we discussed the case of $\sigma_0^2 = 1$). The nested χ^2 test, when used for the point estimation, has the ability to control the probability of the identified orders those exceeding the true order. It is, all in

Chapter 11. Information Criteria and the Nested χ^2 Test

all, a method suited to determine the lower limit of a confidence set of the model order and any test-oriented order determination would not pertain to determining the upper limit. The reason for this is that, for a set of nested hypotheses, it is more logical to test a simpler hypothesis against a more complex one.

For all the three methods, the variation of the disturbance variance does not have a significant effect on the distribution of the estimated orders exceeding the true order. The nested χ^2 test tends to underestimate the order with comparably larger probability when the disturbance variance is large compared with the magnitude of variation of the regressor part. On the other hand, the AIC (and the GIC) generally tends to overestimate the order. In view of these results, we proposed a mixed statistic for the identification of the BCT model, which, as expected, successfully combined the good properties of the AIC and the nested χ^2 test.

The numerical calculations for the nested χ^2 test were performed by the Fortran program NEST94 written by the author [see Yao (1996a)].

11.1 Comparison of the Three Methods

We first conducted a Monte Carlo investigation of the BCT polynomial regression model in order to show some of the properties of the GIC and the AIC. The identified models here are the second-order BCT model (11.1) and a third-order BCT polynomial regression model (10.3), in which ε is $i.i.d. N(0, \sigma_0^2)$.

The 'true' BCT parameter λ_0 is chosen to be $0.0, 0.1, 0.2$, respectively. Because the properties indicated by the experiment on the BCT model (11.1) and on the BCT model (10.3) are very similar, we only give the simulation results based on the BCT model (11.1) for $\lambda_0 = 0.1, 0.5$.

Let us consider the following kth ($k = 1, 2, 3, 4, 5$) order BCT polynomial regression model:

$$y_i^{[\lambda]} = \beta_0 + \beta_1 x_i + \cdots + \beta_i^k \quad i = 1, 2, \cdots, 100. \tag{11.2}$$

We will identify the best fitted BCT polynomial regression model by the GIC and the AIC as well as the nested χ^2 test, i.e., for the given generated data set

11.1. Comparison of the Three Methods

$\{y_i, x_i\}_{i=1}^{100}$, we need to determine a pair of parameter $(\hat{\lambda}_g, \hat{k}_g)$ which determined by the GIC, or $(\hat{\lambda}_a, \hat{k}_a)$ which determined by the AIC, or $(\hat{\lambda}_n, \hat{k}_n)$ which is determined by the nested χ^2 test method, respectively.

For each model, we first conducted 2,000 runs of the Monte Carlo experiment for the GIC and the AIC methods, respectively. The same simulation was also conducted by the nested χ^2 method with the significance level $\alpha_0 = 0.1$. The simulation results are formulated in Table 11.1 for the two information criterion methods and the nested χ^2 method. The numbers in Table 11.1 show the distribution of the estimated frequencies for the BCT parameter and for the selected order k of the polynomial regression model in 2,000 replication Monte Carlo experiments. The 'mean $\hat{\lambda}$' here is the weighted mean of $\{\hat{\lambda}_j\}_{j=1}^{n_1}$ defined by (10.8) ($n_1 = 9$ in this experiment).

From the two upper parts of Table 11.1, we can see that both of the two information criterion methods, the GIC and the AIC, have reasonable identification power. They both select the order of the BCT polynomial regression model effectively. This conclusion also applies to the estimated parameters, for both of the estimators are very near the true values, and the weights that determine the estimator of the BCT parameter λ have almost the same distribution. This result is coincident with the results shown in the preceding chapter.

The simulation results are also plotted into three-dimensional graphs. Plot N1 in Figure 11.1 shows the distribution of the estimated frequencies in the 2,000-times replicated simulation experiment by the nested χ^2 method. Plot A1 shows the distribution of the estimated frequencies in the 2,000-times replicated simulation experiment by the AIC method. Plots N2 and A2 also shows the same simulation results as those expressed by Plots N1 and A1 respectively, but from a different angle of the three-dimensional graphs. These figures demonstrate that, compared to the nested χ^2 test, the AIC is very likely to overestimate the order of the BCT model. On the contrary, the nested χ^2 test is likely underestimate the order of the BCT model. Furthermore, the power of true-order identification of the nested χ^2 test is higher than that of the AIC. This conclusion can be seen by the fact that the peak at the true model determined by the nested χ^2 test is higher than that determined by the AIC.

Chapter 11. Information Criteria and the Nested χ^2 Test

Table 11.1 Simulaton for Polynomial Regression Model for 2,000-Times Iterated Monte Carlo Experiment

λ	$k=1$	$k=2$	$k=3$	$k=4$	$k=5$	Tatol
		GIC	Method			
-0.20	2	0	1	0	1	4
-0.15	4	10	5	1	4	24
-0.10	19	107	28	10	16	180
-0.05	4	315	53	31	45	448
$\lambda_0 = 0.1$	0	464	82	64	80	690
0.05	0	320	59	42	56	477
0.10	0	92	19	21	16	148
0.15	0	13	5	4	4	26
0.20	0	0	3	0	0	3
$N(k)$	29	1321	255	173	222	2000
Mean λ	-0.0069	0.0994	0.0992	0.1121	0.1016	0.0992
		AIC	Method			
-0.20	5	0	1	0	1	7
-0.15	7	9	2	1	2	21
-0.10	11	113	30	9	9	172
-0.05	1	345	56	27	24	453
$\lambda_0 = 0.1$	0	498	82	60	28	668
0.05	0	364	59	42	24	489
0.10	0	109	24	17	11	161
0.15	0	15	5	4	2	26
0.20	0	0	3	0	0	3
$N(k)$	24	1453	262	160	101	2000
Mean λ	-0.0333	0.101	0.1015	0.1125	0.1	0.1003
		Nested χ^2	Method			
-0.20	10	0	0	0	0	10
-0.15	41	8	2	1	1	53
-0.10	62	97	10	1	6	176
-0.05	24	360	23	10	12	429
$\lambda_0 = 0.1$	1	593	32	32	14	672
0.05	1	433	31	13	8	486
0.10	0	132	8	4	5	149
0.15	0	17	2	3	1	23
0.20	0	0	2	0	0	2
$N(k)$	139	1640	110	64	47	2000
Mean λ	-0.0115	0.1052	0.1055	0.1117	0.0936	0.0970

This is the simulation results of model (11.1) with $\sigma_0^2 = 0.5$.

11.1. Comparison of the Three Methods

Figure 11.1 Distribution of the Estimated Frequencies in the 2,000-Times Replicated Simulation Experiment

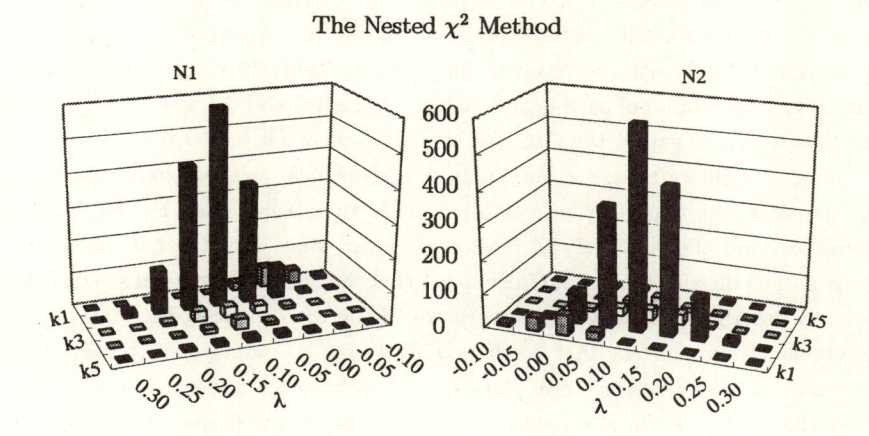

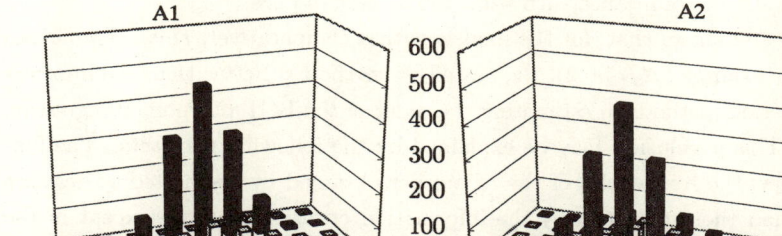

The Nested χ^2 Method

The AIC Method

1. The true model is model (10.1) with $\lambda_0 = 0.1, \sigma_0^2 = 0.5$.
2. The significance level for the nested χ^2 test is $\alpha_0 = 0.1$.

Chapter 11. Information Criteria and the Nested χ^2 Test

11.2 The Nested χ^2 Test and the Mixed Estimate

For further investigation of the nested χ^2 test, we conduct 2,000 times replicated simulation experiments to the cases of the disturbance variance $\hat{\sigma}^2 = 0.1, 1.0$, the BCT parameter $\lambda_0 = 0.0, 0.1, 0.2$, and the given significance level $\alpha_0 = 0.05$, $0.10, 0.15, 0.20, 0.25, 0.30$, respectively. As the results are very near for different λ, so that we only list the result of $\lambda_0 = 0.1$ at Table 11.2. The part A and part B are the results of setting the variance to be 1.0 and 0.1 respectively. The simulation results get by the GIC and the AIC are also listed there.

Table 11.2 shows that, for both part A and part B, as the significance level α_0 increases, the frequency of a selected order that is less than the true order decreases, and the frequency of a selected order great than the true order increases. The distribution of the frequencies that are less than or equal to the true order is greatly dependent on the variance of the disturbance term. This may be explained by the fact that as the variance of the random disturbance term decreases, the second-order term plays a much more important rule in the model. From this table, we can also see that the percentage of the frequencies exceeding the true order increases as the significance level increases. The value of the d_{α_0} is very close to the percentage of the significance level α_0, namely $100\alpha_0$. This result is just in accordance with what the p-value implies.

Table 11.2 shows that, for the models with a comparatively small significance level (for example, $\alpha_0 \leq 0.2$), the nested χ^2 method is better than the information criterion methods in estimating the order of the BCT polynomial regression model. This conclusion may be explained by the following two facts. The first one is that the frequencies of the true order obtained by the nested χ^2 test are larger than those obtained by the information criterion method (except in the case of $\hat{\sigma}_0^2 = 1$, $\alpha_0 = 0.05$). The other fact is listed in the last column of Table 11.2. We can see that the distribution is not heavily dependent on the variations of the variance, and this distribution shows the probability of mistakenly choosing a model order that is greater than the true order. Evidently, the probability determined by the information criterion method is bigger than that determined by the nested χ^2 method.

11.2. The Nested χ^2 Test and the Mixed Estimate

Table 11.2 Selection of Polynomial Regression Model in the 2,000-Times Iterated Monte Carlo Experiment

	\multicolumn{5}{c}{Order}		$d_{\alpha_0}\%$
	$k=1$	$k=2$	$k=3$	$k=4$	$k=5$	Tatol	$k>k_0$
Nested			Part A	$\sigma_0^2=1$			
$\alpha_0=0.05$	630	1276	47	35	12	2000	4.65
$\alpha_0=0.10$	416	1366	112	62	44	2000	10.90
$\alpha_0=0.15$	323	1359	159	88	71	2000	15.90
$\alpha_0=0.20$	254	1320	190	127	109	2000	21.30
$\alpha_0=0.25$	200	1257	223	160	160	2000	27.20
$\alpha_0=0.30$	162	1196	255	171	216	2000	32.10
GIC	167	1206	252	165	210	2000	31.35
AIC	176	1314	249	161	100	2000	25.50
Nested			Part B	$\sigma_0^2=0.1$			
$\alpha_0=0.05$	4	1889	59	34	14	2000	5.35
$\alpha_0=0.10$	0	1781	103	72	44	2000	11.00
$\alpha_0=0.15$	0	1658	160	101	81	2000	17.10
$\alpha_0=0.20$	0	1546	200	130	124	2000	22.70
$\alpha_0=0.25$	0	1432	232	164	172	2000	28.40
$\alpha_0=0.30$	0	1329	261	191	219	2000	33.55
GIC	0	1344	258	183	215	2000	32.80
AIC	0	1461	257	167	115	2000	26.95

The true model is (11.1), $k_0=2, \lambda_0=0.1$

In view of Table 11.2, for the models with comparatively small disturbance variance, we can see that the nested χ^2 test is much better than the information criteria in estimating the order of the BCT polynomial regression model.

We find that, for many practical problems, when the significance level is not to be considered, the AIC method may be more practical than the nested χ^2 method. Furthermore, differently from information criterion method, the nested χ^2 method may be more attractive due to its ability to control the significant level in the model identification procedure. The simulation model of (11.1) by a 2,000-times repetitive Monte Carlo experiment correspond to $\hat{\sigma}_0^2=0.1$, $\lambda_0=0.1$, $\alpha_0=0.1$ is

Chapter 11. Information Criteria and the Nested χ^2 Test

given by
$$Y^{[0.0996]} = 2.1142 + 0.7749X + 0.6735X^2. \tag{11.3}$$

To compare the properties of order estimation by the AIC and the nested χ^2 test, the simulation result for $\sigma_0^2 = 1$ is listed in Table 11.3. From Table 11.3 we can see that for comparably smaller significance level α (say, less than 0.2), the probability of $[\hat{k}_{n,\alpha} \leq \hat{k}_a]$ will be 1, where $\hat{k}_a$ is the order determined by the AIC and $\hat{k}_{n,\alpha}$ is the order determined by the nested χ^2 method under the significance level λ. These characteristics of the two methods suggest the use of the interval $[\hat{k}_{n,\alpha}, \hat{k}_a]$ for a (very rough) $(1 - \alpha)$ confidence level set of the model order since the interval makes sense for small α. In practice, only the comparatively small significance level α is interesting. In view of Shibata's (1976) asymptotic distribution of $\hat{k}_a$, at least for large sample problems, our conclusion is correct.

The experiments are also conducted for different σ_0^2 and for different orders of the polynomial regression model, all of the results support the above conclusion.

Mixed estimate: As for the point estimation of the order of the BCT regression model, we might be able to improve the power of the AIC and the nested χ^2 test by the following mixed estimate. Set the mixed estimator by

$$k_m = \begin{cases} \hat{k}_{n,\alpha} + [\mu(\hat{k}_a - \hat{k}_{n,\alpha})] & \hat{k}_a \geq \hat{k}_{n,\alpha} \\ \hat{k}_a & \hat{k}_a < \hat{k}_{n,\alpha} \end{cases} \tag{11.4}$$

where $[f]$ implies the largest integer not exceeding f, and $0 \leq \mu < 1$. That is to say, as long as $\hat{k}_a < \hat{k}_{n,\alpha}$, the estimate is equal to $\hat{k}_a$, but if $\hat{k}_a > \hat{k}_{n,\alpha}$, put the nested estimate towards to the AIC estimate. For different μ, we conducted a 5,000-times Monte Carlo experiment based on the BCT model (11.1) for the case of $\lambda_0 = 0.1$ and $\alpha_0 = 0.1$ (see Table 11.4). For example, for the case of $\mu_0 = 0.5$, the frequencies of the estimated order determined by the mixed estimate truly combine the good properties of the AIC and the nested χ^2 method. The statistical properties of the mixed estimate will be studied in details in the future..

Table 11.3 Distribution of the Frequencies in
the 2,000-Times Iterated Monte Carlo Experiment

α_0	$k=1$	$k=2$	$k=3$	$k=4$	$k=5$	Tatol	%
			$\hat{k}_{n,\alpha} < \hat{k}_a$				
0.05	–	536	151	90	16	793	39.65
0.10	–	344	111	51	6	512	25.60
0.15	–	236	75	24	3	338	16.90
0.20	–	122	34	0	0	156	7.80
0.25	–	43	1		0	44	2.20
0.30	–	0	0	0	0	0	0
			$\hat{k}_{n,\alpha} = \hat{k}_a$				
0.05	176	960	31	28	12	1207	60.35
0.10	176	1119	90	59	44	1488	74.40
0.15	176	1193	134	88	71	1662	83.10
0.20	175	1245	188	127	100	1835	91.75
0.25	169	1243	223	142	100	1877	93.85
0.30	162	1195	218	128	100	1803	90.15
			$\hat{k}_{n,\alpha} > \hat{k}_a$				
0.05	0	0	0	0	–	0	0
0.10	0	0	0	0	–	0	0
0.15	0	0	0	0	–	0	0
0.20	8	0	0	1	–	9	0.45
0.25	23	23	28	5	–	79	3.95
0.30	78	53	60	6	–	197	9.85

The true model is (11.1) with $\lambda_0 = 0.1, \sigma_0^2 = 1, k_0 = 2$.

11.3 Empirical Examples

In this section, we will deal with some practical problems in the application of the information criterion methods and the nested χ^2 method. We will identify the BCT regression model by the three methods and observe some of their characteristics. For the details of the following examples, see Yao (1992, 1994, 1995).

Chapter 11. Information Criteria and the Nested χ^2 Test

Table 11.4 Distribution of the Orders in the 5,000-Times Replacated Monte Carlo Experiment

	$k=1$	$k=2$	$k=3$	$k=4$	$k=5$	$k<k_0$	$k\geq k_0$
Nested	1063	3406	273	143	115	21.26	10.62
$\mu_0 = 0.3$	1048	3421	273	143	115	20.96	10.62
$\mu_0 = 0.4$	1013	3372	357	143	115	20.26	12.30
$\mu_0 = 0.5$	946	3257	519	163	115	18.92	15.94
$\mu_0 = 0.6$	946	3257	519	163	115	18.92	15.94
$\mu_0 = 0.7$	946	3222	470	247	115	18.92	16.64
$\mu_0 = 0.8$	946	3222	455	262	115	18.92	16.64
AIC	423	3361	615	355	246	8.46	24.32

The true model is (11.1) with $\lambda_0 = 0.1, \sigma_0^2 = 1, \alpha_0 = 0.1$

Example 11.1. Table 11.5 shows 31 pairs of a number (y_i) of earthquakes with intensity (x_i) over 5 magnitude (5M) in the region of north latitude $25° \sim 48°N$ and east longitude $125° \sim 150°E$ during the period 1961-1985 in Japan [see *National Astronomical Observatory, Chronological Scientific Tables (1990)*]. We will consider the kth order BCT polynomial regression model, say model

$$Y^{[\lambda]} = \beta_0 + \beta_1 X + \beta_2 X^2 + \cdots + \beta_k X^k + \varepsilon, \quad (11.5)$$

where the BCT is defined by (8.1) and $y_t^{[\lambda]} = (y_t/100)^{[\lambda]}/\dot{Y}^{(\lambda-1)}$, $\dot{Y}$ is the geometric mean of $\{y_t/100)^{[\lambda]}\}_{t=1}^{31}$. We intend to determine the BCT parameter $\hat{\lambda}$ and the order $\hat{p}$ that makes the model best fit the data. The estimated values of the AIC for three different BCT polynomial models are plotted in Figure 11.2, and part of the data are also listed in Table 11.6.

In view of the AIC method, the distribution of estimated AIC shows that the minimum AIC is reached at $\hat{\lambda}_{a,2} = 0.3$ and minAIC(2,0.3)= -188.31. The identified model is

$$Y^{[0.3]} = 9.638 - 2.581X + 0.159X^2. \quad (11.6)$$

11.3. Empirical Examples

Then for $p = 1, 2, \cdots, k$, where k is the upper limit of the order, we consider the family of p-th order polynomial regression model (11.5). We will identify the BCT parameter λ and the order p of the polynomial regression model simultaneously by the nested χ^2 test. For $k = 3$, the p-values are $p_1 = 0.000005$ and $p_2 = 0.235$, respectively. The notable jump of the p-value in the second-order model shows that the nested χ^2 test does not support using the first-order BCT model in this example.

1. If we use the significance level of $\alpha_0 = 0.1$, we know that the p-value exceeds α_0 at the second-order model for the first time. According to the rule discussed in Section 9.2, the estimators of the BCT parameter and the order of the polynomial regression model are simultaneously determined as: $\hat{\lambda}_{n,\hat{p}} = 0.3$ and $\hat{p} = 2$. The identified BCT model is the same as that in (11.6), which is obtained by the AIC method.

2. If we use the significance level of $\alpha_0 = 0.25$, we see that the p-value is less than α_0 for the first- or the second-order model, so that the corresponding best BCT polynomial regression model is:

$$Y^{[0.4]} = 21.649 - 7.786X + 0.903X^2 - 0.035X^3. \tag{11.7}$$

Table 11.5 The Earthquake Observation

No.	X	Y	No.	X	Y	No.	X	Y
1	5.0	457	11	6.0	64	21	7.0	12
2	5.1	405	12	6.1	52	22	7.1	9
3	5.2	333	13	6.2	44	23	7.2	5
4	5.3	273	14	6.3	31	24	7.3	2
5	5.4	215	15	6.4	24	25	7.4	2
6	5.5	202	16	6.5	17	26	7.5	3
7	5.6	125	17	6.6	22	27	7.6	3
8	5.7	151	18	6.7	18	28	7.7	3
9	5.8	110	19	6.8	10	29	7.8	2
10	5.9	82	20	6.9	10	30	7.9	2
						31	8.0	1

X: the intensity of earthquke (Magnitude)
Y: the observated frequency of earthquke

Chapter 11. Information Criteria and the Nested χ^2 Test

Table 11.6 The Estimated AIC for the Earthquke Data

λ	Order 1	Order 2	Order 3
-0.6	-70.4863	-95.9995	-94.9191
-0.5	-85.7856	-110.0597	-108.3348
-0.4	-101.8364	-123.3480	-121.3509
-0.3	-119.0726	-135.7590	-133.9400
-0.2	-137.8092	-147.2543	-146.0168
-0.1	-156.8887	-157.8952	-157.3916
0.0	<u>-168.7098</u>	-167.7009	-167.6288
0.1	-162.7001	-177.0062	-176.4719
0.2	-144.4881	-184.7229	-183.0236
0.3	-124.9380	<u>-188.3066</u>	-186.8468
0.4	-106.8166	-183.4150	<u>-187.7154</u>
0.5	-90.0919	-169.0726	-185.6484
0.6	-74.3366	-149.4829	-180.6484

Figure 11.2. The Plot of the Estimated AIC for the Earthquake Data

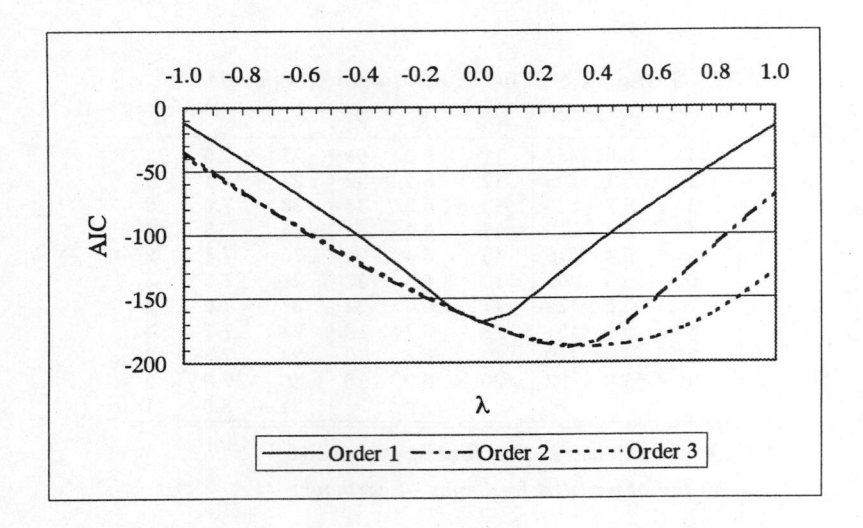

11.3. Empirical Examples

Example 11.2. Table 11.7 lists the consumer expenditure data of China for a period of 37 years. The inflation effects are not considered here. In other words, the data listed in Table 11.7 are based on nominal values. The unit is one hundred million Chinese Yuan. We first consider the following fixed order AR(1) BCT model:

$$C_t^{[\lambda]} = \beta_0 + \beta_1 C_{t-1}^{[\lambda]} + \varepsilon, \tag{11.8}$$

where the BCT is defined by (8.1) and $C_t^{[\lambda]} = (C_t/100)^{[\lambda]}/\dot{C}^{(\lambda-1)}, t = 1, 2, \cdots, 38$, and $\dot{C}$ is the geometric mean of $\{(C_t/100)^{[\lambda]}\}_{i=1}^{38}$. The identification is conducted by the GIC method and the MLE method. The estimated values of the GIC and the maximum log-likelihood (MLL) are listed in Table 11.8. We see that the minimum GIC is reached at $\hat{\lambda}_g = -0.04$, and the identified model by the GIC is

$$C_t^{[-0.04]} = 0.099 + 1.041 C_{t-1}^{[-0.04]}. \tag{11.9}$$

The identified model by the MLE method is

$$C_t^{[-0.08]} = 0.101 + 1.036 C_{t-1}^{[-0.08]}. \tag{11.10}$$

In view of the general least squares regression method, we can get the estimated natural logarithm transformation model

$$\log C_t = 0.097 + 1.045 \log C_{t-1}. \tag{11.11}$$

In view of the identified models (11.9) and (11.10), we see that the performance of the GIC and the ML is almost the same. Both of the identified models are very near to the natural logarithm model that we are usually used.

Now we consider the following BCT autoregressive model by the AIC and the nested χ^2 test:

$$C_t^{[\lambda]} = \beta_0 + \Sigma_{i=1}^{3} \beta_i C_{t-i}^{[\lambda]} + \varepsilon. \tag{11.12}$$

We see the minimum AIC is attained at the third-order model with $\hat{\lambda} = -0.35$, the identified model by the AIC is

$$C_t^{[-0.35]} = -0.051 - 0.046 C_{t-1}^{[-0.35]} - 0.084 C_{t-2}^{[-0.35]} + 1.144 C_{t-3}^{[-0.35]}. \tag{11.13}$$

By use of the nested χ^2 test, we can see that $p_{1,-0.1} = 0.00014$, and $p_{2,-0.3} = 0.294$. So that at the significance level $\alpha_0 = 0.1$, the identified model is the second-order

Chapter 11. Information Criteria and the Nested χ^2 Test

BCT model with $\hat{\lambda} = -0.3$, which is given by

$$C_t^{[-0.3]} = -0.406 - 0.037 C_{t-1}^{[-0.35]} + 1.060 C_{t-2}^{[-0.35]}. \quad (11.14)$$

Table 11.7 Consumer Expenditure of China

Year	c	Year	c	Year	c	Year	c
1951		1961	818	1971	1324	1981	2799
1952	477	1962	849	1972	1404	1982	3054
1953	559	1963	864	1973	1511	1983	3358
1954	570	1964	921	1974	1550	1984	3905
1955	622	1965	982	1975	1621	1985	4879
1956	671	1966	1065	1976	1676	1986	5552
1957	702	1967	1124	1977	1741	1987	6386
1958	738	1968	1111	1978	1888	1988	8038
1959	716	1969	1180	1979	2195	1989	8903
1960	763	1970	1258	1980	2531	1990	

Source: Statistical Yearbook of China, 1990 (in Chinese).

Table 11.8 The Estimated GIC and MLL for Consumer Expenditure of China

λ	GIC	MLL	Trace	Var
-0.10	-189.2573	98.8658	4.2371	0.1767
-0.09	189.3298	98.8764	4.2115	0.1766
-0.08	-189.3888	98.8820	7.1876	0.1766
-0.07	-189.4331	98.8818	4.1652	0.1766
-0.06	-189.4636	98.8766	4.1448	0.1766
-0.05	-189.4780	98.8646	4.1256	0.1767
-0.04	-189.4796	98.8486	4.1088	0.1769
-0.03	-189.4654	98.8263	4.0936	0.1771
-0.02	-189.4379	98.7996	4.0807	0.1774
-0.01	-189.3935	98.7660	4.0693	0.1777
0.00	-189.3342	98.7270	4.0599	0.1781

11.3. Empirical Examples

Example 11.3. In this example we give a further investigation of the Tokyo stock price index which has been discussed in Example 10.2. We use the original data which was listed in Table 10.4. We consider the following BCT regression model

$$P_t^{[\lambda]} = \beta_0 + \Sigma_{i=1}^k \beta_i P_{t-i}^{[\lambda]} + \varepsilon \tag{11.15}$$

with the transformation $P_t^{[\lambda]} = (P_t/100)^{[\lambda]}/\dot{P}^{(\lambda-1)}$, $t = 1, 2, \cdots, 120$, where $\dot{P}$ is the geometric mean of $\{P_t/100)^{[\lambda]}\}_{t=1}^{120}$.

We conduct a model identification by the AIC and the nested χ^2 method. By the calculation result we can see the minimum AIC is attained at $\hat{k} = 2$ and $\hat{\lambda} = -0.5$. The estimated AIC for λ ($\lambda = -1.0, -0.9, \cdots, 0.0$) are listed in Table 11.9. The distribution of the estimated AIC for λ ($\lambda = -1.0, -0.9, \cdots, 0.0$) are plotted on Figure 11.3. The identified BCT model by the AIC is

$$P_t^{[-0.5]} = 0.579 - 0.374 C_{t-1}^{[-0.5]} + 1.363 C_{t-2}^{[-0.5]}. \tag{11.16}$$

For fixed $k = 5$, denoting the $p_{\hat{k},\hat{\lambda}}$ the p-value at the estimated order $\hat{k}$ and the estimated BCT parameter $\hat{\lambda}$, the estimated p-values are: $p_{1,-0.5} = 0.00004, p_{2,-0.5} = 0.1188, p_{3,-0.5} = 0.1520, p_{4,-0.5} = 0.2741$. If we give the significance level $\alpha_0 = 0.1$, then by the nested χ^2 test, we should choose the BCT model with $\hat{k} = 2$ and $\hat{\lambda} = -0.5$. The identified model is just the same as that obtained by the AIC, (11.6). If we set the given critical value $\alpha_0 = 0.15$, then $p_{2,-0.5} = 0.1188$ and $p_{3,-0.5} = 0.1520$ suggest selecting the BCT model with $\hat{k} = 3$ and $\hat{\lambda} = -0.5$. Now, the identified model becomes a AR(3) BCT model given by

$$P_t^{[-0.5]} = 0.587 - 0.147 C_{t-1}^{[-0.5]} - 0.577 C_{t-2}^{[-0.5]} + 1.421 C_{t-3}^{[-0.5]}. \tag{11.17}$$

Chapter 11. Information Criteria and the Nested χ^2 Test

Table 11.9 The Estimated AIC for the Tokyo Stock Price Index

λ	Order 1	Order 2	Order 3
-1.0	-164.6497	-171.7262	-168.6327
-0.9	-170.1823	-178.8312	-175.3873
-0.8	-175.3469	-184.5998	-180.8293
-0.7	-179.0621	-188.9473	-184.8982
-0.6	-181.2770	-191.8116	-187.5497
-0.5	<u>-181.9717</u>	<u>-193.1708</u>	<u>-188.7208</u>
-0.4	-181.1663	-193.0017	-188.4329
-0.3	-178.8888	-191.3267	-186.6916
-0.2	-175.2080	-188.2085	-183.5474
-0.1	-170.2188	-183.7264	-179.1083
0.0	-164.0180	-177.9639	-173.4297

Figure 11.3 The Plot of the Estimated AIC for Tokyo Stock Price Index

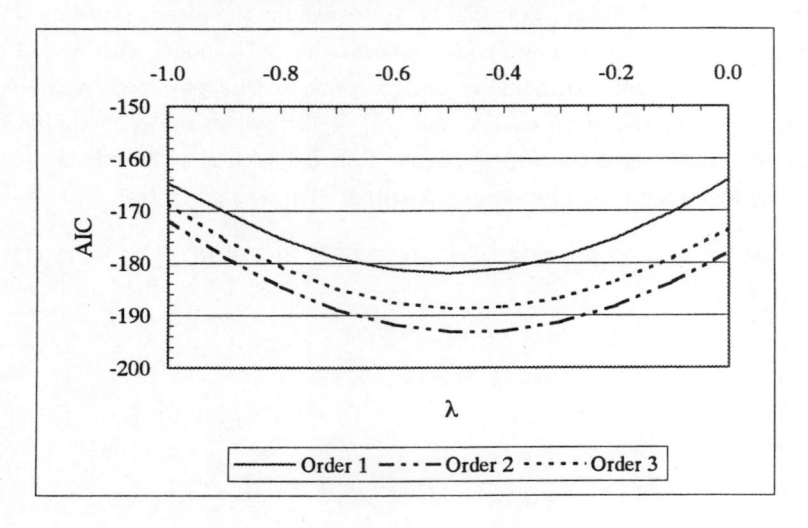

Chapter 12

Nonlinear Model Simulation

In the former chapters, we discussed the properties of the GIC and the AIC as well as the nested χ^2 test in identifying the BCT regression model. At this point, discussions on the BCT model identification are very limited. The Monte Carlo simulations are conducted on the sole basis of the polynomial BCT regression models. The main problem is that of fitting the observation data by the BCT polynomial regression model, where the data-generating process (DGP) belongs to the same family of the fitting model. In the econometric or statistical analysis of economics or business, as the dynamic economic system becomes more complex, we often meet some macroeconomic data that do not satisfy the linear regression model.

Even though the BCT method has proved very useful in the investigation of non-linear processes, it is still critical to know the performance of our approach when applied to the investigation of complex economic phenomena. This chapter presents some simulation results obtained when applying the information criteria and the nested χ^2 test to the BCT model identification. We will investigate the performance of fitting a data set where the DGP does not belong to the same family of the fitting model. We will mainly discuss the performance of fitting the data set generated from an exponential regression model and a logistic regression model by the k-th order BCT polynomial regression model. The results are mainly based on Yao (1996c, 1998).

Chapter 12. Nonlinear Model Simulation

12.1 The Information Criteria for Model Choice

This section is concerned with the properties of fitting the k-th order BCT polynomial regression model in view of the information criteria to data whose DGP does not belong to the family of the BCT polynomial regression model. The investigation is based on a 5,000-times iterated Monte Carlo experiment for three models with three levels of disturbance term variance per model. The Monte Carlo experiment shows that there is no significant difference between the GIC and the AIC. One characteristic is observed when fitting a BCT polynomial regression model to simulate the logistic regression model: the variance of the estimated order relies on the variance of the true logistic regression model.

12.1.1 Models and Simulations

Three regression models are considered in this section. Except a second order polynomial regression model, the other two models are an exponential regression model and a logistic regression model. These models will be used in the Monte Carlo experiment.

We consider the following three models:

$$\text{ModelA}: \quad y = 5 + 0.8x + 0.64x^2 + \varepsilon, \tag{12.1}$$

$$\text{ModelB}: \quad y = 5 + 2^x + \varepsilon, \tag{12.2}$$

$$\text{ModelC}: \quad y = 5 + \frac{1}{1+\exp(-x)} + \varepsilon, \tag{12.3}$$

where ε is random disturbance term generated by $i.i.d.N(0,\sigma^2)$. Here the Model B is an exponential regression model, and Model C is a logistic regression model. It is clearly that Model B and Model C do not belong to the family of the BCT polynomial regression model. We fit the k-th order BCT polynomial regression model

$$Y^{[\lambda]} = \beta_0 + \beta_1 X^1 + \beta_1 X^2 + \cdots + \beta_p X^p + \varepsilon, \tag{12.4}$$

to data generated by the above three models, where λ is the BCT parameter. For the k-th order BCT polynomial regression model and for a set of n generated observations $\{y_i, x_i\}_{i=1}^n$, the AIC and the GIC are respectively given by

$$\text{AIC}(Y,X|\lambda) = \mathcal{C} + \mathcal{C}_2 + 2(p+2), \tag{12.5}$$

12.1. The Information Criteria for Model Choice

$$\text{GIC}(Y, X|\lambda) = \mathcal{C} + \mathcal{C}_2 + 2tr(p, \lambda). \tag{12.6}$$

Where

$$\mathcal{C} = n(1 + \log 2\pi), \quad \mathcal{C}_2 = n\log \hat{\sigma}^2(Y, X|\lambda) - 2(\lambda - 1)\sum_{t=1}^{n} \log y_t.$$

The $tr(p, \lambda)$ can be calculated by the same way as (9.10) if only we set $X_0 = (1, 1, \cdots, 1)^*$ be a n elements column vector and rewrite the index i to be the i-th component.

We conducted the Monte Carlo experiment for the simulation of model (12.1), model (12.2), and model (12.3). The numerical calculation was performed by the Fortran programs presented by Yao (1992, 1996a).

To evaluate the performances of the GIC and the AIC by the Monte Carlo experiment, a random data set was required. Therefor, we first constructed the random data set $\{\varepsilon_{it}\}_{t=1}^{T}$, the values of ε_{it} ($i = 1, 2, 3$) are random numbers and obtained from $N(0, \sigma_0^2)$. The independent variables are defined as $x_t = t/40$, $t = 1, 2, \cdots, T$. For a given data set $\{x_t\}_{t=1}^{T}$, based on the following three models

$$y_{1t} = 5 + 0.8x_t + 0.64x^2 + \varepsilon_{1t}, \tag{12.7}$$

$$y_{2t} = 5 + 2^{x_t} + \varepsilon_{2t}, \tag{12.8}$$

$$y_{3t} = 5 + \frac{1}{1 + \exp(-x_t)} + \varepsilon_{3t}, \tag{12.9}$$

we have constructed experiment data set $\{y_{it}, x_t\}_{t=1}^{T}$, $i = 1, 2, 3$.

The simulation experiment attempted to identify the order of the BCT polynomial regression model and the BCT parameter by a large number of replications. All Monte Carlo experiments were conducted for the three models with the same sample size, $T = 100$. We fitted the BCT polynomial regression model (12.4) to the data generated by the above Model (12.7), Model (12.8), and Model (12.9), respectively. The largest order of the BCT polynomial regression model used in the simulation was chosen to be 7. Then, for all the estimated orders, those that were no less than 7 were put to be 7. The Monte Carlo experiments were performed for all three models with 5,000 replications. For both the GIC and the AIC, the experiments were performed for the three levels of the disturbance term variance, $\sigma_0^2 = 0.5, 1.0, 1.5$.

Chapter 12. Nonlinear Model Simulation

For each created sample set and an initial given BCT parameter λ_0, we need to calculate $\text{GIC}(k,\lambda), k = 1,2,\cdots,7$, $\lambda_j = \lambda_0 + [(n_\lambda + 1)/2 - j]\Delta\lambda$ for $j = 1,2,\cdots,n_\lambda$, where n_λ is a given odd number and $\Delta\lambda$ is a given real value (in this experiment we choose $\Delta\lambda = 0.25$). According to the minimum principle of the information criteria, we can simultaneously get the estimators of k and λ. The estimator $(\hat{k}, \hat{\lambda})$ specifies the optimal BCT regression model.

For the iterated Monte Carlo experiment, the estimated BCT parameter λ_k (for order $k = 1,2,\cdots,7$) is the weighted mean of $\{\lambda_j\}_{j=1}^{n_\lambda}$, namely,

$$\hat{\lambda}_k = \sum_{j=1}^{n_\lambda} \lambda_j \times \frac{N_k(\lambda_j)}{N_k}, \qquad (12.10)$$

where $N_k(\lambda_j)$ is the number of the estimated frequency at λ_j and order k,

$$N_k = \sum_{j=1}^{n_\lambda} N_k(\lambda_j). \qquad (12.11)$$

The estimated BCT parameter $\hat{\lambda}$ is the weighed mean of $\{\lambda_j\}_{j=1}^{n_\lambda}$, namely

$$\hat{\lambda} = \sum_{j=1}^{n_\lambda} \lambda_j \times \frac{N(\lambda_j)}{N}, \qquad (12.12)$$

where $N(\lambda_j)$ is the number of the estimated frequency at λ_j, and

$$N(\lambda_j) = \sum_{k=1}^{7} N_k(\lambda_j), \qquad j = 1,2,\cdots,n_\lambda. \qquad (12.13)$$

For intuitional appreciation of the simulation process and the estimated results, and for the sake of brevity, we only give a distribution of the estimated GIC for one experiment. Then we give the frequencies distribution of the estimated order in the 5,000-times iterated Monte Carlo experiment for model (12.8) in the case of $\sigma_0^2 = 0.5$. The results were listed respectively in Table 12.1 and Table 12.2, respectively.

Table 12.1 shows that the minimum GIC is reached at the BCT parameter $\lambda_8 (= 0.75)$ and order 6, $\min\text{GIC}(6,\lambda_8) = 53.52$. That is to say in this experiment, the BCT regression model best fitted to the data set which generated from model (12.8) is a 6-th order BCT polynomial regression model with the BCT parameter

12.1. The Information Criteria for Model Choice

$\lambda = 0.75$. This experiment gives a contribution of 1 to Table 12.2 at $(6, \lambda_8)$. As for Table 12.2, the first seven data listed at the last line are the estimated BCT parameter $\hat{\lambda}_k$ ($k = 1, 2, \cdots, 7$). The last data at the same line, 0.9794, is the estimated BCT parameter $\hat{\lambda}$ that defined by (12.12). The other simulation results are summarized and given at the following Table 12.3 and Figure 12.1 to Figure 12.7.

Table 12.3 gives the results of the estimated order when fitting the BCT regression model to simulate the models (12.7), (12.8), and (12.9). The percentage listed in the first column is the estimated result for model (12.7). The frequencies of the estimated order in the 5,000-times iterated Monte Carlo experiment by the GIC and the AIC are expressed in a percentage form. As for the GIC method,

Table 12.1 Distribution of the Estimated GIC in Fitting the BCT Polynomial Regression Model to Model (12.8)

		Order						
j	λ_j	1	2	3	4	5	6	7
1	-1.00	-32.73	-33.26	-32.07	-31.16	-32.21	-35.98	-35.85
2	-0.75	-36.56	-38.14	-36.75	-36.13	-37.21	-40.52	-40.10
3	-0.50	-39.53	-42.35	-40.75	-40.44	-41.54	-44.42	-43.72
4	-0.25	-41.59	-45.86	-44.06	-44.07	-45.20	-47.63	-46.70
5	0.00	-42.71	-48.65	-46.65	-47.00	-48.16	-50.16	-49.02
6	0.25	<u>-42.88</u>	-50.67	-48.52	-49.20	-50.41	-52.00	-50.66
7	0.50	-42.07	-51.91	-49.65	-50.68	-51.94	-53.12	-51.62
8	0.75	-40.29	<u>-52.33</u>	<u>-50.02</u>	<u>-51.42</u>	-52.73	<u>-53.52</u>	<u>-51.88</u>
9	1.00	-37.54	-51.92	-49.63	-51.41	<u>-52.79</u>	-53.20	-51.45
10	1.25	-33.84	-50.66	-48.49	-50.65	-52.10	-52.16	-50.31
11	1.50	-29.22	-48.54	-46.59	-49.15	-50.68	-50.40	-48.46
12	1.75	-23.70	-45.55	-43.93	-46.90	-48.52	-47.93	-45.92
13	2.00	-17.33	-41.70	-40.52	-43.92	-45.64	-44.75	-42.68
14	2.25	-10.16	-36.99	-36.37	-40.21	-42.03	-40.88	-38.74
15	2.50	-2.23	-31.42	-31.49	-35.78	-37.71	-36.32	-34.12
16	2.75	6.42	-25.02	-25.88	-30.64	-32.69	-31.09	-28.83
17	3.00	15.73	-17.81	-19.57	-24.80	-26.98	-25.19	-22.88

The variance of the disturbance term is: $\sigma_0^2 = 0.5$.

Chapter 12. Nonlinear Model Simulation

the data in the top three lines are the results corresponding to the different levels of the disturbance term variance, $\sigma_0^2 = 0.5, 1.0, 1.5$. This is indicated by the data listed in the first column of Table 12.3. The rest two parts are the estimated results for simulation of model (12.8) and model (12.9) respectively, by the GIC and the AIC in different levels of the disturbance term variance.

Figure 12.1 shows the distribution of the estimated BCT parameter against the estimated order for fitting the data generated from model (12.7) by the BCT polynomial regression model. The iteration number of the Monte Carlo experiment is 5,000. The three curves in plot 12.1.1 are the results by the GIC method

Table 12.2 Distribution of the Estimated Frequencies in the 5,000-Times Iterated Monte Carlo Experiment

j	λ_j	Order							Total
		1	2	3	4	5	6	7	
1	-1.00	0	0	0	0	0	0	0	0
2	-0.75	1	0	0	0	0	0	0	1
3	-0.50	2	2	0	1	0	0	0	5
4	-0.25	2	5	2	0	0	2	2	13
5	0.00	12	32	9	4	3	2	4	66
6	0.25	22	151	30	15	13	9	12	252
7	0.50	11	400	83	34	29	29	32	618
8	0.75	10	675	141	62	46	40	51	1025
9	1.00	1	761	208	102	50	52	65	1239
10	1.25	1	561	154	91	57	49	49	962
11	1.50	0	247	118	46	32	39	42	524
12	1.75	0	113	51	18	16	14	18	230
13	2.00	0	20	12	7	6	4	6	55
14	2.25	0	2	3	2	1	1	0	9
15	2.50	0	0	1	0	0	0	0	1
16	2.75	0	0	0	0	0	0	0	0
17	3.00	0	0	0	0	0	0	0	0
N_k		62	2969	812	382	253	241	281	5000
$\hat{\lambda}_k$		0.2984	0.9487	1.0520	1.0510	1.0425	1.0488	1.0302	0.9794

1. Fit BCT polynomial regression model to simulate model (12.8).
2. The variance of the disturbance term is: $\sigma_0^2 = 0.5$.

12.1. The Information Criteria for Model Choice

for three levels of the disturbance variance. The three curves in plot 12.1.2 are the result estimated by the AIC method. Plot 12.2.1 and plot 12.2.2 give the estimated BCT parameter against the estimated order for the data generated by model (12.8). Plot 12.3.1 and plot 12.3.2, on the other hand, give the estimated BCT parameter against the estimated order for model (12.9).

Table 12.3 Distribution of the Estimated Order in the 5,000-Times Iterated Monte Carlo Experiment

σ_0^2	1	2	3	Order 4	5	6	7	Total
Model A				GIC				
0.5	1.56	64.10	11.90	7.26	4.94	4.88	5.36	100
1	7.48	59.12	11.52	7.02	4.84	4.74	5.28	100
1.5	14.24	53.58	10.90	6.80	4.66	4.66	5.16	100
				AIC				
0.5	1.84	69.28	11.68	6.34	4.08	3.42	3.36	100
1	8.52	63.36	11.26	6.24	4.00	3.32	3.30	100
1.5	15.82	57.40	10.52	5.88	3.90	3.24	3.24	100
Model B				GIC				
0.5	1.24	59.38	16.24	7.64	5.06	4.82	5.62	100
1	7.26	57.06	13.92	7.14	4.68	4.68	5.26	100
1.5	14.76	51.36	12.76	6.80	4.62	4.46	5.24	100
				AIC				
0.5	1.48	64.10	16.44	6.70	4.24	3.42	3.62	100
1	8.14	60.92	13.70	6.50	4.02	3.32	3.40	100
1.5	16.56	54.94	11.92	6.22	3.98	3.16	3.22	100
Model C				GIC				
0.5	65.52	12.20	6.66	4.50	3.64	3.48	4.00	100
1	66.12	11.84	6.48	4.46	3.62	3.50	3.98	100
1.5	66.44	11.50	6.54	4.40	3.64	3.52	3.96	100
				AIC				
0.5	69.92	12.22	6.22	3.62	2.78	2.58	2.66	100
1	70.74	11.50	6.10	3.64	2.84	2.52	2.66	100
1.5	70.68	11.56	6.08	3.68	2.86	2.52	2.62	100

Chapter 12. Nonlinear Model Simulation

Figure 12.1 Distribution of the Estimated BCT Parameter in the 5,000-Times Replicated Experiment

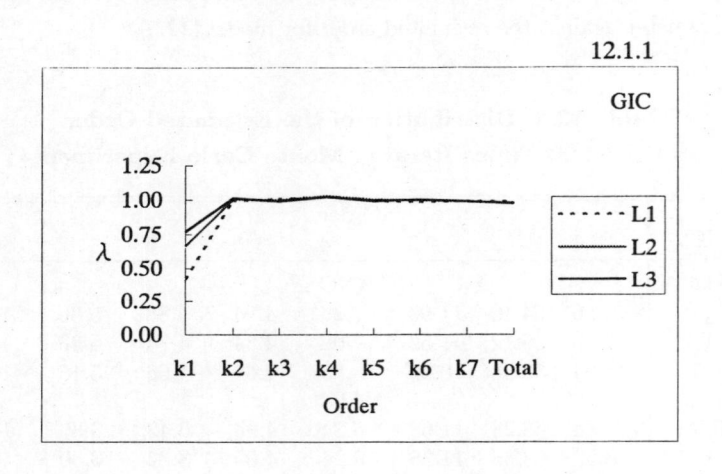

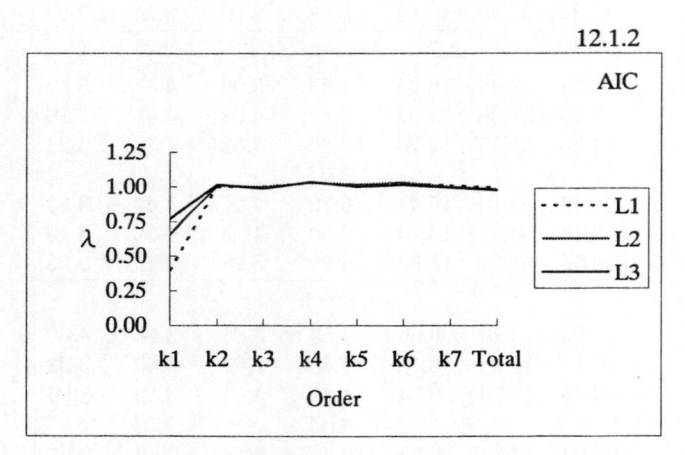

12.1.1
GIC

12.1.2
AIC

1. The true model is Model (12.7).
2. L1, L2, L3 denote the cases with different variances.

12.1. The Information Criteria for Model Choice

Figure 12.2 Distribution of the Estimated BCT Parameter in the 5,000-Times Replicated Experiment

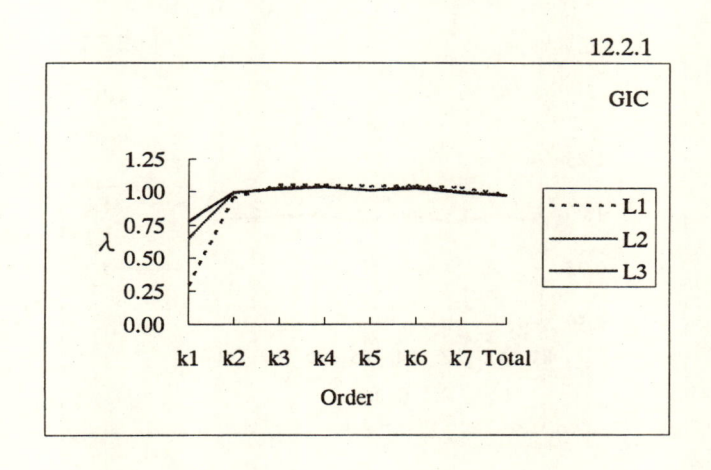

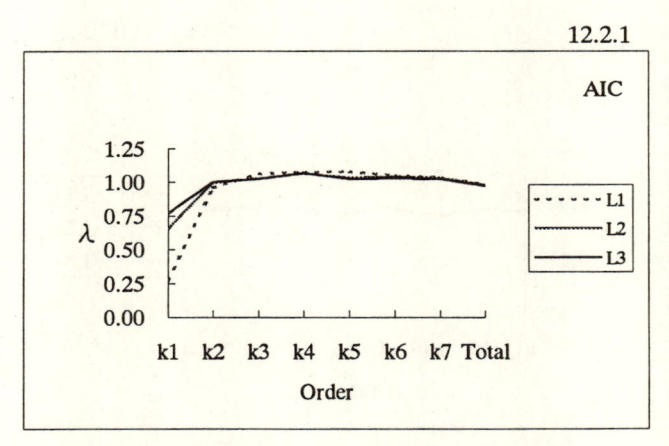

12.2.1
GIC

[Chart: λ vs Order (k1, k2, k3, k4, k5, k6, k7, Total) with curves L1 (dotted), L2, L3; y-axis 0.00 to 1.25]

12.2.1
AIC

[Chart: λ vs Order (k1, k2, k3, k4, k5, k6, k7, Total) with curves L1 (dotted), L2, L3; y-axis 0.00 to 1.25]

1. The true model is Model (12.8).
2. L1, L2, L3 denote the cases with different variances.

Chapter 12. Nonlinear Model Simulation

Figure 12.3 Distribution of the Estimated BCT Parameter in the 5,000-Times Replicated Experiment

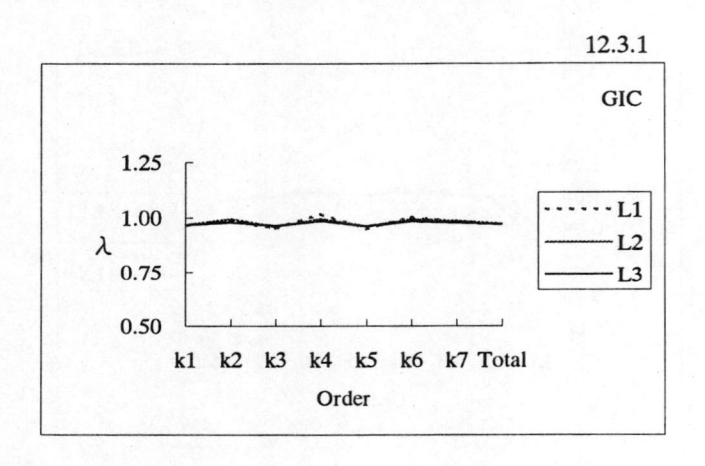

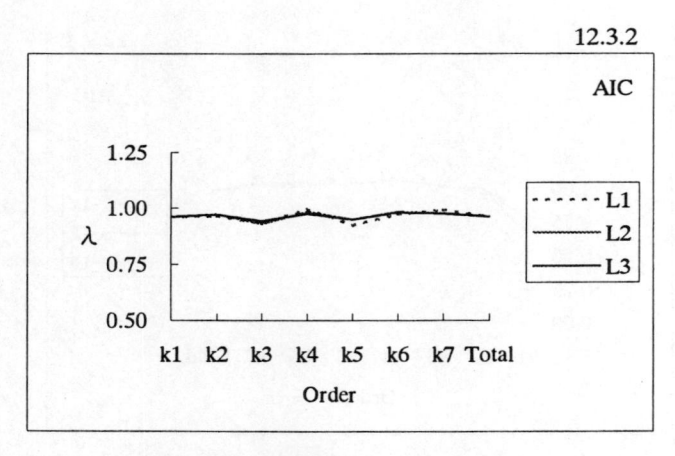

12.3.1

[Chart: GIC — λ vs Order (k1–k7, Total); lines L1, L2, L3]

12.3.2

[Chart: AIC — λ vs Order (k1–k7, Total); lines L1, L2, L3]

1. The true model is Model (12.9).
2. L1, L2, L3 denote the cases with different variances.

12.1. The Information Criteria for Model Choice

12.1.2 Evaluation of the Simulation Results

Based on the above Monte Carlo experiments, we evaluate the simulation results in this section to see the performance of the GIC and the AIC when used for model selection.

The upper column in Table 12.3 shows that both the GIC and the AIC offered good identification of the true second-order polynomial regression model. The variation of the disturbance term variance has an effect on the estimated orders which are over the true order. In other words, the percentage of the estimated orders over the true order is almost fixed regardless of the changes in the disturbance term variance. The higher the disturbance term variance is, the lower the estimated percentage of the true order is. As for the comparison of the GIC and the AIC in the identification of the same model, the conclusion is the same as that obtained in earlier investigations [see Yao (1992, 1996a)]. The data on line 1 and line 4, or on line 2 and line 5, or on line 3 and line 6 provide a clear explanation to the conclusions.

The middle column in Table 12.3 lists the simulation results of fitting a BCT regression model to data generated from the exponential regression model (12.8). For the two information criterion methods, the change of the disturbance term variance does not have a significant effect on the distribution of the estimated orders which exceed the true order. The simulation results show that there is not a significant difference between the GIC and the AIC.

The column at the bottom of Table 12.3 lists the experiment results of fitting a BCT polynomial regression model to simulate the logistic regression model (12.9). In view of the distribution of the estimated order in the 5,000-times iterated experiment for three levels of the variance, we can see that the best fitted model is the BCT regression model with order 1. Considering of the properties of the logistic curve, this conclusion is exactly as what we had anticipated.

Figure 12.1 through Figure 12.3 are plotted according to the estimated results of the BCT parameter. We first give the experiment results for the data generated from polynomial regression model (12.7). Plot 12.1.1 shows the estimated BCT parameters against the order of the BCT regression model by the GIC method. The estimated BCT parameter in the 5,000-times iterated Monte Carlo experi-

Chapter 12. Nonlinear Model Simulation

ment is shown by the index Total. The estimated result by the AIC method is shown in plot 12.1.2.

The three curves indicate that L1 corresponds to the model with the variance of $\sigma_0^2 = 0.5$; L2 corresponds to the model with the variance of $\sigma_0^2 = 1.0$; and L3 corresponds to the model with the variance of $\sigma_0^2 = 1.5$. Except for order 1, the estimated $\hat{\lambda}_k$ ($k = 2, \cdots, 7$) and $\hat{\lambda}$ which for the total 5,000 times experiments are very near to 1. In discussing the estimated order of the BCT regression model, what we are interested in is the $\hat{\lambda}_k$, the estimated BCT parameter corresponding to the estimated order $\hat{k}$. In this example, $\hat{k} = 2$ and $\hat{\lambda}_2 \approx 1$. There is not a significant difference between the GIC and the AIC in the identification of the BCT regression model. The changing of the disturbance term variance do not have significant effects on the estimated BCT parameter.

Plot 12.2.1 and plot 12.2.2 show the estimated BCT parameters of fitting a BCT regression model to data generated from the exponential regression model (12.8). Different from the model (12.7), model (12.8) does not belong to the family of the BCT polynomial regression model. As for the same simulated model (with the same disturbance term variance), the estimated BCT parameter against the estimated order decided by the GIC is slightly lower (compared with the conclusion for model (12.7)) than that determined by the AIC. We observed that the changes of the variance have an effect on the estimate of the BCT parameter against the estimated order, especially for the AIC method. For model (12.8), if the variance of the disturbance term is large, the estimated $\hat{\lambda}_k$ is also large. Comparatively, this effect is very small on the estimator $\hat{\lambda}$.

Plot 12.3.1 and plot 12.3.2 show the estimated BCT parameters when fitting a BCT regression model to data generated from the exponential regression model (12.9). The estimated BCT parameters against the estimated order are comparatively stable for both information criterion methods. The changes of the variance of the disturbance term have almost no effect on the estimator of the BCT parameter. The above discussion demonstrates that the estimated order of the BCT regression model is $\hat{k} = 1$. The estimated BCT parameters that we get here for both information criterion methods and the three levels of variance are in the region of (0.959, 0.9568).

Thirty three-dimensional graphs are summarized in five figures from Figure

12.1. The Information Criteria for Model Choice

12.4.1 to Figure 12.6. Those are the results for two information criterion methods and three models with three levels of the disturbance term variance in the 5,000-times iterated Monte Carlo experiment. A number of properties of the Monte Carlo simulation can be obtained by a detailed observation of those graphs.

Figure 12.4.1 gives the details of the three-dimensional graphs of the estimated frequencies. This is the result of fitting the BCT polynomial regression model to data generated from model (12.7) in the 5,000-times iterated experiment. The graphs are divided into two groups, the G group and the A group. Each group has three graphs, for example, G1, G2, and G3. The three indexes show the three data-generating models with disturbance term variance $\sigma_0^2 = 0.5, 1.0, 1.5$, respectively. The simulation performances of the two information criteria for the three different variance levels can be inferred from the peak of the column and the symmetry property against the BCT parameter λ_i. Figure 12.4.2 is a view of Figure 12.4.1 from the opposite direction. An observation of Figure 12.4.1 and Figure 12.4.2 reveals that the two information criterion methods have no significant differences.

The six graphs in Figure 12.5.1 give the details of the three-dimensional graphs of the estimated frequencies of fitting the BCT polynomial regression model to data generated from model (12.8) in the 5,000-times iterated experiment. Figure 12.5.2 gives the same simulation results as Figure 12.5.1 viewed from the opposite direction. We can see that there is a slight difference between the two information criteria methods when fitting a BCT polynomial regression model to the exponential regression model. As for the model with the same variance, the peak of the column determined by the AIC is a slightly higher than that of determined by the GIC. If we select the second-order BCT models with $\sigma^2 = 0.5$, there are about 72% and 67% of the selected models (in the 5,000-times iterated experiment) with the BCT parameter in (0.5, 1.5), respectively, for the AIC and the GIC. This shows that the data generated from exponential regression model (12.8) can be fitted very well by the second- or third-order BCT polynomial regression model with the BCT parameter near 1. The simulation results suggest that the best-fitting model is the second polynomial regression model (with $\hat{\lambda} = 1$).

The graphs in Figure 12.6 give the details of the three-dimensional graphs of the estimated frequencies to fit the data generated from model (12.9) by the BCT

Chapter 12. Nonlinear Model Simulation

polynomial regression model. The Monte Carlo experiments suggest selecting the first-order BCT model to fit the data generated from the logistic regression model. Careful observation of Figure 12.6 reveals that there is little difference between the two information criterion methods. The variance of the estimated order relies on the variance of the true logistic regression model. The changes of the variance of the estimated BCT model are in the converse direction of what the data DGP (12.9) does.

12.1.3 Conclusions

Based on the 5,000-times iterated Monte Carlo experiment for three models, each of them with three levels of disturbance term variance, the simulation results capture quite well the basic characteristics of the two information criteria as applied to the fitting of the BCT polynomial regression model to data whose DGP does not belong to the family of the BCT polynomial regression model.

There is not a significant difference between the GIC and the AIC in model selection. The data generated from the exponential regression model (12.8) can be fitted very well by the second- or third-order BCT polynomial regression model with the BCT parameter near 1. The estimated BCT parameters determined by the AIC are more concentrated to $\hat{\lambda} = 1$ than those determined by the GIC. The Monte Carlo experiments suggest using the first-order BCT model with the BCT parameter near 1 to fit the data generated from the logistic regression model (12.9). When fitting the BCT polynomial regression model to data generated from the logistic regression model, the changes of the disturbance term variance have comparatively large effects on both information criterion methods.

12.1. The Information Criteria for Model Choice

Figure 12.4 Distribution of the Estimated Frequencies in the 5,000-Times Iterated Monte Carlo Experiment

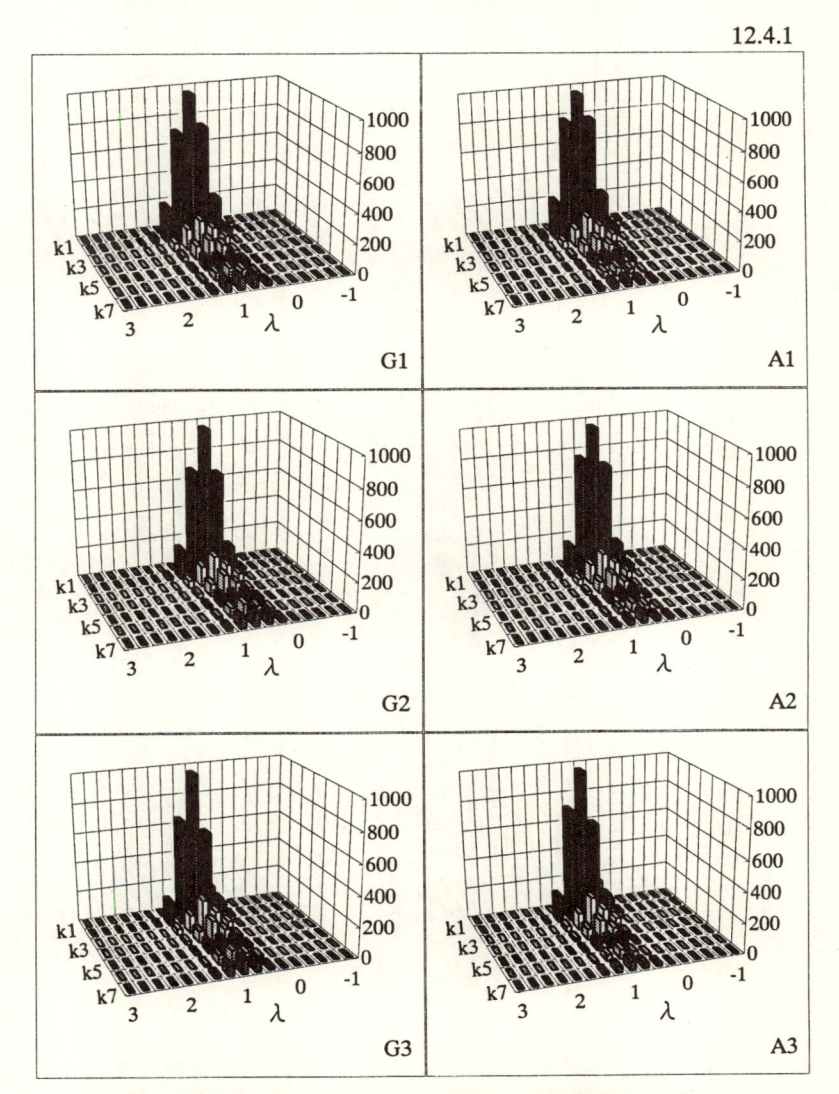

12.4.1

G1

A1

G2

A2

G3

A3

Note: Fitting Model (12.4) to Data Generated by Model (12.7).

Chapter 12. Nonlinear Model Simulation

Figure 12.4 Continued

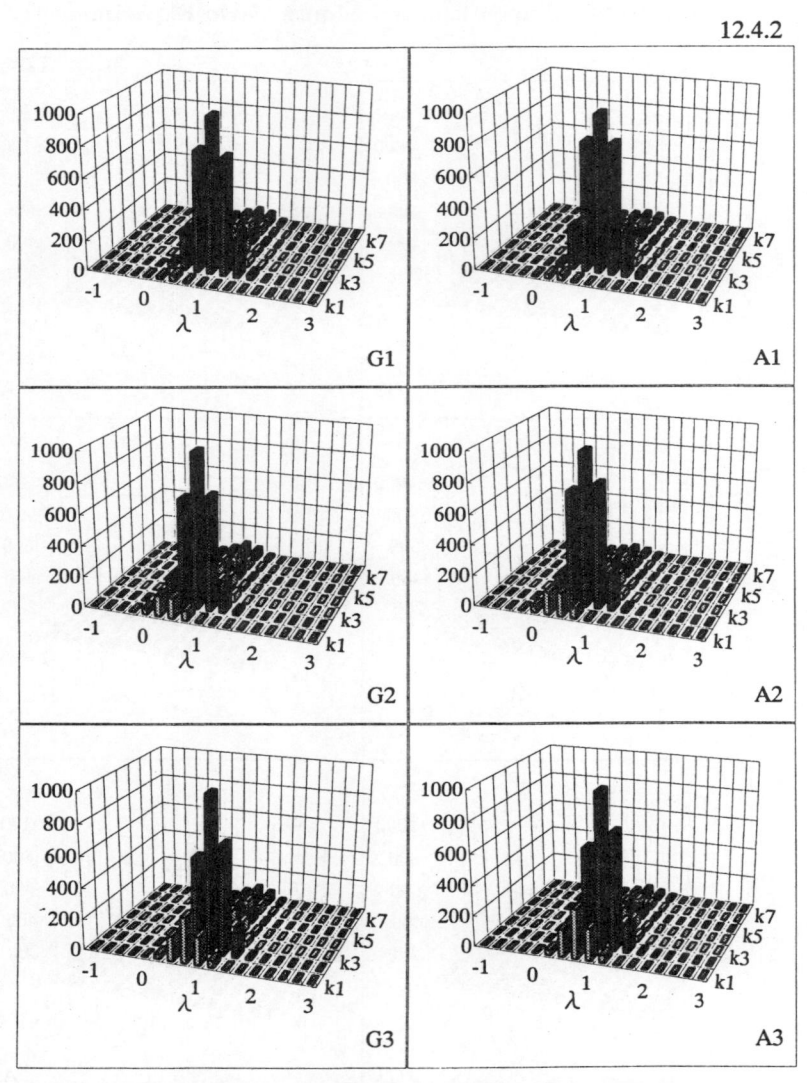

12.4.2

G1

A1

G2

A2

G3

A3

Note: Fitting Model (12.4) to Data Generated by Model (12.7).

12.1. The Information Criteria for Model Choice

Figure 12.5 Distribution of the Estimated Frequencies in the 5,000-Times Iterated Monte Carlo Experiment

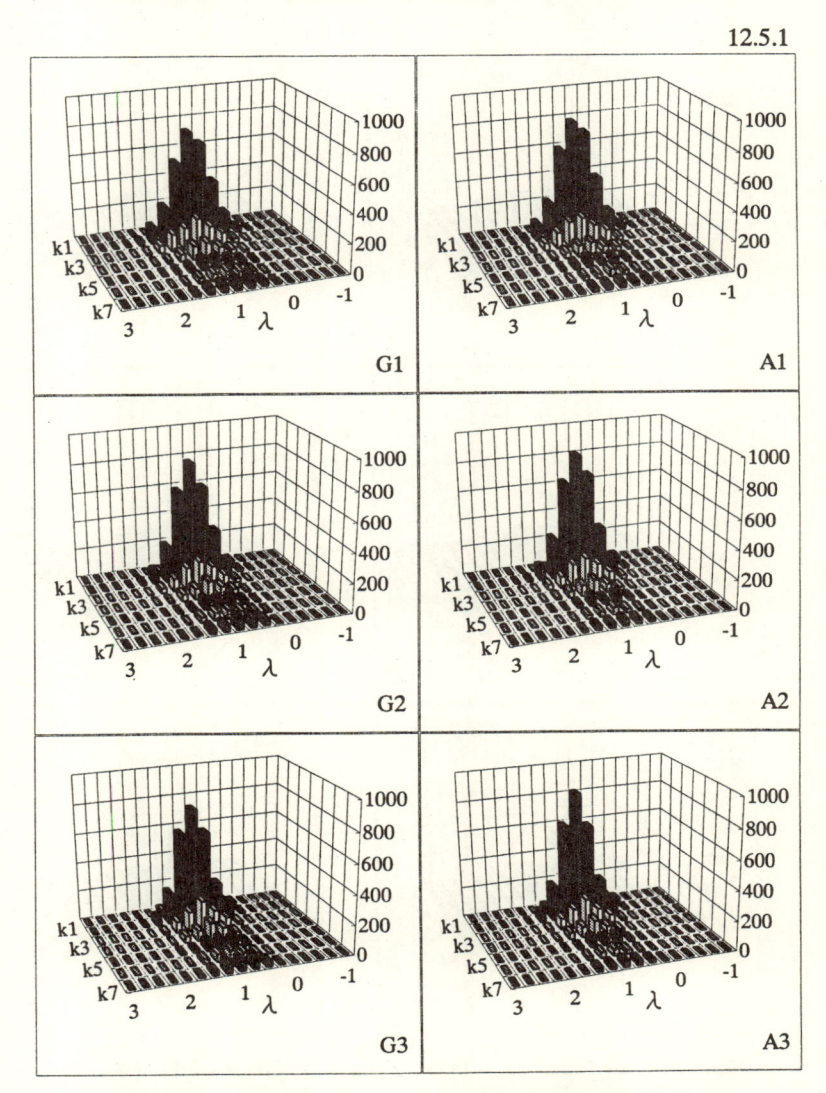

12.5.1

Note: Fitting Model (12.4) to Data Generated by Model (12.8).

Chapter 12. Nonlinear Model Simulation

Figure 12.5 Continued

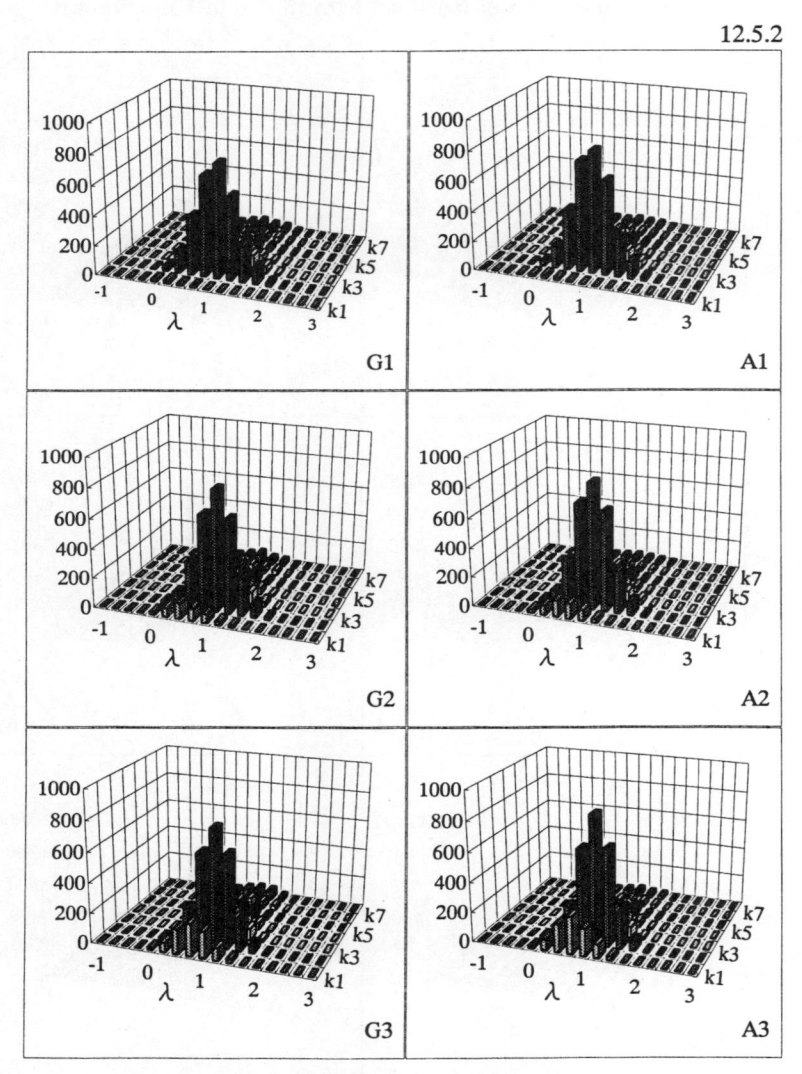

12.5.2

Note: Fitting Model (12.4) to Data Generated by Model (12.8).

12.1. The Information Criteria for Model Choice

Figure 12.6 Distribution of the Estimated Frequencies in the 5,000-Times Iterated Monte Carlo Experiment

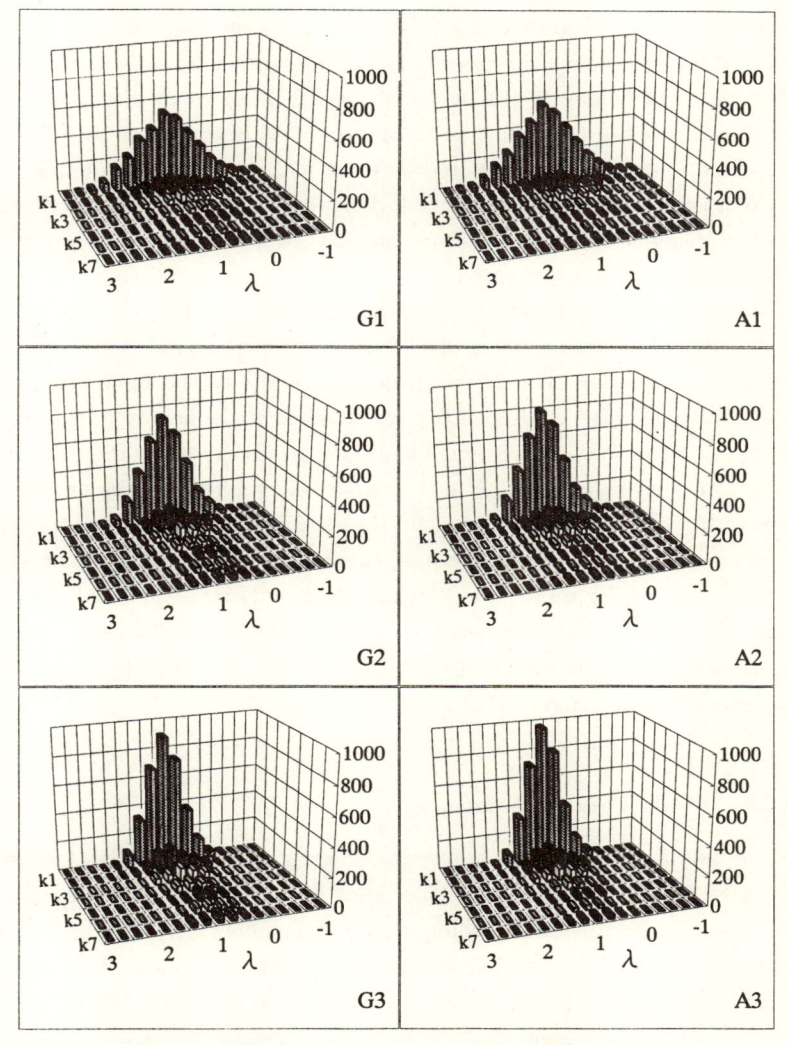

Note: Fitting Model (12.4) to Data Generated by Model (12.9).

Chapter 12. Nonlinear Model Simulation

12.2 The Nested χ^2 Test and the AIC for Model Choice

This section presents some of the simulation results of the nested χ^2 test in the simultaneous identification of the BCT model. It focuses on the investigation of fitting a BCT polynomial regression model to data generated by a nonlinear model which does not belong to the family of the BCT regression models. The three nonlinear models are the same as those introduced in the above section. Except for a second order polynomial regression model, the rest two models are the exponential regression model and the logistic regression model. The performances when applying the nested χ^2 test and the AIC to the simultaneous identification of the BCT model are compared.

Our simulation results show that both the nested χ^2 test and the AIC have good performance when fitting the BCT polynomial regression model to data generated by the two models which do not belong to the family of the BCT polynomial regression models. It is reconfirmed that the nested χ^2 test has good ability to control the probability of identifying orders exceeding the true order. It is also shown that the nested χ^2 test tends to select a higher order, especially for cases with a larger sample variance. In the identification of the true model order, for comparatively small critical values, the nested χ^2 test is deemed superior to the AIC. Concerning those cases in which the true order of the BCT polynomial regression model is underestimated, a properly estimated BCT parameter might compensate for the information loss caused by the underestimated order. This is true for both methods.

12.2.1 Models and Simulations

This section investigates the properties of applying the nested χ^2 test to fit a k-th order BCT polynomial regression model to the data generated by the three models as discussed in the preceding section [see model (12.7), (12.8), and (12.9)] to each model with three levels of disturbance term variance. The purpose is to investigate the properties of the nested χ^2 test and the AIC when fitting the BCT polynomial regression model (12.4) to data generated by the above

12.2. The Nested χ^2 Test and the AIC for Model Choice

mentioned nonlinear regression models. The numerical calculation is conducted by the FORTRAN programs, Nest94 [see Yao (1992, 1996a)].

In view of model (12.7), (12.8) and (12.9), for the sample size $T = 100$, we first create random data set $\{\varepsilon_{it}\}_{i=1}^{T}$ ($i = 1, 2, 3$) which are random numbers and obtained from $N(0, \sigma_0^2)$. The independent variables are defined as $x_t = t/40$, $t = 1, 2, \cdots, T$, and we constructed experiment data set $\{y_{it}, x_t\}_{i=1}^{T}$, $i = 1, 2, 3$. We fit the BCT polynomial regression model (12.4) to data generated by the above three models, respectively. For both the nested χ^2 test and the AIC, the experiments are performed for three levels of the disturbance term variance, $\sigma_0^2 = 0.5, 1.0, 1.5$. For each of the cases, Monte Carlo experiment is conducted for 5,000-times replication. Furthermore, the critical value used in the nested χ^2 test are chosen in five levels from 0.10 to 0.30 by a fixed step of 0.05. The usually used 0.05 critical value is not discussed in this paper because Yao (1995) pointed out that the comparatively small critical value (for example 0.05) makes the nested χ^2 test underestimating the true model order. The largest order of the BCT polynomial regression model used in the simulation is chosen to be 7. Then, for all the estimated orders exceeding 7 are put to be 7.

In the Monte Carlo simulation, for each of the generated data sets and an initial given BCT parameter λ_0, we need to estimate the p-value (and the AIC) for order $k = 1, 2, \cdots, 7$ and the BCT parameter $\lambda_j = \lambda_0 + ((n_\lambda + 1)/2 - j)\Delta\lambda$, $j = 1, 2, \cdots, n_\lambda$, where n_λ is a given (odd) number and $\Delta\lambda$ is a given real value. The initial given λ_0 and n_λ as well as $\Delta\lambda$ should be determined by a pre-test or based on some prior information about the BCT parameter and the pattern of the frequency distribution. In the following experiments, we choose $\lambda_0 = 1.0$, $n_\lambda = 17$ and $\Delta\lambda = 0.25$. In view of the nested χ^2 test and according to the minimum principle of the AIC, we can simultaneously get the estimates of $\hat{k}$ and $\hat{\lambda}$ for both of the two methods. The estimator $(\hat{k}, \hat{\lambda})$ can determine the best fitted BCT regression model for the generated data set. We can choose an enough large n_λ to satisfy any required precise of the estimated BCT parameter.

Remark 12.1 For the space of this book, in the following Tables 12.5 to 12.7, we only listed the simulation results for $n_\lambda = 15$. It gives no effects on the BCT regression model identification because the estimated frequencies are zero at the

Chapter 12. Nonlinear Model Simulation

BCT parameter of -1 or 3.

To show the simultaneous identification processes, we only give a distribution of the estimated ML and the estimated p-values for one experiment (in the 5,000-times iteration) of fitting the BCT polynomial regression model (12.4) to data generated by the nonlinear regression model (12.7). In Table 12.4 the estimated minimum ML values for the seven orders in levels of the BCT parameter are underlined. Based on these estimated ML values, the p-value can be estimated for the corresponding order. This information is listed in the last row. For the given 0.1 critical value, for example, it can be seen that the p-value is first over 0.1 at the second-order, and the corresponding estimated BCT parameter is λ_8 ($= 0.75$). In other words, in this experiment, the best-fitted BCT regression model to the data generated by model (12.7) is the second-order BCT polynomial regression model with the estimated BCT parameter 0.75. This experiment gives a contribution of '1' to the upper block of Table 12.5 at (0.75, 2). The upper block in Table 12.5 is the results of repeating the experiment by 5000 times.

Table 12.5 shows the distribution of the estimated frequencies in the 5,000-times replicated Monte Carlo experiment by the nested χ^2 test and the AIC. The simulation result by use of the nested χ^2 test is only one of the results of fitting the BCT polynomial regression model to data generated by model (12.7) in the case of choosing $\sigma^2 = 1.0$ and the critical value $\alpha = 0.15$.

The estimator of the order of the BCT model should be determined by

$$\hat{k} = (k \mid N_{\hat{k}} = \max_{k}\{N_k\}). \tag{12.14}$$

If there exists one more estimated orders, i.e. for example $N_{\hat{k}_1} = N_{\hat{k}_2}$, we usually choose the larger one, $\hat{k} = \max(k_1, k_2)$.

The results of the simulation experiment for fitting the BCT polynomial regression model to data generated by the exponential regression model (12.8) and the logistic regression model (12.9) in the same situation are summarized and given in the following Table 12.6 and Table 12.7, respectively.

To investigate the performance of applying the nested χ^2 test to model identification when there is a change in the disturbance term variance and the given critical values, we summarize 45 three-dimensional graphs in nine figures, from Figure 12.7.1 to Figure 12.9.3. They are the simulation results of fitting the BCT

12.2. The Nested χ^2 Test and the AIC for Model Choice

Table 12.4 Distribution of the Estimated MLL and the p-values by the Nested χ^2 Test

j	λ_j	Orders 1	2	3	4	5	6	7
1	-1.00	-26.13	-26.13	-24.78	-23.74	-22.30	-18.73	-17.08
2	-0.75	-20.96	-20.90	-19.62	-18.48	-17.06	-13.81	-12.47
3	-0.50	-16.58	-16.34	-15.17	-13.93	-12.51	-9.60	-8.54
4	-0.25	-13.07	-12.48	-11.45	-10.11	-8.70	-6.13	-5.31
5	0.00	-10.47	-9.35	-8.50	-7.06	-5.65	-3.42	-2.81
6	0.25	-8.82	-7.00	-6.34	-4.79	-3.38	-1.47	-1.04
7	0.50	<u>-8.15</u>	-5.43	-4.97	-3.31	-1.90	-0.30	-0.01
8	0.75	-8.47	<u>-4.68</u>	<u>-4.40</u>	<u>-2.63</u>	<u>-1.20</u>	<u>0.11</u>	<u>0.29</u>
9	1.00	-9.74	-4.74	-4.61	-2.73	-1.28	-0.23	-0.13
10	1.25	-11.93	-5.61	-5.57	-3.58	-2.11	-1.30	-1.24
11	1.50	-14.99	-7.28	-7.28	-5.16	-3.67	-3.05	-3.03
12	1.75	-18.84	-9.72	-9.68	-7.44	-5.91	-5.47	-5.46
13	2.00	-23.42	-12.91	-12.75	-10.38	-8.81	-8.50	-8.50
14	2.25	-28.65	-16.80	-16.45	-13.93	-12.31	-12.12	-12.12
15	2.50	-34.46	-21.36	-20.74	-18.07	-16.39	-16.28	-16.27
16	2.75	-40.78	-26.54	-25.57	-22.75	-21.00	-20.94	-20.94
17	3.00	-47.55	-32.31	-30.93	-27.94	-26.10	-26.09	-26.08
	p-value	0.0162	0.1122	0.0638	0.1177	0.1538	0.5444	—

Fit BCT model (12.4) to data generated by model (12.7), $\sigma_0^2 = 1.0$.

polynomial regression model (12.4) to the data sets generated by the three nonlinear models mentioned above. Figure 12.7.1 to Figure 12.7.3 show the results of fitting the BCT polynomial regression model (12.4) to the data set generated by model (12.7) in three levels of the disturbance term variance $\sigma_0^2 = 0.5, 1.0, 1.5$, respectively. In each of the figures, we give five plots corresponding to the critical values α from 0.10 to 0.30 with a fixed step 0.05. Each of the three-dimensional bar graphs is based on the distribution of the estimated frequencies $N(\lambda_j, k)$ in the 5,000-times replicated Monte Carlo experiment. Table 12.5 focuses on one of the plots in Figure 12.7.2 for $\alpha = 0.15$. All of the simulations for data set generated by the exponential regression model (12.8) are conducted by the same way,

Chapter 12. Nonlinear Model Simulation

the results are plotted in Figures 12.8.1, 12.8.2, 12.8.3 for three levels of variance and five levels of critical values, respectively. The Monte Carlo experiment results for fitting the data generated by the logistic regression model (12.9) are plotted in Figure 12.9.1, Figure 12.9.2, and Figure 12.9.3. In each of the figures, the simulation result by the AIC method is also listed for the model and the disturbance term variance indicated. Then the difference of the performances between the nested χ^2 test and the AIC can be observed visually. A number of properties of the Monte Carlo simulations can be obtained by a detailed observation of those graphs. This will be discussed in detail in the next section.

For further investigation of the nested χ^2 method, we then summarize the distribution of the estimated frequencies and the BCT parameter in the 5,000-times replicated Monte Carlo experiment for a nonlinear model (12.8) in the three cases of $\sigma_0^2 = 0.5, 1.0, 1.5$, with five levels of critical values, $\alpha = 0.10, 0.15, 0.20, 0.25, 0.30$. The results are listed in Table 12.8 for the two methods, respectively. In Table 12.8, the upper block shows the frequency distribution of the estimated N_k [see (12.11)] in percentage form for a different order k ($k = 1, 2, \cdots, 7$). The simulation results in view of the AIC are listed on the last three lines. The last column to the right of this block lists the estimated percentage values exceeding the true order. We denote them as $d(\alpha, \sigma^2)\%$ and, in the tables, as %. As the true model is the second-order BCT regression model (12.7), $d(0.1, 0.5) = 12.08$ is the sum of the percentage from the third order to the seventh order. The lower block shows the estimated BCT parameters $\hat{\lambda}_k$ ($k = 1, 2, \cdots, 7$) [see (12.4)] for the models distinguished by three levels of variance and five critical values which were used in the nested χ^2 test. The last three lines are the simulation results estimated by the AIC method. The last column to the right of this block lists the estimated BCT parameters defined by (12.12).

The distribution of the estimated order and the BCT parameters used for fitting model (12.4) to data generated by exponential regression model (12.8) are listed in Table 12.9. The same Monte Carlo simulation results for logistic regression model (12.9) are summarized in Table 12.10. The $d\%$ in these two tables shows the percentage of the estimated frequencies exceeding the estimated order which is determined by (12.14).

12.2. The Nested χ^2 Test and the AIC for Model Choice

Table 12.5 The Estimated Frequencies in the 5,000-Times Iterated Experiment by the Nested χ^2 Test and the AIC

λ_j	1	2	3	Order 4	5	6	7	Total
			Nested	χ^2				$N(\lambda_j)$
-0.75	0	0	0	0	0	0	0	0
-0.50	0	0	0	0	0	0	0	0
-0.25	2	0	0	0	0	0	0	2
0.00	10	0	0	1	0	0	1	12
0.25	77	16	4	1	2	1	2	103
0.50	280	165	29	13	9	8	16	520
0.75	332	691	67	33	36	24	25	1208
1.00	136	1237	108	63	28	40	46	1658
1.25	25	901	66	49	32	22	32	1127
1.50	2	250	33	9	11	7	9	321
1.75	0	31	4	5	3	1	3	47
2.00	0	1	1	0	0	0	0	2
2.25	0	0	0	0	0	0	0	0
2.50	0	0	0	0	0	0	0	0
2.75	0	0	0	0	0	0	0	0
N_k	864	3292	312	174	121	103	134	5000
λ_k	0.6690	1.0326	1.0088	1.0230	1.0062	0.9903	0.9851	0.9651
				AIC				$N(\lambda_j)$
-0.75	0	0	0	0	0	0	0	0
-0.50	0	0	0	0	0	0	0	0
-0.25	1	0	0	0	0	0	0	1
0.00	6	1	0	1	0	0	1	9
0.25	41	20	7	1	2	1	2	74
0.50	145	185	49	21	16	9	19	444
0.75	152	740	125	59	50	36	33	1195
1.00	70	1183	198	118	56	63	53	1741
1.25	10	803	133	82	56	39	38	1161
1.50	1	211	43	25	14	16	15	325
1.75	0	24	6	5	6	2	4	47
2.00	0	1	2	0	0	0	0	3
2.25	0	0	0	0	0	0	0	0
2.50	0	0	0	0	0	0	0	0
2.75	0	0	0	0	0	0	0	0
N_k	426	3168	563	312	200	166	165	5000
λ_k	0.6585	1.0100	1.0004	1.0313	1.0175	1.0301	0.9985	0.9809

1. Fit BCT model (12.4) to data generated by model (12.7), $\sigma_0^2 = 1.0$.
2. The Nested χ^2 test used the critical value $\alpha = 0.15$.

Table 12.6 The Estimated Frequencies in the 5,000-Times Iterated Experiment by the Nested χ^2 Test and the AIC

λ_j	1	2	3	Order 4	5	6	7	Total
			Nested	χ^2				$N(\lambda_j)$
-0.75	2	0	0	0	0	0	0	2
-0.50	0	0	0	1	0	0	0	1
-0.25	7	2	0	0	0	1	0	10
0.00	47	12	2	0	0	0	3	64
0.25	132	82	16	6	5	3	1	245
0.50	225	316	33	14	17	9	22	636
0.75	226	695	61	40	28	20	27	1097
1.00	144	912	94	53	19	29	33	1284
1.25	54	741	93	31	32	24	27	1002
1.50	14	333	52	25	18	14	15	471
1.75	1	100	26	12	5	3	8	155
2.00	0	16	4	5	2	1	1	29
2.25	0	2	2	0	0	0	0	4
2.50	0	0	0	0	0	0	0	0
2.75	0	0	0	0	0	0	0	0
N_k	852	3211	383	187	126	104	137	5000
λ_k	0.6408	1.0117	1.0770	1.0602	1.0278	1.0313	0.9982	0.9557
			AIC					$N(\lambda_j)$
-0.75	0	0	0	0	0	0	0	0
-0.50	1	1	0	1	0	0	0	3
-0.25	2	2	0	0	0	2	0	6
0.00	25	14	4	0	1	0	3	47
0.25	60	90	27	10	4	5	3	199
0.50	109	315	65	24	24	15	24	576
0.75	101	708	133	56	48	27	32	1105
1.00	71	850	185	98	37	50	39	1330
1.25	27	673	152	73	52	34	32	1043
1.50	10	284	78	42	24	25	23	486
1.75	1	91	35	16	5	7	12	167
2.00	0	16	4	5	6	1	2	34
2.25	0	2	2	0	0	0	0	4
2.50	0	0	0	0	0	0	0	0
2.75	0	0	0	0	0	0	0	0
N_k	407	3046	685	325	201	166	170	5000
λ_k	0.6529	0.9924	1.0288	1.0654	1.0336	1.0407	1.0309	0.9791

1. Fit BCT model (12.4) to data generated by model (12.8), $\sigma_0^2 = 1.0$.
2. The Nested χ^2 test used the critical value $\alpha = 0.15$

12.2. The Nested χ^2 Test and the AIC for Model Choice

Table 12.7 The Estimated Frequencies in the 5,000-Times Iterated Experiment by the Nested χ^2 Test and the AIC

λ_j	1	2	3	4	5	6	7	Total
			Nested	χ^2				$N(\lambda_j)$
-0.75	1	1	1	0	0	0	0	3
-0.50	11	1	0	0	0	0	0	12
-0.25	33	4	2	3	1	0	2	45
0.00	117	19	5	2	3	3	4	153
0.25	248	20	10	10	3	3	9	303
0.50	503	29	21	11	16	9	13	602
0.75	826	56	17	15	14	13	20	961
1.00	936	62	31	26	14	22	23	1114
1.25	731	60	24	23	15	17	19	889
1.50	450	39	19	15	7	9	15	554
1.75	208	15	11	8	8	3	6	259
2.00	58	6	4	4	0	4	2	78
2.25	20	1	0	1	0	1	1	24
2.50	1	0	0	0	1	0	0	2
2.75	0	0	0	0	1	0	0	1
N_k	4143	313	145	118	83	84	114	5000
λ_k	0.9584	0.9433	0.9741	1.0169	0.9819	1.0387	0.9583	0.9610
			AIC					$N(\lambda_j)$
-0.75	1	1	1	0	0	0	0	3
-0.50	10	2	0	0	0	0	0	12
-0.25	28	6	5	3	1	2	2	47
0.00	102	18	9	4	6	5	5	149
0.25	209	41	22	13	7	6	9	307
0.50	432	56	41	21	23	16	16	605
0.75	698	108	57	28	27	20	24	962
1.00	798	123	64	45	34	29	26	1119
1.25	624	104	51	34	18	22	20	873
1.50	391	70	35	15	12	15	19	557
1.75	179	32	14	12	10	5	6	258
2.00	48	10	6	7	1	5	5	82
2.25	16	4	0	0	1	1	1	23
2.50	1	0	0	0	1	0	0	2
2.75	0	0	0	0	1	0	0	1
N_k	3537	575	305	182	142	126	133	5000
λ_k	0.9588	0.9722	0.9295	0.9835	0.9489	0.9841	0.9774	0.9603

1. Fit BCT model (12.4) to data generated by model (12.9), $\sigma_0^2 = 1.0$
2. The Nested χ^2 test used the critical value $\alpha = 0.15$.

Chapter 12. Nonlinear Model Simulation

Table 12.8 Distribution of the Estimated Order and the BCT Paramater for Data Generated by Model (12.7)

α	σ_0^2	1	2	3	order 4	5	6	7	d % k > 2
				Nested	χ^2				
0.10	0.5	7.56	80.36	4.72	2.40	1.62	1.44	1.90	12.08
	1.0	22.98	65.22	4.56	2.38	1.58	1.42	1.86	11.80
	1.5	35.26	53.34	4.26	2.28	1.56	1.42	1.88	11.40
0.15	0.5	4.90	77.82	6.52	3.48	2.42	2.12	2.74	17.28
	1.0	17.28	65.84	6.24	3.48	2.42	2.06	2.68	16.88
	1.5	27.86	55.80	5.92	3.44	2.26	2.00	2.72	16.34
0.20	0.5	3.54	73.82	8.18	4.08	3.26	3.02	4.10	22.64
	1.0	13.52	64.20	8.02	4.00	3.28	2.96	4.02	22.28
	1.5	23.00	55.26	7.78	3.86	3.18	2.90	4.02	21.74
0.25	0.5	2.74	68.76	9.28	5.56	3.92	4.08	5.66	28.50
	1.0	10.74	61.66	8.96	5.38	3.76	4.04	5.46	27.60
	1.5	19.46	53.96	8.58	5.06	3.74	3.86	5.34	26.58
0.30	0.5	2.04	64.70	10.18	6.38	4.56	4.84	7.30	33.26
	1.0	8.50	58.98	10.00	6.22	4.42	4.70	7.18	32.52
	1.5	15.84	52.74	9.46	5.96	4.28	4.58	7.14	31.42
					AIC				
	0.5	1.84	69.28	11.68	6.34	4.08	3.42	3.36	28.88
	1.0	8.52	63.36	11.26	6.24	4.00	3.32	3.30	28.12
	1.5	15.82	57.40	10.52	5.88	3.90	3.24	3.24	26.78
				Nested	χ^2				$\hat{\lambda}$
0.10	0.5	0.411	1.023	0.995	1.021	0.963	0.993	1.016	0.974
	1.0	0.672	1.042	0.991	1.011	0.975	1.014	1.005	0.952
	1.5	0.767	1.048	0.994	1.024	0.962	1.004	0.995	0.943
0.15	0.5	0.403	1.014	1.018	1.030	1.015	1.000	1.006	0.984
	1.0	0.669	1.033	1.009	1.023	1.006	0.990	0.985	0.965
	1.5	0.770	1.037	0.998	1.026	0.998	0.990	0.982	0.956
0.20	0.5	0.400	1.007	1.010	1.038	1.032	1.007	1.013	0.988
	1.0	0.666	1.024	0.996	1.035	1.023	1.020	0.998	0.973
	1.5	0.772	1.027	0.990	1.039	1.006	1.002	0.991	0.963
0.25	0.5	0.394	1.003	1.009	1.039	1.017	1.017	1.006	0.990
	1.0	0.664	1.015	0.996	1.042	1.015	1.019	1.014	0.977
	1.5	0.767	1.022	0.983	1.041	0.996	1.019	1.009	0.968
0.30	0.5	0.392	1.000	1.012	1.021	1.011	1.013	1.013	0.992
	1.0	0.659	1.011	0.999	1.023	1.015	1.017	1.001	0.980
	1.5	0.766	1.016	0.996	1.020	0.994	1.014	1.002	0.973
					AIC				
	0.5	0.400	1.000	1.003	1.030	1.017	1.023	1.009	0.993
	1.0	0.659	1.010	1.000	1.031	1.018	1.030	0.999	0.981
	1.5	0.768	1.016	0.989	1.037	1.001	1.014	0.994	0.974

Replicated Monte Carlo Experiment by 5,000 Times.

12.2. The Nested χ^2 Test and the AIC for Model Choice

Table 12.9 Distribution of the Estimated Order and the BCT Paramater for Data Generated by Model (12.8)

α	σ_0^2	1	2	3	order 4	5	6	7	$d\%$ $k>2$
				Nested	χ^2				
0.10	0.5	6.28	78.26	7.76	2.70	1.62	1.56	1.82	15.46
	1.0	23.42	63.24	6.08	2.30	1.56	1.52	1.88	13.34
	1.5	36.40	51.30	5.22	2.26	1.46	1.44	1.92	12.30
0.15	0.5	4.00	74.40	9.72	4.18	2.60	2.16	2.94	21.60
	1.0	17.04	64.22	7.66	3.74	2.52	2.08	2.74	18.74
	1.5	28.90	53.84	6.84	3.52	2.36	1.94	2.60	17.26
0.20	0.5	2.76	70.08	11.28	4.92	3.46	3.04	4.46	27.16
	1.0	13.04	62.46	9.38	4.80	3.26	2.90	4.16	24.50
	1.5	24.06	53.22	8.04	4.46	3.24	2.88	4.10	22.72
0.25	0.5	1.98	65.24	13.36	5.86	4.04	3.78	5.74	32.78
	1.0	10.58	59.88	10.76	5.58	3.88	3.82	5.50	29.54
	1.5	20.06	52.16	9.56	5.38	3.84	3.80	5.20	27.78
0.30	0.5	1.50	59.82	14.78	6.88	4.50	4.88	7.64	38.68
	1.0	8.46	56.48	12.32	6.42	4.40	4.60	7.32	35.06
	1.5	16.62	50.62	10.92	6.08	4.28	4.40	7.08	32.76
				AIC					
	0.5	1.24	59.38	16.24	7.64	5.06	4.82	5.62	39.38
	1.0	7.26	57.06	13.92	7.14	4.68	4.68	5.26	35.68
	1.5	14.76	51.36	12.76	6.80	4.62	4.46	5.24	33.88
				Nested	χ^2				$\hat{\lambda}$
0.10	0.5	0.312	0.974	1.160	1.135	1.006	1.010	1.047	0.954
	1.0	0.651	1.021	1.083	1.109	0.987	1.020	1.021	0.940
	1.5	0.779	1.026	1.050	1.095	1.007	1.021	1.016	0.938
0.15	0.5	0.314	0.965	1.131	1.078	1.081	1.056	1.026	0.967
	1.0	0.641	1.012	1.077	1.060	1.028	1.031	0.998	0.956
	1.5	0.771	1.022	1.039	1.047	1.015	1.031	1.010	0.951
0.20	0.5	0.288	0.960	1.102	1.089	1.085	1.038	1.046	0.975
	1.0	0.641	0.999	1.065	1.079	1.045	1.028	1.043	0.967
	1.5	0.767	1.015	1.029	1.061	1.026	1.009	1.044	0.960
0.25	0.5	0.268	0.959	1.066	1.090	1.068	1.078	1.051	0.981
	1.0	0.642	0.994	1.045	1.069	1.040	1.060	1.035	0.973
	1.5	0.769	1.006	1.025	1.067	1.017	1.041	1.034	0.967
0.30	0.5	0.293	0.956	1.072	1.068	1.050	1.036	1.041	0.986
	1.0	0.644	0.993	1.030	1.053	1.035	1.037	1.029	0.979
	1.5	0.773	1.002	1.014	1.049	1.025	1.023	1.025	0.971
				AIC					
	0.5	0.274	0.959	1.065	1.073	1.078	1.048	1.035	0.984
	1.0	0.653	0.992	1.029	1.065	1.034	1.041	1.031	0.979
	1.5	0.769	1.002	1.023	1.066	1.023	1.029	1.025	0.972

Replicated Monte Carlo Experiment by 5,000 Times.

Chapter 12. Nonlinear Model Simulation

Table 12.10 Distribution of the Estimated Order and the BCT Paramater for Data Generated by Model (12.9)

α	σ_0^2	1	2	3	order 4	5	6	7	$d\%$ $k>2$
				Nested	χ^2				
0.10	0.5	87.94	4.86	1.94	1.54	1.00	1.16	1.56	12.06
	1.0	88.36	4.50	1.96	1.54	0.96	1.16	1.52	11.64
	1.5	88.46	4.44	1.98	1.50	0.94	1.12	1.56	11.54
0.15	0.5	82.48	6.66	2.90	2.48	1.58	1.66	2.24	17.52
	1.0	82.86	6.26	2.90	2.36	1.66	1.68	2.28	17.14
	1.5	82.88	6.20	2.96	2.28	1.64	1.76	2.28	17.12
0.20	0.5	77.10	8.12	4.06	2.62	2.42	2.30	3.38	22.90
	1.0	77.52	7.72	4.10	2.62	2.36	2.32	3.36	22.48
	1.5	77.66	7.58	4.06	2.62	2.38	2.32	3.38	22.34
0.25	0.5	72.04	9.06	4.94	3.46	3.02	2.92	4.56	27.96
	1.0	72.40	8.76	4.88	3.46	3.04	2.98	4.48	27.60
	1.5	72.48	8.60	4.76	3.56	3.06	3.00	4.54	27.52
0.30	0.5	66.94	10.18	5.82	4.14	3.44	3.62	5.86	33.06
	1.0	67.34	9.70	5.82	4.06	3.52	3.70	5.86	32.66
	1.5	67.46	9.54	5.74	4.12	3.58	3.70	5.86	32.54
				AIC					
	0.5	69.92	12.22	6.22	3.62	2.78	2.58	2.66	30.08
	1.0	70.74	11.50	6.10	3.64	2.84	2.52	2.66	29.26
	1.5	70.68	11.56	6.08	3.68	2.86	2.52	2.62	29.32
				Nested	χ^2				$\hat{\lambda}$
0.10	0.5	0.955	0.977	1.034	1.104	0.910	1.047	1.010	0.961
	1.0	0.955	0.983	1.015	1.046	0.943	1.056	1.020	0.961
	1.5	0.958	0.988	0.995	1.030	0.931	1.040	1.016	0.963
0.15	0.5	0.959	0.937	0.990	1.061	0.930	1.051	0.958	0.962
	1.0	0.958	0.943	0.974	1.017	0.982	1.039	0.958	0.961
	1.5	0.961	0.943	0.980	1.000	0.979	1.026	0.963	0.963
0.20	0.5	0.960	0.950	0.953	0.998	0.942	0.967	0.988	0.961
	1.0	0.959	0.964	0.916	1.013	0.960	0.974	0.993	0.961
	1.5	0.962	0.962	0.932	1.000	0.943	0.963	0.991	0.962
0.25	0.5	0.956	0.975	0.929	1.006	0.916	0.964	1.007	0.960
	1.0	0.959	0.968	0.932	0.984	0.942	0.966	0.992	0.960
	1.5	0.961	0.962	0.956	0.979	0.933	0.958	0.990	0.962
0.30	0.5	0.957	0.972	0.936	1.004	0.935	0.956	0.969	0.959
	1.0	0.958	0.976	0.947	0.991	0.947	0.955	0.968	0.960
	1.5	0.959	0.972	0.957	0.992	0.950	0.945	0.968	0.961
				AIC					
	0.5	0.961	0.964	0.931	0.996	0.923	0.973	0.993	0.961
	1.0	0.959	0.972	0.930	0.984	0.949	0.984	0.977	0.960
	1.5	0.961	0.971	0.942	0.974	0.948	0.980	0.975	0.962

Replicated Monte Carlo Experiment by 5,000 Times.

12.2. The Nested χ^2 Test and the AIC for Model Choice

12.2.2 Evaluation of the Simulation Results

The simulation results of fitting the BCT model (12.4) to data generated by the second-order polynomial regression model (12.7) for the case of $\sigma_0^2 = 1.0$ are listed in Table 12.5. The critical value $\alpha = 0.15$ is used in the nested χ^2 test. The distributions of the estimated frequencies in the 5,000-times replicated experiment by the nested χ^2 and the AIC are shown in two blocks, respectively.

This shows that both methods have good performance when fitting the BCT polynomial regression model to the data generated by a polynomial regression model. In the 5,000-times replicated experiment by the nested χ^2 test, there are 1,237 replications perfectly fitted the true model (12.7), and 1,183 replications fitted the AIC. Concerning the identification of the model order, the model order was identified 3,292 times out of the 5,000 replications by the nestedχ^2 test and 3,168 times by the AIC. Each of the above four frequencies represents the maximum value of the case presented. The frequencies of fitting the true model or identifying the true model order by the nested χ^2 test are larger than those by the AIC. In view of the nested χ^2 test, the percentage of the overestimated frequency exceeding the true model order is 16.88% (approximately equal to the critical value $\alpha = 0.15$). However, the percentage of the overestimated frequency by the AIC is 28.12%, which is significantly higher than that determined by the nested χ^2 test.

As for the estimation of the BCT parameter, the AIC seems better than the nested χ^2 test but the difference is not very large. Concerning the AIC method, the estimate of the BCT parameter is 1.01, which is the weighted mean determined by the frequencies against the identified true model order 2, $N(\lambda_j, 2)$. This is better than that determined by the nested χ^2 method, which is 1.03. If we choose the BCT parameter by the weighted mean determined by N_{λ_j}, the result is 0.98 by the AIC method and 0.97 by the nested χ^2 method. On the whole, for comparatively small critical values ($\alpha < 0.25$), the nested χ^2 method is superior to the AIC method in the identification of the true model order, but it is the reverse in the estimation of the BCT parameter.

Table 12.6 shows the simulation result of fitting the BCT model (12.4) to data

Chapter 12. Nonlinear Model Simulation

generated by the exponential regression model (12.8) for the case of $\sigma_0^2 = 1.0$, and the critical value $\alpha = 0.15$ is also used in the nested χ^2 test. An observation of the two blocks tells us that the performances of the two methods in model selection are very similar to the case of fitting the data generated from model (12.7), as discussed above. The nested χ^2 test suggests choosing the second-order BCT polynomial regression model with the BCT parameter 1.01 to fit the data generated from model (12.8). The AIC suggests choosing the second-order BCT polynomial regression model with the BCT parameter 0.99 to fit the same model. Table 12.7 shows the distributions of the estimated frequencies by the nested χ^2 test and the AIC for fitting the BCT model (12.4) to data generated by the logistic regression model (12.9). For the case of $\sigma_0^2 = 1.0$, both methods suggest using the order 1 BCT polynomial regression model with the BCT parameter 0.96 to fit the data set generated by model (12.9). In view of the nested χ^2 test, the estimated frequency 4,143 suggests choosing the order 1 BCT model. This estimated frequency is much larger than that estimated by the AIC (3,537). In this sense, we can say that the power of the nested χ^2 test is higher than that of the AIC, at least in this case.

The plots in Figure 12.7.1, for five levels of critical values, respectively, give details of the estimated frequencies in fitting the BCT polynomial regression model (12.4) to data generated by model (12.7) with disturbance term variance $\sigma_0^2 = 0.5$. The last graph is the result given by the AIC method. The simulation performances for different critical values can be observed by the peak of the column and the symmetry against the BCT parameter $\lambda \, (= -1, 0, \cdots, 3)$. When using the nested χ^2 test for the identification of the BCT regression model order, it is better to choose the lower critical value 0.10. The power will be degenerate as the critical value increased. The symmetry of the frequency distribution against the BCT parameter tells us that a high critical value gives a good estimation of the BCT parameter. The performance of the AIC is almost the same as that of the nested χ^2 test when choosing critical value 0.25. Figure 12.7.2 and Figure 12.7.3 give the results for the cases of disturbance term variance $\sigma_0^2 = 1.0, 1.5$, respectively. The performances of the two methods in the identification of the BCT model can be compared by the plots with the same critical value in three figures. An observation of these figures shows that both methods tend to

12.2. The Nested χ^2 Test and the AIC for Model Choice

underestimate the order of the BCT regression model as the disturbance term variance increase. The nested χ^2 test is more sensitive to the variations of the disturbance term variance.

The plots in Figure 12.8.1, for five levels of the critical values, respectively, give the details of the estimated frequencies in fitting the BCT polynomial regression model to data generated by exponential model (12.8). It is the case of the disturbance term variance of $\sigma_0^2 = 0.5$. Figure 12.8.2 and Figure 12.8.3 give the same simulation results for the case the disturbance term variance $\sigma_0^2 = 1.0, 1.5$, respectively. The properties are very similar to the above discussions concerning Figure 12.7.1 to Figure 12.7.3. For both data sets generated by model (12.7) and the exponential model (12.8), in the case of the disturbance term variance is large, for example, $\sigma_0^2 = 1.5$, the performance of the AIC in estimating the true order seems better than the nested χ^2 test. This can be observed by Figure 12.7.3 and Figure 12.8.3, as the peak of the column at the second order with the BCT parameter $\lambda = 1$ determined by the AIC is higher than that determined by the nested χ^2 test for all of the given critical values.

The plots in Figure 12.9.1, for five levels of critical values, respectively, give the details of the estimated frequencies in fitting the BCT polynomial regression model (12.4) to data generated by the logistic model (12.9) for $\sigma_0^2 = 0.5$. The simulation result by using the AIC is listed on the last of this figure. Figure 12.9.2 and Figure 12.9.3 show the simulation results for the case of the disturbance term variance $\sigma_0^2 = 1.0, 1.5$, respectively. These three figures show that there is almost no difference between the two methods in estimating the BCT parameter. All these cases suggest choosing the first-order BCT polynomial regression model to fit the logistic model (12.9). The power of estimating the simulation model order by the nested χ^2 test with lower critical values is higher than that of by the AIC. The performance of the AIC is almost the same as that of the nested χ^2 test with a critical value $\alpha = 0.25$ for all the three cases of model (12.9) specified by $\sigma_0^2 = 0.5, 1.0, 1.5$.

The upper block in Table 12.8 shows that the nested χ^2 test can give a good estimation of the BCT model order in fitting the data generated by model (12.7). The changes of the disturbance term variance only have an effect on the distribution of the estimated frequencies when the identified order is less than the true

Chapter 12. Nonlinear Model Simulation

order. The larger the disturbance term variance is, the smaller the estimated percentage at the true order is. It is the reverse for the percentage of the underestimated order. Furthermore, the percentage of the estimated orders exceeding the true order is almost fixed regardless of the changes in the disturbance term variance. Table 12.8 shows that, as the critical value α increases, the estimated frequency of the identified order that is less than the true order decreases and the frequency of the identified order exceeding the true order increases. From this table, we can also see that the percentage of the frequencies exceeding the true order increases as the significance level increases. The value of $d(\alpha, \sigma^2)$ is very near the given critical value α. This result is exactly in accordance with what the p-value implies. The AIC method tends to overestimate the model order. By selecting the critical value, the nested χ^2 test retains the good property of controlling the levels of overestimating model order. We can also see that, for a comparatively small critical value (for example, $\chi^2 \leq 0.2$), the nested χ^2 test is better than the AIC in identifying the order of the BCT polynomial regression model. The above result is coincidence with the conclusion reached in the earlier investigations [see Yao (1995, 1996b)]. The estimated results of the BCT parameter listed in the lower block show that except for the case of order 1, the estimator $\hat{\lambda}_k$ ($k = 2, \cdots, 7$) and $\hat{\lambda}$ which is estimated by all 5,000-times replicated experiment, are very near 1. The changes of the disturbance term variance do not have a significant effect on the estimate of the BCT parameter. There is no significant difference between the nested χ^2 method and the AIC method.

As for the case of underestimating the true order of the BCT model, the estimated BCT parameter seems to be enough compensation for the information loss caused by the underestimated order. The virtues of simultaneous identification of the BCT regression model by the use of the nested χ^2 test or the AIC can be seen here. In case of underestimating the true order, the estimate of the BCT parameter is very sensitive to the disturbance term variance. This conclusion is true for both the nested χ^2 test and the AIC.

Table 12.9 shows the estimators of the BCT parameter in fitting the BCT regression model (12.4) to data generated from the exponential regression model (12.8). The patterns of the percentage distribution of the estimated order and the BCT parameter are very similar to the results shown in Table 12.8. The sim-

12.2. The Nested χ^2 Test and the AIC for Model Choice

ulation result suggests using the second-order BCT polynomial regression model with the BCT parameter $\hat{\lambda}_2 \approx 0.98$ to fit model (12.8). The estimated BCT parameters that we get here for the three levels of variance are in the interval of $(0.96, 1.0)$. Furthermore, it can be seen that for each of the given critical value α for all three levels of the disturbance term variance especially for the lower variance, the estimator of $d(\alpha, \sigma^2)$ is much higher than α. To some extent, this seems to be in conflict with the property of the nested χ^2 test, but it may be explained by the fact that the divergence between the BCT polynomial regression model and the exponential regression model is too large. A proper explanation would require further investigation; thus, we will leave it as an open question. Table 12.10 lists the experiment results obtained when fitting the BCT polynomial regression model (12.4) to data generated by the logistic regression model (12.9). In view of the distribution of the estimated order in the 5,000-times replicated experiment for three levels of variance, we can see that the best-fitted model is the first-order BCT polynomial regression model. The changes of the variance have almost no effect on the estimation of the BCT parameter. Both methods suggest choosing the BCT parameter $\hat{\lambda}_1 \approx 0.96$.

12.2.3 Conclusions

To investigate the basic characteristics of the nested χ^2 test and the AIC in the application of fitting the BCT polynomial regression model to data generated by nonlinear models which do not belong to the family of the BCT polynomial regression models, we conducted 5,000-times replicated Monte Carlo experiment for three nonlinear models, a second-order polynomial regression model, and exponential regression model as well as a logistic regression model. For each of the models, in view of the nested χ^2 test, we discussed three levels of disturbance term variance as well as five levels of critical values. The simulation results capture the characteristics of the nested χ^2 test and the AIC quite well. Concerning the information criterion methods in model selection, as the performances of the GIC and the AIC are not so different, we only discuss the AIC.

When fitting the BCT polynomial regression model to data generated by models that do not belong to the family of the BCT polynomial regression models,

Chapter 12. Nonlinear Model Simulation

simulation results show that both methods have good performances in model identification. The nested χ^2 test has the ability to control the probability of identifying orders exceeding the true order, but it tends to underestimate the true order, especially when there is a larger disturbance term variance. To avoid overestimating the order of the BCT regression model, we suggest selecting a comparatively small critical value or, conversely, a larger critical value. The AIC, in general, tends to overestimate the true order of the model. When the true order of the BCT regression model is underestimated, a properly estimated BCT parameter seems to be enough compensation for the information loss caused by the underestimated order. This is true for both methods. For comparatively small critical values, the nested χ^2 test has better performance than the AIC in the estimation of the true model order. Furthermore, simulation results show that both methods suggest using the second-order BCT polynomial regression model with the BCT parameter $\hat{\lambda}_2 \approx 0.98$ to fit the exponential regression model (12.8), and using the first-order BCT polynomial regression model with the BCT parameter $\hat{\lambda}_2 \approx 0.96$ to fit the logistic regression model (12.9).

When fitting a data set generated by the exponential regression model, it is seen that, for all given critical values α and for three levels of disturbance term variance, especially for the case with lower variance, the percentage of the estimated frequencies exceeding the true order is much higher than 100α. This result seems in conflict with the property of the nested χ^2 test. We will leave it as an open question. The reached conclusions should be tempered for the stochastic specifications which have been made and the general nature of Monte Carlo experimentation. The robustness of our conclusions, seems difficult to prove but very important, should also be discussed in the future.

Due to some constraints in the computation, concrete simulation models could not be presented in this paper. The discussion based on the concrete simulation models may contribute to the comparison of the nested χ^2 test and the AIC. Moreover, the mixed estimate based on the nested χ^2 test and the AIC [see Yao (1995)] may play an important role in model identification. Our forthcoming paper will discuss these issues.

12.2. The Nested χ^2 Test and the AIC for Model Choice

Figure 12.7.1 Distribution of the Estimated Frequencies in the 5,000-Times Iterated Monte Carlo Experiment

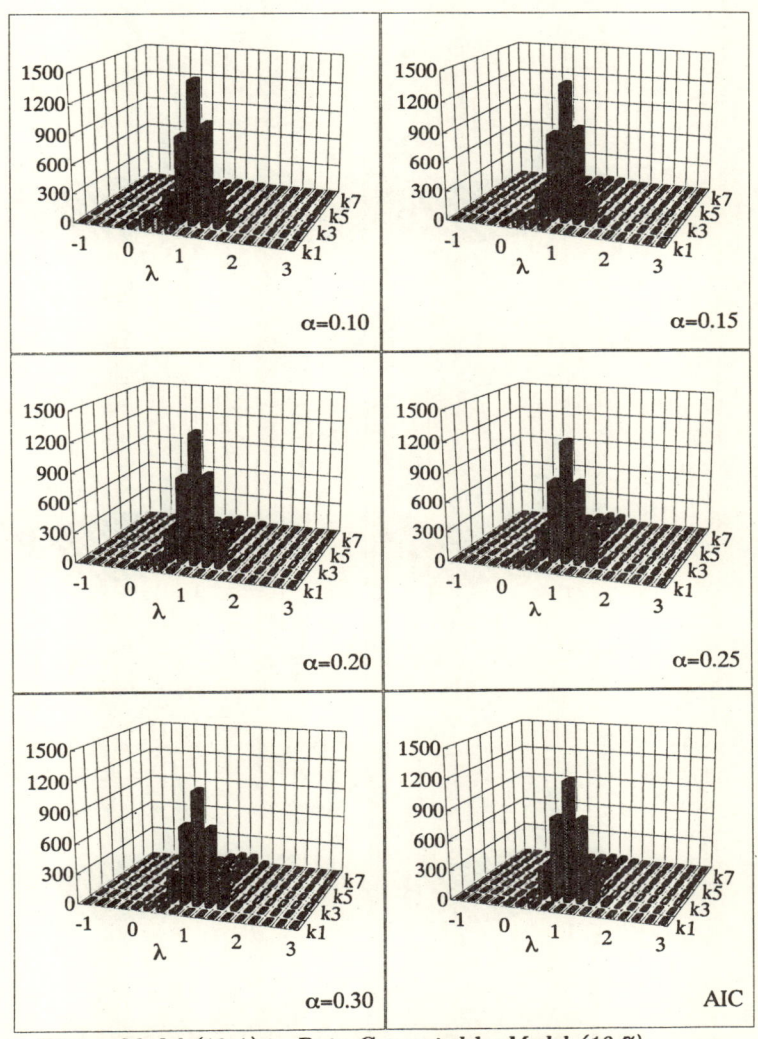

Fitting Model (12.4) to Data Generated by Model (12.7) for the case of $\sigma_0^2 = 0.5$.

Chapter 12. Nonlinear Model Simulation

Figure 12.7.2 Distribution of the Estimated Frequencies in the 5,000-Times Iterated Monte Carlo Experiment

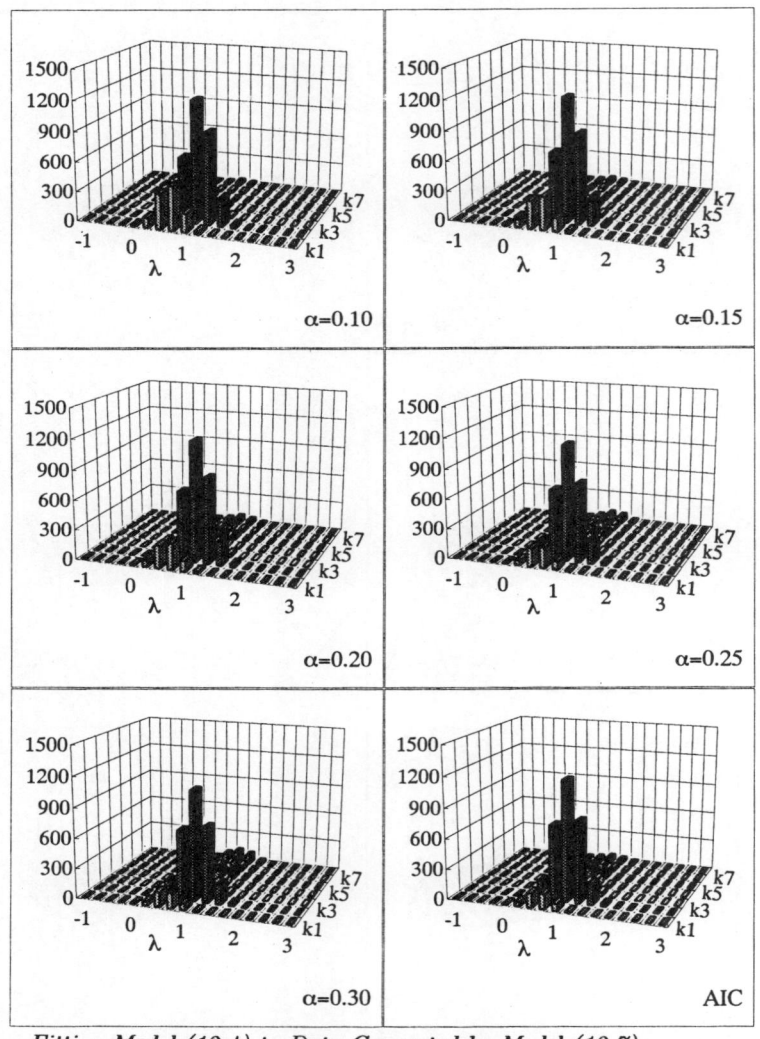

Fitting Model (12.4) to Data Generated by Model (12.7) for the case of $\sigma_0^2 = 1.0$.

12.2. The Nested χ^2 Test and the AIC for Model Choice

Figure 12.7.3 Distribution of the Estimated Frequencies in the 5,000-Times Iterated Monte Carlo Experiment

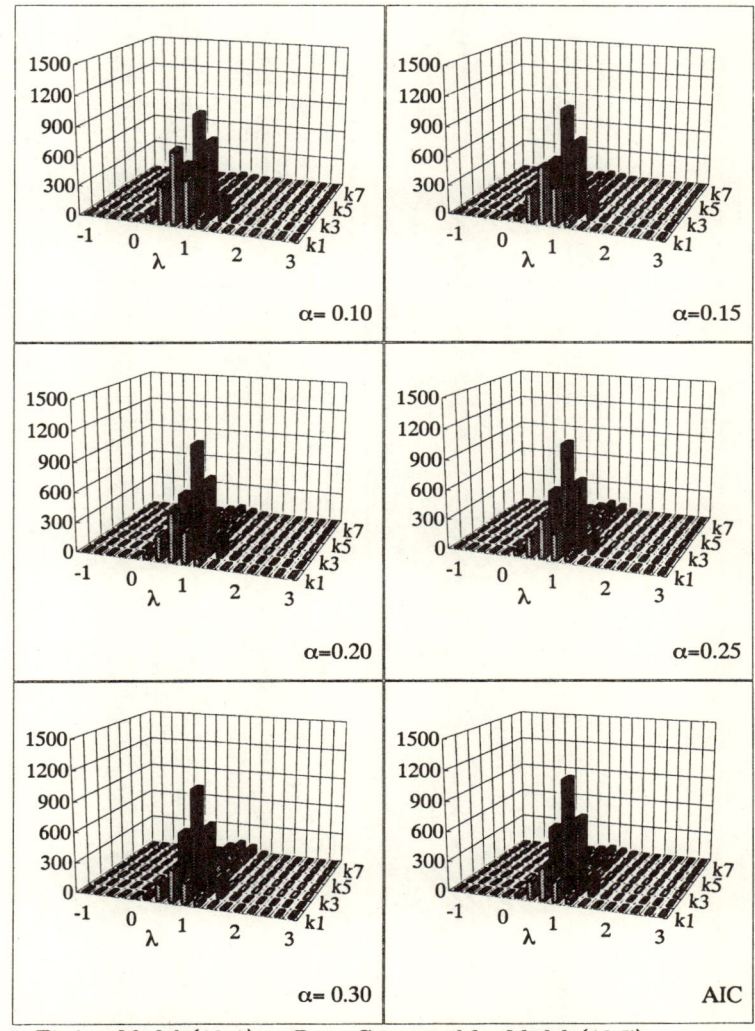

Fitting Model (12.4) to Data Generated by Model (12.7) for the case of $\sigma_0^2 = 1.5$.

Chapter 12. Nonlinear Model Simulation

Figure 12.8.1 Distribution of the Estimated Frequencies in the 5,000-Times Iterated Monte Carlo Experiment

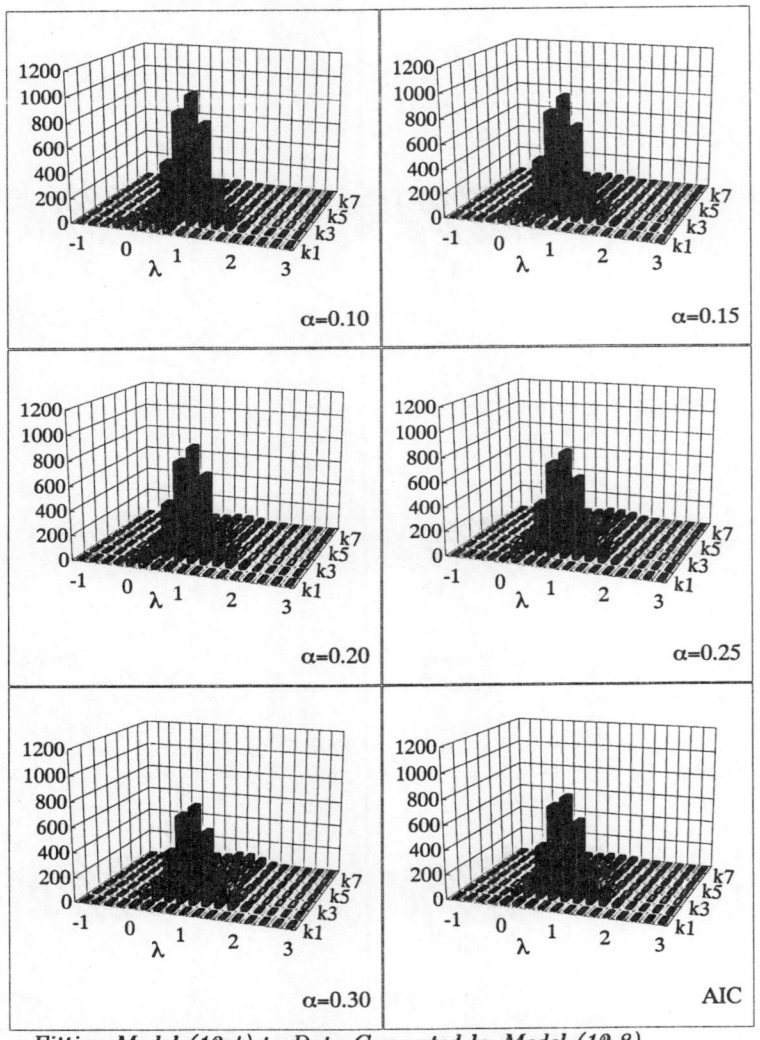

Fitting Model (12.4) to Data Generated by Model (12.8) for the case of $\sigma_0^2 = 0.5$.

12.2. The Nested χ^2 Test and the AIC for Model Choice

Figure 12.8.2 Distribution of the Estimated Frequencies in the 5,000-Times Iterated Monte Carlo Experiment

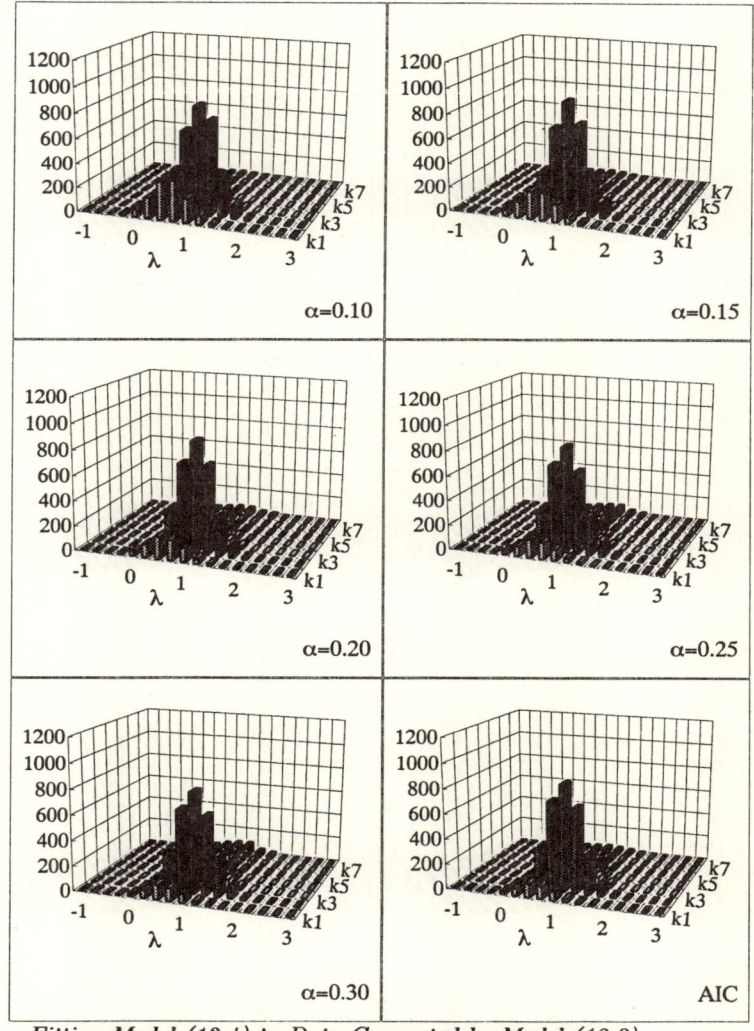

Fitting Model (12.4) to Data Generated by Model (12.8) for the case of $\sigma_0^2 = 1.0$.

Chapter 12. Nonlinear Model Simulation

Figure 12.8.3 Distribution of the Estimated Frequencies in the 5,000-Times Iterated Monte Carlo Experiment

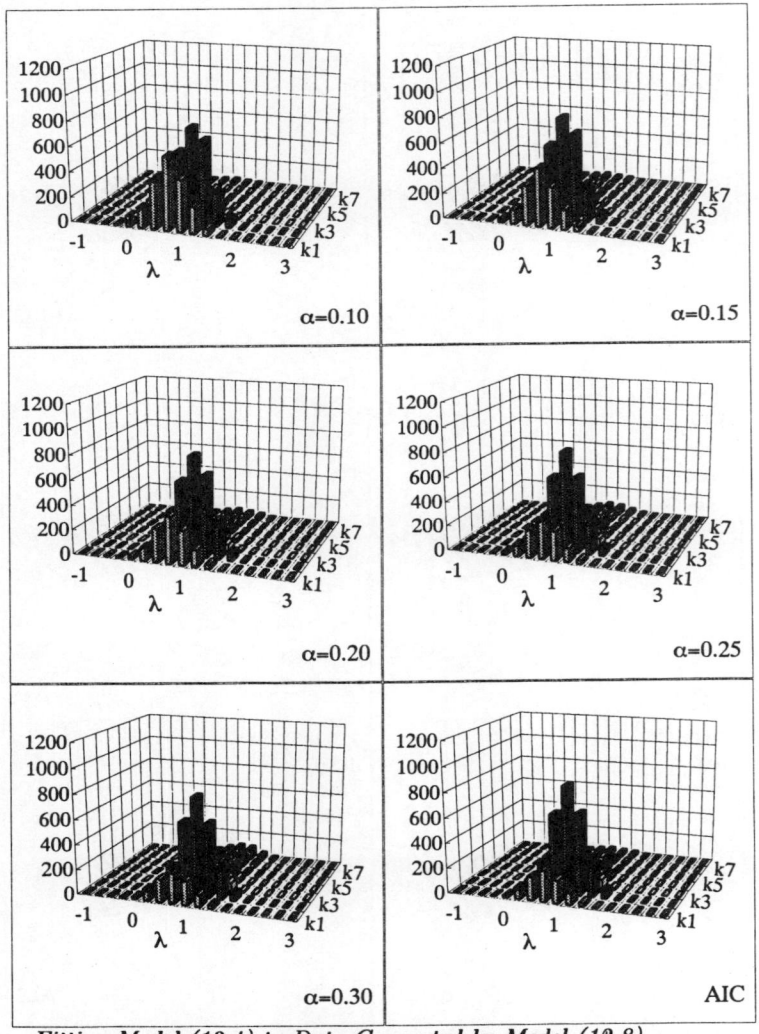

Fitting Model (12.4) to Data Generated by Model (12.8) for the case of $\sigma_0^2 = 1.5$.

12.2. The Nested χ^2 Test and the AIC for Model Choice

Figure 12.9.1 Distribution of the Estimated Frequencies in the 5,000-Times Iterated Monte Carlo Experiment

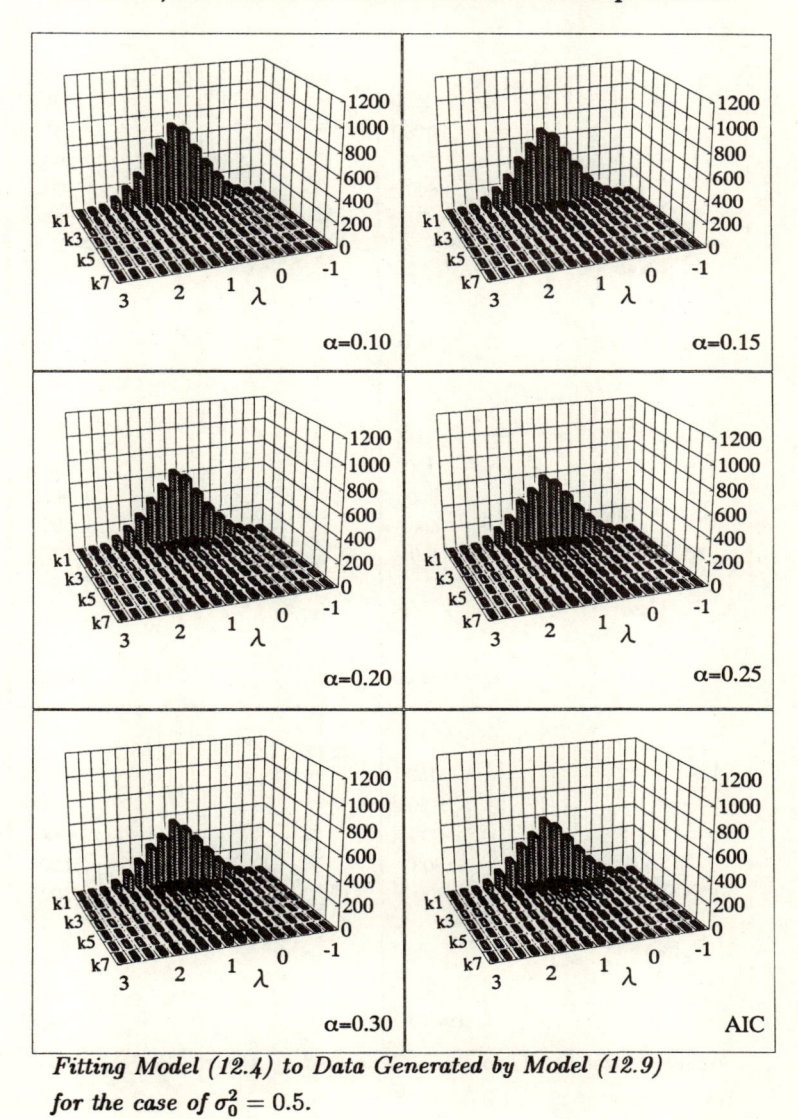

Fitting Model (12.4) to Data Generated by Model (12.9) for the case of $\sigma_0^2 = 0.5$.

Figure 12.9.2 Distribution of the Estimated Frequencies in the 5,000-Times Iterated Monte Carlo Experiment

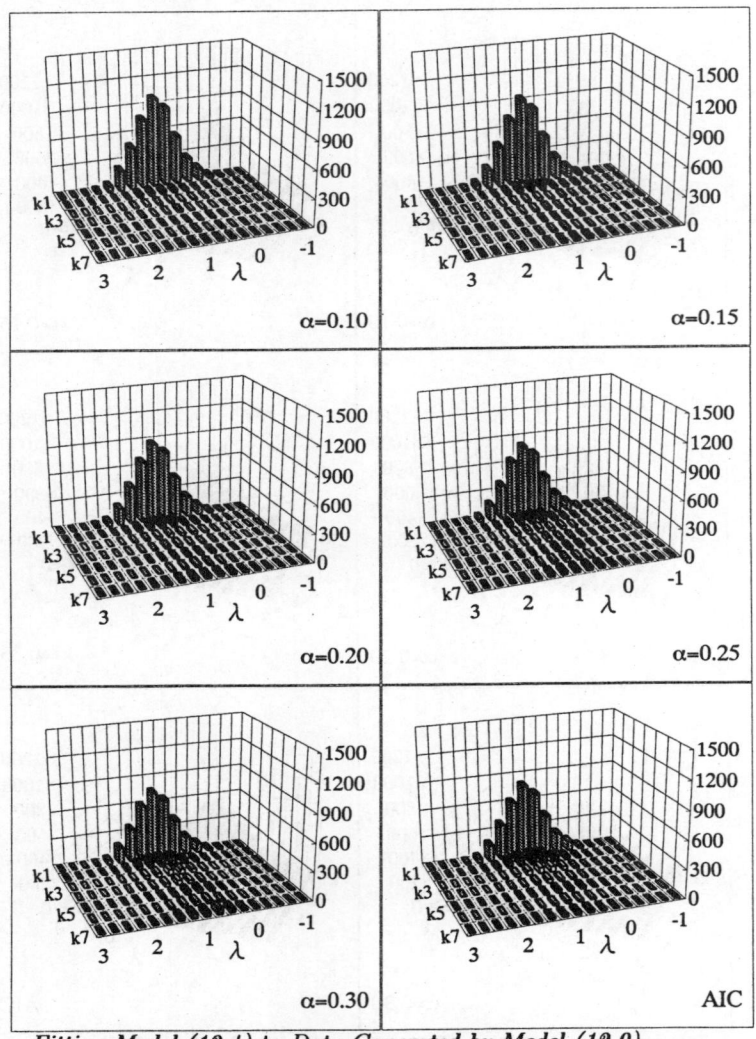

Fitting Model (12.4) to Data Generated by Model (12.9) for the case of $\sigma_0^2 = 1.0$.

12.2. The Nested χ^2 Test and the AIC for Model Choice

Figure 12.9.3 Distribution of the Estimated Frequencies in the 5,000-Times Iterated Monte Carlo Experiment

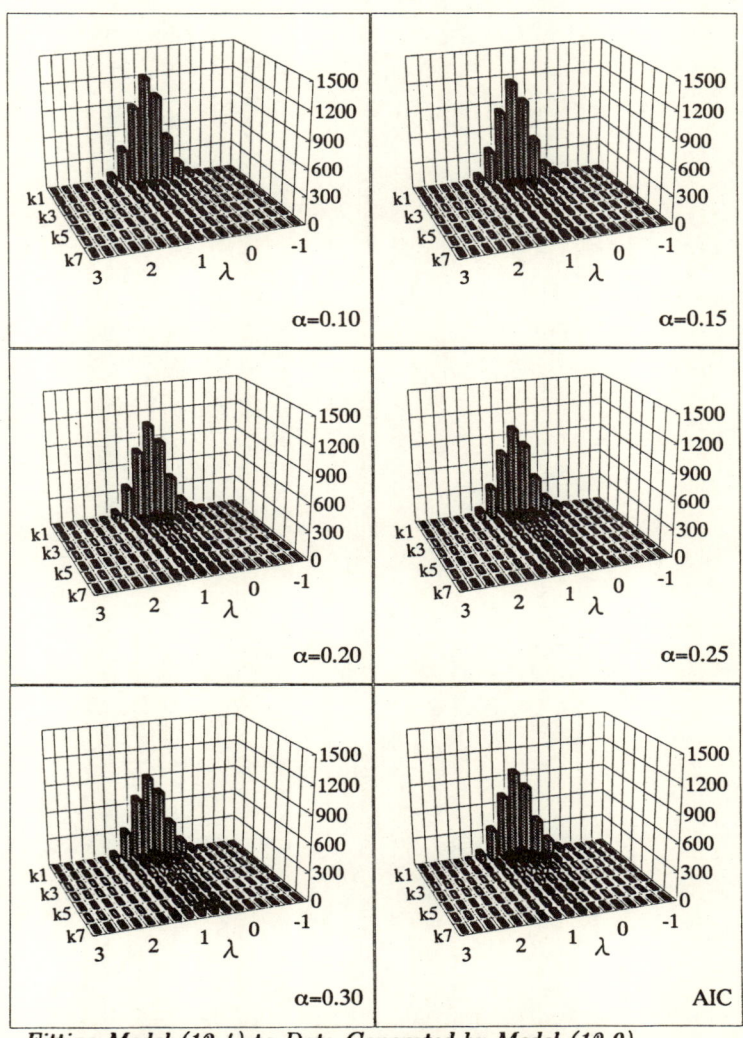

Fitting Model (12.4) to Data Generated by Model (12.9) for the case of $\sigma_0^2 = 1.5$.

211

References

Ahn, S.K. and Reinsel. G.C., 1990, Estimation of partially nonstationary multivariate autoregressive models, *Journal of the American Statistical Association*, Vol.85, pp.813-23.

Akaike, H., 1968, On the use of a linear model for the identification of feedback system, *Annals of the Institute of Statistical Mathematics*, Vol.20.

Akaike, H., 1973, Information theory and an extension of the maximum likelihood principle, 2nd International Symposium on Information Theory, Eds. B.P. Petrov and F. Csaki, pp.267-81, Budapest: Akademia Kiado.

Basman, R.L., 1963, The causal interpretation of non-triangular systems of economic relations, *Econometrica*, Vol.31, pp.439-48.

Bickel, P.J and Doksum, K.A., 1981, An analysis of transformations revisited, *Journal of the American Statistical Association*, Vol.76, pp.296-311.

Bewley. R.A. and Orden. D., 1994, Alternative methods for estimating long-run responses with applications to Australia import demand, *Econometric Reviews*, Vol.13, No.2, pp.179-204.

Bossaerts, P., 1988, Common nonstationary components of asset prices, *Journal of Economic Dynamics and Control*, Vol. 12, pp.347-64.

Box, G.E.P. and Cox, D.R., 1964, An analysis of transformations, *Journal of the Royal Statistical Society*, B26, pp.211-43.

Box, G.E.P. and Cox, D.R., 1982, An analysis of transformations revisited, rebutted, *Journal of the American Statistical Association*, Vol.77, pp.209-10.

Box, G.E.P. and Jenkins, G.M., 1970, *Time Series Analysis: Forecasting and Contro.* San Francisco: Holden Day (revised edition 1976).

References

Box, G.E.P. and Tiao, G.C., 1977, A canonical analysis of multiple time series, *Econometrica*, Vol.64, pp.355-65.

Caines, P.E. and Chan, C.W., 1975, Feedback between stationary stochastic processes, *IEEE Transaction Automatic Control*, Ac-20, pp.498-508.

Chang, H.S., 1977, Functional forms and the demand for meat in the United States, *The Review of the Economics and Statistics*, Vol.59, pp.355-9

Chang, H.S., 1980, Functional forms and the demand for meat in the United States: A Reply, *The Review of the Economics and Statistics*, Vol.62, pp.148-50.

China Statistical Yearbook, 1990 (in Chinese), State Statistical Bureau of the P.R.C., China Statistical Publishing House.

Chow, G.C., (1983), Econometrics, New York: McGraw-Hill.

D'Agostino, R.B., (1970), Transformation to normality of the null distribution of g_1, *Biometrika*, Vol.57, pp.679-81.

Doornik, J.A. and Hansen, H., 1994, An omunibus test for univariate and multivariate normality, mimeo, Nuffield College, Oxford.

Dufour, J.M. and Renault, E., 1998, Short run and long run causality in time series: Theory, *Econometrica*, Vol.66, No.5, pp.1099-125.

Engle, R.F. and Granger, C.W.J., 1987, Co-integration and error correction: representation, estimation and testing, *Econometrica*, Vol.55, No.2, pp.251-76.

Engle, R.F. and Yoo, B.S., 1989, Cointegrated economic time series: A survey with new results, Discussion Paper 87-26R, University of California, San Diego, CA.

Fishman, G.S., 1969, Spectral Methods in Econometrics, Harvard University Press, Cambridge.

Frideman, B.M. and Kuttner, K.N., 1993, Another look at the evidence on money-income causality, *Journal of Econometrics*, Vol.57, pp.189-203.

Gel'fand, I.M. and Yaglom, A.M., 1959, Calculation of the amount of information about a random function contained in another such function, *Transactions of the American Mathematical Society*, Vol.57, Ser.2 No.12, pp.199-246.

References

Gemmill, G., 1980, Using the Box-Cox transformation form for estimation demand: A Comment, *The Review of the Economics and Statistics*, Vol.62, pp.147-8.

Geweke, J., 1982, Measurement of linear dependence and feedback between multiple time series. *Journal of the American Statistical Association*, Vol.77, No.378, pp.304-13.

Geweke, J., 1983, The Superneutrality of money in the United States: An Interpretation of the Evidence, Working Paper No.70-82-83, Carnegie-Mellon University, Graduate School of Industrial Administration.

Geweke, J., 1984, Measure of conditional linear dependence and feedback between time series, *Journal of the American Statistical Association*, Vol.79, No.388, pp.907-15.

Granger, C.W.J., 1963, Economic process involving feedback. *Information and Control*, Vol.6, No.1, pp.28-48.

Granger, C.W.J., 1969, Investigating causal relations by cross-spectrum methods. *Econometrica*, Vol.39, No.3, pp.424-38.

Granger, C.W.J., 1980, Testing for causality: a personal view-point. *Journal of Economic Dynamics and Control*, Vol.2, No.4, pp.329-52.

Granger, C.W.J., 1981, Some properties of time series data and their use in econometric model specification, *Journal of Econometrics*, Vol.16, pp.121-30.

Granger, C.W.J., 1983, Co-integrated variables and error-correcting models, Discussion paper 83-13, University of California, San Diego,CA.

Granger, C.W.J., 1990, Causal Inference, in Econometrics, 45-49, Eds. Eatwell, J., Milgate, M., Newman, P., the Macmillan Press Ltd.

Granger. C. W. J. and Hatanaka M., 1964, Spectral Analysis of Economic Time Series, Princeton University Press.

Granger. C. W. J. and Weiss A.A., 1983, Time series analysis of error-correction models in *Studies in Econometrics: Time Series and Multivariate Statistics*, Eds S. Karlin and T. Amemiya and L.A. Goodman, New York: Academic Press.

References

Granger, C.W.J. and Lin, J.L. 1995, Causality in the long run. *Econometric Theory*, Vol.11, No.3, pp.530-36.

Gonzalo, J., 1994, Five alternative methods of estimating long-run equilibrium relationships, *Journal of Econometrics*, Vol.60, pp.203-33.

Hansen, B. and Phillips, P.C.B., 1990, Estimation and inference in models of cointegration: a simulation study, *Advances in Econometrics*, Vol.8, pp.225-48.

Hosking, J.R.M. (1980), The multivariate portmanteau statistics, *Journal of the American Statistical Association*, Vol.75, pp.602-8.

Hosoya, Y., 1977, On the Granger·condition for non-causality. *Econometrica*, Vol.45, No.7, pp.1735-6.

Hosoya, Y., 1983, Some results related to model selection based on estimated risk, Discussion Paper No.44, Faculty of Economics, Tohoku University.

Hosoya, Y., 1984, Information criteria and tests-series models, Time Series Analysis: Theory and Practice 5, 39-50, Ed. Anderson O.D., Elsevier Science Publishers, Amsterdam.

Hosoya, Y., 1986, A simultaneous test in the presence of nested alternative hypotheses, *Journal of Applied Probability*, 23A, pp.187-200.

Hosoya, Y., 1989, Hierarchical statistical models and generalized likelihood ratio test, *Journal of Royal Statistical Society*, B51, pp.435-47.

Hosoya, Y., 1991, The decomposition and measurement of the interdependency between second-order stationary processes. *Probability Theory and Related Fields*, Vol.88, pp.429-44.

Hosoya, Y., 1997, Causal analysis and statistical inference on possibly non-stationary time series, in *Advances in Economics and Econometrics: theory and application, 7th World Congress Vol.III*, Eds D.M. Keps and K.F. Wallis, Cambridge: Cambridge University press.

Hosoya, Y. and Taniguchi, M., 1982, A central limit theorem for stationary processes and the parameter estimation of linear processes. *The Annals of Statistics*, Vol.10, No.1, pp.132-53; 1993. Correction. *The Annals of Statistics*, Vol.21, No.2, pp.1155-7.

References

Hosoya, Y. and Katayama, S., 1987, A p-value algorithm for a nested χ^2 test, *Annual Report of the Economic Society*, Tohoku University, Vol.49, No.1, pp.83-90.

Hosoya Y. and Yao, F., 1999, Statistical Causal Analysis and its Application to Time-Series, *Proceedings of 1999 NBER/NSF Time Series Conference*, Session VIII, Academia Sinica, Taipei.

Hosoya, Y. and Takimoto, T., 2000, Testing cointegration rank in the presence of structural changes, *Annual Report of the Economic Society*, Tohoku University, Vol.61, No.4, pp.78-99.

Hsiao, C., 1982, Time series modeling and causal ordering of Canadian money, income and interest rates, in *Time Series Analysis: Theory and Practice I*, Ed. O.D. Anderson, pp.671-98. Amsterdam: North-Holland.

Hsiao, C., 1997, Cointegration and dynamic simultaneous equations model, *Econometrica*, Vol.65, No.3, pp.647-70.

Huang, C.J. and Grawe, O.R., 1980, Functional forms and the demand for meat in the United States: A Comment, *The Review of the Economics and Statistics*, Vol.62, pp.144-6.

Huang, C.J. and Kelingos, A., 1979, Conditional mean function and a general specification of the disturbance in regression analysis, *Southern Economic Journal*, Vol.45, pp.710-7.

James, B.R. and Davied, S.M., 1982, Analysis of income and food expenditure distributions: A Flexible Approach, *The Review of the Economics and Statistics*, Vol.64, pp.104-9.

Johansen, S., 1988, Statistical analysis of cointegration vectors. *Journal of Economic Dynamic and Control*, Vol.12, No.213, pp.231-54.

Johansen, S., 1991, Estimation and Hypothesis testing of cointegration vectors in Gaussian vector autoregressive models. *Econometrica*, Vol.59, No.6, pp.1551-80.

Johansen, S., 1992, A representation of vector autoregressive processes integrated of order 2, *Econometric Theory*, Vol.8, pp.188-202.

Johansen, S., 1995, *Likelihood-based Inference in Cointegrated Auto-regressive Models*, Oxford University Press, New York.

References

Johansen, S. and Juselius, K., 1990, Maximum likelihood estimation and inference on cointegration with application to the demand for money, *Oxford Bulletin of Economics and Statistics*, Vol.52, No.2, pp.169-210.

Johansen, S. and Juselius, K., 1992, Testing structural hypotheses in a multivariate cointegration analysis of the PPP and the UIP for UK, *Journal of Econometrics*, Vol.53, pp.211-44.

Johansen, S. and Juselius, K., 1994, Identification of the long-run and the short-run structure: An Application to the ISLM Model, *Journal of Econometrics*, Vol.63, pp.7-36.

Johansen, S. and Nielsen, B.G., 1994, Asymptotics for tests for cointegrating rank in the presence of intervention dummies: manual for the simulation program DisCo, Discussion Paper, University of Copenhagen.

Juselius, K., 1994, On the duality between long-run relations and common trends in the I(1) versus I(2) model: An application to aggregate money holdings, *Econometric Reviews*, Vol.13, No.2, pp.151-78.

Juselius, K., 1995, Do purchasing power parity and uncovered interest rate parity hold in the long-run? An example of likelihood inference in a multivariate time series model, *Journal of Econometric*, Vol.69, pp.211-40.

Kunitomo, N., 1996, Tests of unit roots and cointegration hypotheses in econometric model, *The Japanese Economic Review*, vol.47, no.1, pp.79-109.

Ljung, G.M. and G.E.P. Box, 1978, On a measure of lack of fit in time series models, Biometrika, Vol.65, pp.297-303.

Lütkepohl, H., 1993, Granger-causality in cointegrated VAR processes. *Economics Letters*, Vol.40, No.3, pp.263-8.

Lütkepohl, H. and Reimers, H.-E., 1992, Granger-causality in cointegrated VAR processes. *Economics Letters*, Vol.40, No.3, pp.263-8.

Magnus J.R. and H. Neudecker, 1988, Matrix Differential Calculus with Applications in Statistics and Econometrics, John Wiley & Sons, New York.

McAleer, M. and McKenzie, C.R. and Pesaran, M.H., 1994, Cointegration and direct test of the rational expectations hypothesis, *Econometric Reviews*, Vol.13, No.2, pp.231-58.

References

Mallela, P. 1980, Distribution between linear and logarithmic forms: A Note, *The Review of the Economics and Statistics*, Vol.62, pp.142-4.

Morimune, K. and Zhao, G.Q., 1997, Unit root analysis of the causality between Japanese money and income, *The Japanese Economic Review*, Vol.48, No.4, pp.343-67.

Mosconi, R. and Giannini, C., 1992, Non-causality in cointegration systems: Representation, Estimation and Testing, *Oxford Bulletin of Economics and Statistics*, Vol.54, No.3, pp.399-417.

National Astronomical Observatory, 1990, Chronological Scientific Tables, (in Japanese), Maruzen Co. Ltd., Tokyo.

Nelson, C.R. and Schwert, G.W., 1982, Tests for predictive relationships between time series variables, *Journal of the American Statistical Association*, Vol.77, pp.11-8.

Osterwald-Lenum, M., 1992, A note with quantiles of the asymptotic distribution of the maximum likelihood cointegration rank test, *Oxford Bulletin of Economics and Statistics*, Vol.54, pp.461-71.

Phillips, P.C.B., 1990, Spectral regression for cointegrated time series, in *Nonparametric and Semiparametric Methods in Economic Process*, Ed. W. Barnett, New York, California University Press.

Phillips, P.C.B., 1991, Optimal inference in cointegrated systems, *Econometrica*, Vol.59, pp.283-306.

Phillips, P.C.B. and Loretan, M., 1991, Estimating long run economic equilibria, *Review of Economic Studies*, Vol.58, pp.407-96.

Pierce, D.A., 1979, R^2 measures for time series, *Journal of the American Statistical Association*, Vol.74, pp.901-10.

Pierce, D.A. and Haugh, L.D., 1977, Causality in temporal systems, *Journal of Econometrics*, Vol.5, pp.265-93.

Poirier, D.J., 1978, The use of the Box-Cox transformation in limited dependent variable models, *Journal of the American Statistical Association*, Vol.73, pp.284-7.

Poirier, D.J. and Melino, A., 1978, A note on the interpretation of regression coefficients within a class of truncated distributions, *Econometrica*, Vol.46,

References

pp.1207-9.

Rozanov, Y.A., 1967, Stationary Random Processes. San Francisco: Holden-Day.

Salmon. M., 1982, Error correction mechanisms, *The Economic Journal*, Vol.92, pp.615-29.

Sakamoto, Y. and Isiguro, M. and Kitagawa, G., 1986, Akaike information criterion statistics, D. Reidel Publishing Company, Tokyo.

Saikkonen, P., 1991, Asymptotically efficient estimation of cointegration regression, *Econometric Theory*, Vol.7, pp.1-21.

Seaks, T.G. and Layson, S.K., 1983, Box-Cox estimation with standard econometric problems, *The Review of the Economics and Statistics*, Vol.65, pp.160-4.

Shibata, R., 1976, Selection of the order of an autoregressive model by Akaike's information criterion, *Biometrica*, Vol.63, pp.117-26.

Simon, H. A.1953, Causal ordering and identifiability, Studies in Econometric Method, Eds. W. C. Hood and T. C. Koopmans, Cowles Commission Monograph 14, New York.

Sims, C.A., 1972, Money, income and causality, *American Economic Review*, Vol.62, No.4, pp.540-52.

Sims, C.A., 1980, Macroeconomics and reality, *Econometrica*, Vol.48, pp.1-48.

Sims, C.A. and Stock, J.H. and Watson, M.W., 1990, Inference in linear time series models with some unit roots, *Econometrica*, Vol.58, pp.113-44.

Spitzer, J.J., 1978, A Monte Carlo investigation of the Box-Cox transformation in small samples, *Journal of the American Statistical Association*, Vol.73, pp.488-95

Spitzer, J.J., 1982, A Fast and efficient algorithm for the estimation of parameters in models with the Box-Cox transformation , *Journal of the American Statistical Association*, Vol.77, pp.760-6.

Stock. J.H., 1987, Asymptotic properties of least squares estimators of cointegrating vectors, *Econometrica*, Vol. 55, pp.1035-56.

Stock. J.H. and Watson, M.W., 1988, Testing for common trends, *Journal of the American Statistical Association*, Vol.83, pp.1097-107.

References

Stock. J.H. and Watson, M.W., 1989, Interpreting the evidence on money-income causality, *Journal of Econometrics*, Vol.40, pp.161-82.

Strotz, R.H. and Wold, T.C., 1960, Recursive versus non-recursive systems: an attempt at synthesis, *Econometrica*, Vol.28, pp.417-27.

Takeuchi, K., 1976, The distribution of information statistics and the criterion of goodness of fit of models, Suri Kagaku, (in Japanese), Vol.153, pp.12-18.

Terui, N., 1990, An F-type small sample simulation test for nested linear regression models, Communications in Statistics: Theory and Methods, A19, No.2, pp.703-22.

Toda, H. and Phillips, P.C.B., 1993, Vector autoregressions and causality. *Econometrica*, Vol.61, No.6, pp.1367-93.

Toda, H. and Phillips, P.C.B., 1994, Vector autoregression and causality: a theoretical overview and simulation study, *Economic Review*, Vol. 13(2), pp.259-85.

Tse, Y.K., 1984, Testing for linear and log-linear regressions with heteroscedasticity, *Economics Letters*, Vol.16, pp.63-9.

Tso, M.K.S., 1981, Reduced-rank regression and canonical analysis, *Journal of the Royal Statistical Society*, Series B, Vol.83, pp.183-9.

Tsukuda, Y. and T. Miyakoshi, 1998, Granger causality between money and income for the Japanese economy in the presence of a structural change, *The Japanese Economic Review*, Vol.49, No.2, pp.191-209.

White, K.J., 1972, Estimation of the liquidity trap with a generalized functional form, *Econometrica*, Vol.40, pp.193-9.

Whittle, P., 1963, Prediction and Regulation by Linear Least-Square Methods, D. Van Nostrand, Princeton.

Wiener, N., 1956, The theory of prediction, Modern Mathematics for Engineers, Series I, Chapter 8, Ed. Beckenback, E. F..

Yao, F., 1992, Analysis of the Box-Cox Transformation with general information criterion and Akaike information criterion, Master Degree Thesis, Graduate School of Economics and Management, Tohoku University, Japan.

References

Yao, F., 1994, Analysis of the Box-Cox transformation with general information criterion and Akaike information criterion, *Annual Report of the Economic Society*, Tohoku University, Vol.56, No.1, pp.123-39.

Yao, F., 1995, Information criteria and the nested χ^2 method for the Box-Cox data transformation, *Annual Report of the Economic Society*, Tohoku University, Vol.57, No.2, pp.85-99.

Yao, F., 1996a, Econometric Analysis of Nonlinear and Nontationary Relationships: Inference and Computational Methods, *Doctoral Thesis* presented to Graduate School of Economics and Management, Tohoku University, Japan.

Yao, F., 1996b, Causal analysis of Japanese Money and International Trade, *Statistical Analysis of Time Series: Theory and Application*, The Institute of Statistical Mathematics Cooperative Research Report, No.90, pp.119-30.

Yao, F., 1996c, Investigation of the Information Criteria in the Box-Cox Transformation Model, *Kagawa University Economic Review*, the Institute of Economic Research, Kagawa University, Vol.69, No2·3, pp.267-95.

Yao, F., 1998, Investigation of Nested Chi-square Test and AIC in the Box-Cox Transformation Model, *Kagawa University Economic Review*, the Institute of Economic Research, Kagawa University,. Vol.71, No.3, pp.217-56

Yao, F., 1999, Empirical analysis of the Causal Relations in Japanese and Chinese macroeconomic Data, *Annals of Economic Studies*, Kagawa University, No.39, pp.145-91.

Yao, F., 2000, Testing the one-way effect in the presence of trend breaks, mimeo.

Yao, F. and Hosoya, Y., 1994, Statistical model identification in the Box-Cox data transformation, Discussion Paper No.109, Faculty of Economics, Tohoku University.

Yao, F. and Hosoya, Y., 1995, Empirical causality analysis of Japanese macro economic data. *Statistical Analysis of Time Series: Theory and Application*, The Institute of Statistical Mathematics Cooperative Research Report, No.79, pp.85-96.

Yao, F. and Y. Hosoya, 2000, Inference on one-way effect and evidence in Japanese macroeconomic data, *Journal of Econometrics*, Vol.98, No2, pp.225-55.

References

Yao, Y.C., 1985, Nyquist frequency, *Encyclopedia of Statistical Sciences*, Vol.6, pp.393-95, Eds. Kotz, S. and Johanson, N.L., John Wikey & Sons, New York.

Zarembka, P., 1968, Functional form in the demand for money, *Journal of the American Statistical Association*, Vol.63, pp.502-11.

Zarembka, P., 1974, Transformation of variables in econometrics, Frontiers of Econometrics, 81-104, Ed. Zarembka, P., Academic Press, New York.

Zarembka, P., 1990, Transformation of variables in econometrics, in Econometrics, pp.261-64, Eds. Eatwell, J., Milgate, M., Newman, P., the Macmillan Press Ltd.

List of Abbreviations

AIC: Akaike Information Criterion
AR: Autoregressive or Autoregression
ARMA : Autoregressive Moving-average
BCT: Box-Cox Transformation
DGP: Data-generating Process
ECM: Error-correction Model
Ec: The Exports to China
Ex: Exports
FMO: Frequency Measure of One-way effect
GIC: General Information Criterion
I(d): Integrated of order d
Im: Imports
Ic: The Imports from China
LR: Likelihood Ratio
M: M2+CD
MA: Moving-average
$M_{V \to U}$: The one-way effect measure of V to U
$M_{U,V}$: The measure of association between U and V
$M_{U.V}$: The measure of reciprocity between U and V
$M_{V \to U}(\lambda)$: The one-way effect of V to U at frequency λ
$M_{U,V}(\lambda)$: The measure of association between U and V at frequency λ
$M_{U.V}(\lambda)$: The measure of reciprocity between U and V at frequency λ
ML: Maximum Likelihood
MLE: Maximum Likelihood Estimate
MLL: Maximum Log-Likelihood

NBER: National Bureau of Economic Research
NSF: National Science Foundation
OMO: Overall Measure of One-way effect
R: Call Rates
var: variance
VAR: Vector Autoregressive or Vector Autoregression
Y: GDP; Gross Domestic Production

Author's Profile:

Dr. Feng YAO
Born 1960, Chang-Chun, China.

1983/7, Bachelor of Science. Jilin University, China.
1987/7, Master of Law. Jilin University, China.
1993/3, Master of Economics. Tohoku University, Japan.
1996/3, Doctor of Economics. Tohoku University, Japan.

1987-1995, Economist, State Planning Committee, China.
1996-1997, Lecture, Faculty of Economics, Kagawa University, Japan.
1997-present, Associate Professor, Faculty of Economics,
　　　　　　Kagawa University, Japan.

Research and Interest Field:
Econometrics, Economic Statistics, Mathematics, Demography,
Empirical analysis of Japanese and Chinese economy.